THE POTATO MASHER MURDER

TRUE CRIME HISTORY

The Potato Masher Murder

*Death at the Hands of
a Jealous Husband*

Gary Sosniecki

The Kent State University Press

KENT, OHIO

© 2020 by The Kent State University Press, Kent, Ohio 44242
Library of Congress Catalog Number 2020000211
ISBN 978-1-60635-404-9
Manufactured in the United States of America

LIBRARY OF CONGRESS CATALOGING-IN-PUBLICATION DATA
Names: Sosniecki, Gary, author.
Title: The potato masher murder : death at the hands of a jealous husband /
    Gary Sosniecki.
Description: Kent, Ohio : The Kent State University Press, [2020] | Series: True
    crime history | Includes bibliographical references and index.
Identifiers: LCCN 2020000211 | ISBN 9781606354049 (paperback) | ISBN
    9781631014192 (epub) | ISBN 9781631014208 (pdf)
Subjects: LCSH: Ludwig, Albin, 1869-1954. | Ludwig, Cecilia, 1876-1906. |
    Uxoricide--Indiana--Mishawaka--Case studies
Classification: LCC HV6542 .S67 2020 | DDC 364.152/3092--dc23
LC record available at https://lccn.loc.gov/2020000211

24 23 22 21 20   5 4 3 2 1

Contents

LUDWIG NEIGHBORHOOD, MISHAWAKA, 1906

GRAND TRUNK WESTERN RAILWAY

N
W ← → E
S

CHARLES PATTERSON

MARCELLUS GAZE

JOHN WILSON/ BRAND

ALBIN LUDWIG

FRED METZLER

EMMA REHSNEIDER

CHRISTYANN STREET

MARION STREET

ALICE MCNABB

ANNA SPIES

BROADWAY STREET

COTTAGE UNDER CONSTRUCTION

SARAH STREET

DEPOT

ANNA BURKHART

ALIVIA BRUCE MEAT MARKET

BATTELL SCHOOL

BRIDGE STREET

MILTON ROBBINS GROCER

NORTH SIDE DRUG STORE

ST. JOESEPH RIVER & DOWNTOWN MISHAWAKA

map not to scale

The neighborhood of Albin and Cecilia Ludwig, 1906. (Map by Shawna Bradley)

Preface

THE STORY OF MY great-grandmother's murder was forgotten for more than a century because the descendants of Cecilia Henderson Hornburg Ludwig and her second husband (and murderer), Albin Ludwig, were shielded from the sad and sordid details of their troubled marriage and the violent way it ended.

All the time I spent as a child with my maternal grandfather—the day trips to Lake Marie, Illinois, to fish for perch; sitting behind home plate at Wrigley Field while Grandma watched on TV, counting the beers Grandpa drank; picking up a box of hand-rolled cigars in the tobacco-filled backroom of a neighborhood Chicago storefront—he never told me that his mother, my great-grandmother, was murdered by her jealous second husband when Grandpa was fourteen years old and living with his father.

Like me, the descendants of the Henderson and Ludwig families whom I tracked down for this book knew little beforehand about Cecilia's death, one of the most brutal of its era in northern Indiana. Murder was a tasteless and embarrassing subject for families only one and two generations removed from knowing the victim or the perpetrator personally.

"I know that she was a very attractive woman," my ninety-four-year-old mother, Cecilia's granddaughter, told me in 2013, eight months before her death. But Mom didn't know firsthand. An only child, she was born thirteen years after the murder. Charley Hornburg, Cecilia's first husband, was the only grandfather my mother knew as a child. She knew nothing of Albin Ludwig.

Tight-lipped for years about this family secret, Mom finally divulged what little she recalled about Cecilia's death in a 1996 conversation. She didn't know many details, some of what she remembered was wrong, but she knew enough to set me off on my twenty-three-year quest (with job-related interruptions) to learn the facts of the case.

Mom thought the murder had occurred in La Porte, Indiana, which she knew as her father's hometown. And she thought she knew what year. With that information, I wrote Fern Eddy Schultz, La Porte County's state-appointed historian, asking for help. Fern hit a brick wall with her first perusal of newspaper microfilm—Mom had guessed the wrong year—but on her second try she discovered that the murder occurred in 1906, not in La Porte but about thirty-five miles east in Mishawaka. Even though the crime was committed elsewhere, a murder this brutal involving a family with local ties was covered extensively in La Porte's two daily newspapers. The articles Fern mailed me aroused my curiosity even further. Years later when I resumed researching the murder with the idea of a book, I learned that the tragedy was front-page, bold-headlined news throughout northern Indiana for much of a year.

It was fitting that on the last day of my last research trip for this project, July 24, 2018, I had the opportunity to thank Fern in person when we met by chance at the La Porte County Historical Society Museum.

Newspapers were a major source of the story you are about to read, as my University of Missouri journalism professor, Dr. William H. Taft, taught a half century ago when he called newspapers "a tool for historians." (I worry about what future historians will do if newspapers cease to exist.)

As I read more about the case, I was stunned by the brutality Cecilia faced in both marriages. I was stunned to learn how commonplace wife beating was in the early twentieth century before polite society adopted the gender-neutral term of *domestic violence*. I similarly was stunned in researching other cases of the era to learn that *wife murder* was so common that newspapers described virtually every case by that term.

I also was saddened to learn how Cecilia's marital recklessness stoked her husband's temper. Sadly, Cecilia's story is one without heroes. But it is a story that needed to be told—not just as an account of a once-notorious crime that history has forgotten but also as an examination of domestic violence in an earlier era. Husbands still kill wives today, but women now have more places to turn to when a marriage goes bad.

A twenty-year lapse in my research proved fortunate in that it resumed after the launch of genealogy websites. The new technology enabled me to track down previously unknown cousins as well as descendants of Albin Ludwig's family. All were cooperative. All were as interested as I was to learn why and how Cecilia died.

As this project came to a close, I asked once more for their reflections on the case. How did they learn about the murder? How has it affected them? Did their immediate family talk about it? Did anyone know the full story?

In an almost unimaginable coincidence, Kent A. Berridge, whose grandmother was Cecilia's sister Jessie, was born decades later in the same house where the murder occurred. "Neither my brothers or I knew the circumstances of what happened; we did know that it was a home that my father's aunt owned, or so we were told," he wrote.

It wasn't until another aunt died in the late 1980s that Berridge learned the truth.

"As morbid as it was, my late wife Emily and I were walking around the cemetery looking at tombstones of various ancestors when my cousin Judy approached and started telling us that our great-aunt was buried with our great-grandparents, and what had happened to her. So I guess there was a lot of shame in the family about the murder because it was never discussed."[1]

Chuck Ellsworth is the adopted son of Cecilia's nephew Charles, who, as a six-year-old, may have been the murder's only witness. Unknown to each other until my research brought us together, cousin Chuck and I not only have become friends but also have met three times despite living half a country apart.

"If I had not been put in touch with you [through a half sister] I would never have known of Cecilia's murder," Chuck wrote. "[The] Ellsworth family was tight-lipped and iron-fisted. Kind, loving and very intractable once a mission was put in place. I can understand their point of view with all the secrecy. I don't agree with it; especially after so many scores of decades had gone by."[2]

From another distant cousin, one who asked that I not use her name in the book: "I learned about the murder through my great-grandmother,

Cecilia's daughter Lyle. I don't think it has affected me much since it was long before my time. Nobody in the family ever discussed it. I did some research myself and found out the story that was in the newspaper after it happened. My mother only knew she was killed in a fire; no one told the details or wanted to talk about it."[3]

On the Ludwig side of the story, Gretchen L. Marks, who is Albin's first cousin five times removed, learned about the murder while doing her own research. Despite not being related to Cecilia by blood, she has taken the murder personally.

"As a genealogist, it is very informative and very intriguing," she wrote. "As a cousin, I am both sad and mad.

"As I read the newspaper articles, I go through all the emotions. It is hard to believe someone could do such a horrifying act. Knowing that she is a cousin . . . I become so outraged, with many questions and no full answers. Then I become saddened, wondering what her life may have been like if this didn't happen to her. The 'What if?' game. In the end I would say that I mourn for her, and for what she had endured."[4]

I mourn, too, for I was deprived of a great-grandmother. If Cecilia had not been murdered, she might have lived to the age of seventy-four, long enough to see me born. I would have appreciated the chance to know her.

Dramatis Personae

CECILIA "CELIA" BETTIE JOHNSON HENDERSON HORNBURG LUD-
WIG, the second-oldest daughter born after the marriage of James
and Christina Orr Henderson, the wife of Charley Hornburg and
Albin Ludwig, the mother of William and Lyle Hornburg, and the
great-grandmother of the author. She was the victim.

CHRISTINA "AUNT TINA" SHAW WADE DENHAM, daughter born to
Christina Orr before her marriage to James Henderson. The younger
Christina's father, who died shortly before her birth, was a Shaw.

JAMES and CHRISTINA ORR HENDERSON, Scottish immigrants, parents of four daughters, including Cecilia, and a son.

JEAN HENDERSON ELLSWORTH, fourth and youngest daughter born
after the marriage of James and Christina Henderson, estranged wife
of Ora "Orie" Horace Ellsworth, and mother of Lucy and Charles Ellsworth. Jean and the children were living with Albin and Cecilia at the
time of the murder. In later years, Jean was married to William "Billy"
Jones Leigh. Orie's second wife was Anna Ellsworth.

JESSIE LOCKHART HENDERSON BERRIDGE WHEELER, third daughter
born after the marriage of James and Christina Henderson. Jessie's
grandchildren, Paula Steiner, Judy A. Myer, and Kent A. Berridge,
were among the sources for this book.

MARGARET "MAGGIE" ISABELLA CESSFORD HENDERSON FRANCIS
WEED, first daughter born after the marriage of James and Christina
Henderson.

THOMAS ORR HENDERSON, youngest child, only son of James and Christina Henderson. He was their only child born in America.

THE HORNBURG FAMILY

CHARLES "CHARLEY" HENRY HORNBURG, first husband of Cecilia Henderson, father of William and Lyle. His second wife was Eva Wickering.

LYLE ELLEN HORNBURG GEMBERLING, second child of Charley and Cecilia Hornburg. She lived with Albin and Cecilia Ludwig at the time of the murder but was in school when it occurred.

WILLIAM "WILLIE" CHARLES HORNBURG, first child of Charley and Cecilia Hornburg. William lived with his father and stepmother Eva at the time of the murder. He was the maternal grandfather of the author.

THE LUDWIG FAMILY

ALBIN RICHARD LUDWIG, sometimes erroneously called Alvin. He was the son of Wilhelm and Eva, brother of Gustave, and the second husband of Cecilia. Albin was convicted of murdering Cecilia.

GUSTAVE (GUSTAV) "GUS" H. LUDWIG, older brother of Albin. Gustave joined Albin in prison a decade later after pleading guilty to a burglary charge; not to be confused with another Gus Ludwig, an Elkhart businessman and singer.

HEINRICH WILHELM JACOB LUDWIG, referred to as Wilhelm, and EVA IDA SCHUMAN LUDWIG, parents of Gustave and Albin. They were German immigrants.

LOUIS LUDWIG, the first of five brothers to emigrate from Germany to northern Indiana.

KARL "CHARLES" CHRISTOPHER LUDWIG, brother who preceded Wilhelm to Elkhart.

MINNIE ALDINGER LUDWIG, wife of Gustave.

ELLSWORTH CHILDREN

CHARLES THOMAS ELLSWORTH, son of Ora and Jean Ellsworth. Jean and her children were living with Albin and Cecilia Ludwig at the time of the murder. Charles, then six years old, may have witnessed the murder. In 1935, Charles married Floreta Pearl "Flo" Boyd. Their adopted son, Chuck Ellsworth, was a source for this book.

LUCY ELLSWORTH KRUEGER, daughter of Ora and Jean Ellsworth. Jean and her children were living with Albin and Cecilia Ludwig at the time of the murder. Lucy, then nine years old, was believed to be outside when the murder occurred.

NEIGHBORS

CATHERINE BRAND lived with her daughter and son-in-law, Mr. and Mrs. John Wilson, in the first house west of Albin and Cecilia.

ANNA BURKHART lived with her husband on Bridge Street at Marion Street. Albin approached her to buy his dog the morning of the murder. She said no.

MARCELLUS and VERONICA GAZE lived two houses west of Albin and Cecilia.

NETTIE MAY HESS, a former neighbor who testified against Albin.

ALICE MCNABB lived one block south of Albin and Cecilia. A young girl, possibly Lucy Ellsworth, ran to her house after fire broke out at the Ludwig house.

FRED METZLER lived with his wife in the first house east of Albin and Cecilia. He was a close friend of Albin.

CHARLES R. PATTERSON lived with his wife three houses west of Albin and Cecilia.

EMMA REIFSNEIDER lived southeast of Albin and Cecilia on Christyann Street.

ANNA SPIES lived one block south of Albin and Cecilia.

ATTORNEYS

CLINTON N. CRABILL, a Mishawaka attorney hired by Albin Ludwig's brother, Gustave, to locate witnesses for Albin's defense.

WILL G. CRABILL, a partner in the South Bend law firm of Anderson, Parker & Crabill. He was deputy to Samuel Parker in Albin Ludwig's murder trial.

W. B. HILE, an attorney with the Hile and Baker law firm who prepared a divorce case for Cecilia while the Ludwigs lived in Elkhart. The case was not filed.

GEORGE A. KURTZ, Joseph Talbot's predecessor as St. Joseph County state's attorney.

C. L. "CHARLIE" METZGER, a Mishawaka lawyer whom Albin and friend Fred Metzler planned to visit the evening of September 25, 1906, to discuss Albin's marital problems. Albin killed Cecilia before the meeting could occur. Ironically, Metzger was deputy prosecutor when the Ludwig murder case went before the grand jury.

SAMUEL PARKER, a partner in the South Bend law firm of Anderson, Parker & Crabill. One of the best-known attorneys in northern Indiana, he led Albin Ludwig's defense.

ISAAC KANE PARKS, deputy prosecutor to Joseph Talbot in Albin Ludwig's murder trial.

SAMUEL P. SCHWARTZ, prosecuting attorney in the Sixtieth Judicial Circuit in 1919, who wrote the prison warden about Albin Ludwig's parole application.

JOSEPH EDWARD LEO TALBOT, St. Joseph County state's attorney, elected in 1906, who tried Albin Ludwig for murder.

COURT PERSONNEL

FRANK P. CHRISTOPH, clerk of St. Joseph County Circuit Court, who signed Albin Ludwig's commitment paperwork.

WALTER A. FUNK, circuit judge who presided over Albin Ludwig's murder trial. A native of Elkhart County, Funk opened his law practice in South Bend in 1886. He was first elected circuit judge in 1900.

WILLIAM S. GARBER, official reporter in the Marion County Courts, who wrote about the disintegration of marriages in that era.

JOHN H. GILLETT, chief justice of the Indiana Supreme Court, who wrote the opinion rejecting Albin Ludwig's appeal.

HUGH NOEL SEYMOUR HOME, court reporter for Albin Ludwig's trial.

JOHN LAYTON, jury foreman for Albin Ludwig's trial.

MISHAWAKA BUSINESS OPERATORS

ALVIA J. BRUCE, operator of a meat market, possibly known as Landis Meat Market, at Sarah and Broadway, a block and a half from the Ludwig house. Bruce had served in the US Army Hospital Corps and treated Albin Ludwig at the fire scene for his injuries.

JOHN F. GAYLOR, a real estate broker at 126 East Second. He was selling the Marion Street home to the Ludwigs and repossessed it after Cecilia's murder.

LESTER GITRE, druggist at A. P. Graham's North Side Drug Store at the southwest corner of Bridge and Joseph Streets, which in 2018 was a green space along the river. A. P. Graham also owned a drugstore on the south side of the river at 102–104 West Second.

ANNA HERZOG, operator of a boardinghouse at 220 North Main where Fred Young, Jean Henderson's suspected suitor, resided.

MILTON E. ROBBINS, a grocer at 607 North Bridge Street. In 2018, the location was home to a former gas station being used as a car lot.

GEORGE H. WILKLOW, operator of a livery service, who picked up Cecilia's charred body and delivered it to Finch's undertaking room.

LAW ENFORCEMENT

JAMES ANDERSON, Mishawaka patrolman who was approached by Albin Ludwig the evening before the murder.

LOREN A. FOUST, Mishawaka patrolman who found a straight razor at the murder scene and also guarded Albin Ludwig in the hospital. He was a former coworker of Albin Ludwig.

JAMES EDWARD GIRTON guarded Albin Ludwig at the hospital and overheard a nurse ask him about the murder.

ARTHUR HOUSEHOLDER, a constable who guarded Albin Ludwig at the hospital. He admitted to "pumping" him for information.

BENJAMIN F. JARRETT, Mishawaka chief of police. His wife, Grace, also was a witness in Albin Ludwig's trial. John Jarrett, presumably a relative, accompanied the Jarretts and Gustave and Minnie Ludwig to Albin's house the Sunday after the Tuesday murder.

SERGEANT ROBBLES, Elkhart policeman who investigated an altercation at Albin Ludwig's Monument Saloon in Elkhart.

GEORGE H. WHITEMAN served various roles on the Elkhart police force, from patrolman to superintendent. He offered Albin Ludwig a job upon parole.

FIREMEN

ALBERT BUYSSE, Mishawaka fire chief.

OTTO N. GOELLER, Mishawaka fireman who discharged a "chemical apparatus" at the scene.

WILLIAM C. HOSE, a "call man" for Mishawaka Fire Department, meaning he did not sleep at the station.

MEDICAL PERSONNEL

JAMES G. BOSTWICK, Mishawaka city health officer, who filed Cecilia's death certificate.

CHARLES A. DAUGHERTY, a St. Joseph County physician who had no personal involvement in the case but was called as an expert witness.

EDGAR DOANE, a physician who conducted Cecilia's autopsy with Dr. Charles Stroup. He testified before the grand jury but not at Albin's trial.

C. A. DRESCH, a Mishawaka physician who examined Albin Ludwig at the fire scene.

HENRY C. HOLTZENDORF, St. Joseph County coroner, who arrived at the Ludwig house shortly after Cecilia's body was discovered and later that day supervised the autopsy.

M. M. KREIDER, Elkhart County coroner who determined that Wilhelm Ludwig died of sunstroke.

MISS/MRS. McELROY, a nurse who, according to witnesses at the trial, asked Albin why he killed his wife. She did not testify. She was referred to as both "Miss" and "Mrs." during the trial.

CHARLES STROUP, a physician who conducted Cecilia's autopsy with Dr. Edgar Doane. He testified at Albin's trial.

NEWSMEN

EDWARD ALLEN JERNEGAN, publisher of the *Mishawaka Enterprise,* a weekly newspaper, since 1872. As of 2019, the newspaper still was published.

WILLIAM P. O'NEILL, publisher of the *Mishawaka Democrat,* a competing weekly newspaper. Unfortunately, microfilm or digital archives of the *Democrat* during the period of the Ludwig case could not be located.

PETER A. YOUNG, whose daily Mishawaka Department column in the *South Bend Daily Times* was credited to P. A. Young. He covered Cecilia Ludwig's murder more thoroughly than any other reporter.

PRISON PERSONNEL

A. M. COONEY, officer at Indiana State Prison who checked in Albin Ludwig.

EDWARD J. FOGARTY, warden of the Indiana State Prison in Michigan City when Albin Ludwig was paroled.

JAMES D. REID, warden of the Indiana State Prison in Michigan City when Albin Ludwig became an inmate. He explained prison life in a 1903 speech in South Bend. Reid's successor was Edward J. Fogarty.

P. H. WEEKS, physician at Indiana State Prison in Michigan City.

WITNESSES (NOT ENCOUNTERED ELSEWHERE)

DAVID HULL, JAMES FRANCE, and MILTON CARTER, all workers at a cottage under construction on Sarah Street when Cecilia Ludwig was murdered.

ALFRED HEINEY, a painter and paperhanger who repaired the fire damage to the Ludwig home.

FRED YOUNG, childhood friend of Cecilia and Jean Henderson from Kingsbury. He was a widower who was working in Mishawaka and spent time with both women. Albin Ludwig suspected that Young was interested romantically in Cecilia.

D. D. RATHBUN, the first person up the ladder at the Ludwig fire, a missing witness at the trial, referred to as the "stranger." He offered an affidavit in the appeal.

ROBERT F. SCHELLENBERG, fourth man on the scene of the Ludwig fire after hearing the alarm from his home several blocks away.

BERT W. SHAW, second rescuer up the ladder at the Ludwig fire. He did not testify at the trial but offered an affidavit in the appeal.

OTHERS MENTIONED

ACKERMAN, the "bridgeman" whom Albin saw talking to his wife the night before her murder.

DAY ARMSTRONG, an accused murderer whose case had similarities to Albin Ludwig's.

WILLIAM EUGENE COOK, whose unrelated murder trial was postponed at the same time Albin's was.

SYLVESTER HARTMAN rented a barn from Albin Ludwig. The barn was destroyed in a fire.

FRANK LEROY, a widower who employed Jessie Henderson as a servant. Cecilia was a boarder.

GOVERNOR WARREN T. MCCRAY commuted Ludwig's sentence from life to a sentence of sixteen years to life.

"SMOKE" MEINEN, a boarder in the Ludwig home whom Albin caught in a closet with Cecilia, was also referred to as "Spot" Miner.

LOUIS "KING" PATE, an employee of the Monument Saloon when Gustave owned it.

REV. H. B. TOWNSEND employed Cecilia as a domestic when she married Albin Ludwig.

NOAH YODER negotiated but failed to buy the Monument Saloon from Albin Ludwig.

APPENDIX A (THOSE NOT PREVIOUSLY MENTIONED, IN ORDER OF APPEARANCE)

E. C. BORNEMAN, an owner of Borneman & Sons, a hardware store Gustave Ludwig was accused of burglarizing.

MAX SHUMAN/SCHUMAN, whose father was Gustave's cousin. Max was charged with stealing property from his employer in Chicago and shipping it to Gustave under the pseudonym "Frank Boss."

FRANK LEADER, former sheriff of Elkhart County, who helped arrest Gustave.

CAPT. JACK NORTHRUP, Elkhart policeman who helped arrest Gustave.

MARSHAL CHRISTMAN, from Goshen, who helped arrest Gustave.

G. B. PLOWMAN, Chicago officer who brought the arrested Shuman back to Elkhart.

INSPECTOR SCHULER, investigator for American Express Co.

OSCAR JAY, Elkhart County prosecutor.

DAN ROTH, Elkhart fireman who escorted Gustave Ludwig to prison.

E. L. ARNOLD, Gustave's attorney.

EUGENE HOLDEMAN, Elkhart County coroner.

APPENDIX B (THOSE NOT PREVIOUSLY MENTIONED, IN ORDER OF APPEARANCE)

CHARLES F. HOLLER, a South Bend attorney who asked that Joseph Talbot be investigated. Talbot previously charged Holler in connection with his handling of a divorce case.

FRED C. GABRIEL, a South Bend attorney who was charged in the same case as Holler.

MRS. PERRY DICKSON, a Buffalo, New York, woman who applied for divorce.

JOHN W. TALBOT, Joseph Talbot's brother and law partner.

HARRY B. TUTHILL, a special judge from Michigan City who initially handled the case against Talbot.

CYRUS E. PATTEE, a Republican who defeated Joseph Talbot for re-election as St. Joseph County state's attorney in 1908.

HARRY B. WAIR, attorney for the committee that brought disbarment charges against Joseph Talbot.

"YOCK" ALLISON, a one-time prison escapee whom Joseph Talbot was accused of assisting. Allison refused to testify in the case against Talbot.

ANTHONY DEAHL, a special judge from Goshen who took over the disbarment case after it was moved to Elkhart County.

FRANCIS E. LAMBERT, an attorney for the prosecution in the disbarment case.

WILLIAM SHIMP, a St. Joseph County jury commissioner who was prevented from testifying that the Talbots had attempted to pack the jury.

LEONA MASON, a former client and lover of John Talbot. She was acquitted of shooting at Talbot.

CHARLES A. DAVEY, Leona Mason's defense attorney.

NORMAN R. DONATHEN charged in 1909 that Joseph Talbot arrested him and forced him into a marriage with GOLDY BARKMAN.

W. B. WRIGHT, justice of the peace who married Donathen and Barkman.

LENA A. JOSLIN, a Mishawaka woman who sued Leona Mason's husband for breach-of-promise.

Prologue

CECILIA HENDERSON was a battered wife—in both her marriages.

In her divorce complaint, she accused her first husband of striking her on the shoulder with a piece of steel, then, when the blow didn't knock her down, "he followed it up with blows with his hands and knocked her down upon the couch."[1]

On another occasion, Cecilia's husband held a revolver near her head and threatened to kill her. Another time, he beat her with his fist. Still another time, according to the divorce complaint, her husband struck her over the head with a piece of stovepipe. That was the only time Cecilia retaliated, hitting her husband with a broom.

The divorce was granted.

Her second marriage was worse. That husband killed her—brutally, savagely in a murder described in the *La Porte Argus-Bulletin* as "without a parallel in northern Indiana."[2]

The prosecution claimed Cecilia's husband knocked her unconscious with a wooden potato masher before setting her on fire. The defense claimed Cecilia attacked her husband with the potato masher, and he responded with violence.

Cecilia Henderson was not a perfect wife. Though she denied it, she had a reputation for "gadding about," for flirting with other men, maybe going further than flirting. She and her second husband quarreled about her behavior. The last quarrel ended with her death, a murder that a century later has been forgotten despite its notoriety at the time.

Cecilia Henderson was my great-grandmother. This is her story.

CHAPTER 1

The Last Night

IT WAS MONDAY EVENING, and the two sisters went out for a walk as they had many times growing up in rural Kingsbury, Indiana.[1]

They no longer were children, and their worlds no longer were trouble-free. Cecilia Henderson Hornburg Ludwig had turned thirty that summer. Her first marriage had ended badly, and her second marriage, to a man seven years her senior, was disintegrating day by day. Her first child, a fourteen-year-old boy conceived when she was fifteen, lived with his father. The second child, an eleven-year-old girl, divided her time between her grandparents' home back in Kingsbury and the troubled home in Mishawaka, Indiana, where the quarrels between Cecilia and husband Albin were escalating. They didn't have any children together, and, considering the state of their marriage, that was good.

Sister Jean Henderson Ellsworth was four years younger. She had married a local Kingsbury boy whose family owned more land than anyone in town, and the young couple had moved to California, then Nevada, in search of their own fortune.[2] Jean, too, had two children, a nine-year-old girl and a boy who was not quite seven. Jean, too, had a troubled marriage, though unlike her big sister, this was her first. Jean and the children had left husband and father Ora in Nevada earlier in the year, spending much of the summer, including the past three weeks, with Cecilia and Albin.

Divorce was on the horizon for both women.

So was a murder that would end the life of one of them.

September 24, 1906, was a warm evening in Mishawaka as the sisters set off walking around 6:45 P.M. from the Ludwig home on East Marion Street, a short distance from Bridge Street, the main north to south thoroughfare.[3] The Ludwigs were making payments on a two-story frame home with a covered porch in front and enough space upstairs for extended stays by family, like the Ellsworths, or even a boarder. The lots on East Marion were narrow—close to neighbors—but deep, with small front yards facing Marion Street and backyards big enough for summer kitchens, separate buildings that were used for cooking in hot weather to keep the main house cooler. An alley ran east to west behind the homes, with Grand Trunk Western Railway tracks on the north side of the alley. The passenger depot conveniently was just a block away at Bridge Street, which was handy for visits by Cecilia's mother from Kingsbury, twenty-nine miles to the southwest by rail.[4]

Mishawaka was a growing city with a population in the process of doubling from the 5,560 of 1900 to the 11,886 of 1910. Businesses and homes were being built on both sides of the St. Joseph River, which flowed west through the middle of town before turning northwest in nearby South Bend and eventually emptying into Lake Michigan.

"Mishawaka is beautifully situated on the St. Joseph river, one of the most picturesque streams in the world, in the center of a fertile valley, 90 miles east of Chicago," boasted A History of St. Joseph County, Indiana, published in 1907. "It is one of the most healthful and most charming places of residence. It has every modern convenience. While it is a manufacturing city with several of the largest plants of their kind in the world it has retained that simplicity which makes life worth living."[5]

Albin worked at the Mishawaka Woolen Manufacturing Company, with roots that dated to about 1838 when a woolen mill was established. By 1906, it was making rubber boots and shoes and was known to locals simply as "the rubber works."[6]

Although some stores were closer, the Ludwig home was only eight-tenths of a mile—about a fifteen-minute walk—from Mishawaka's main business district on the south side of the river, the sisters' eventual destination that Monday evening.[7]

The stroll was their second of the day. Cecilia and Jean had spent the afternoon shopping—Cecilia wanted a pair of shoes—and they had been

home only about an hour, just long enough for supper, before heading
out again. Their first destination was A. B. Graham's North Side Drug
Store on the southwest corner of Bridge and Joseph Streets, a six-and-
a-half-block walk. Earlier, Cecilia had asked her husband to clean out
a medicine bottle for her to take to the drugstore to fill with iodine and
glycerine, a medicine she applied to her feet. He had done so. She handed
the bottle to one of the clerks, and the clerk filled it and handed it back.

What the sisters did not know was that Albin was watching from
across the street. He later would claim that he had left home around 7:00
P.M., fifteen minutes after the women, in search of his dog, a valuable
black-and-tan hound. He figured the hound was within a few blocks.
But he picked up the trail of his wife and her sister instead of the dog as
they entered the drugstore. He watched them through the window from
across the street while they were inside.

When the women left the store, Albin followed them south across
the river, another five- to ten-minute walk, to the corner of Second and
Main, sometimes called the "Four Corners," considered Mishawaka's
downtown. The sisters' path had taken them past a boardinghouse operated by Mrs. Anna Herzog at 220 North Main Street. Living upstairs
was Fred Young, also a Kingsbury native, who had been a frequent visitor at the Ludwig home in recent weeks. Albin suspected that something
was going on between Young and one of the women. And he feared it
was Cecilia.

It was inappropriate for women to call on a man at a boardinghouse,
but fate handed them a solution as they stood on the northwest corner
of the busy intersection. Jean Ellsworth saw a man she knew was a
friend of Young, a man with the last name of Ackerman. They began a
conversation. Albin, watching from near the southeast corner outside
the Milburn House, a hotel, fumed at the sight of his wife talking to the
man.[8] He stopped James Anderson, a patrolman with the Mishawaka
Police Department, and, pointing, asked if he knew the two women
across the street. "I told him I did not, and he asked me to find out who
they were," Anderson would say later.

Anderson walked closer, then confirmed to Ludwig that it was his
wife and sister-in-law, whom the policeman knew from seeing them on
the street together previously. Albin complained that the women had
wanted him to stay home with Jean's children while they went out, but

he followed them instead—and found them talking to a man. He told Anderson that he wanted him to see what he saw.

Ludwig was angry. "I am going to put a stop to that and if anything happens, I want you to remember it," he told Anderson.

Cecilia and Jean either didn't know Albin was spying on them or didn't care. The women, with Ackerman in tow, walked back up Main Street to the boardinghouse, where Jean asked Ackerman to have the landlady alert Young that they were waiting outside to see him. Later, Young, a widower for more than two years, referred to Jean, whom he knew was married, as "a young friend" and said that he had known the sisters about twenty-three years. By now it was after 8:00 P.M., dusk, more than an hour after the sisters had left the home on East Marion Street.

As an adult, Young was known to the sisters and Albin Ludwig. The entire family, including Jean's two children, was out for a Sunday walk six weeks to two months earlier. As they passed Mrs. Herzog's boardinghouse that day, the sisters recognized their childhood friend Fred Young. After that chance encounter, Young called at the Ludwig home at least a half-dozen times—maybe as many as a dozen. Sometimes he and Jean went out for a stroll, sometimes with her children, sometimes not. Sometimes the visits were on a Sunday, including just the day before. Sometimes they were in the evening. But never, Young would claim later, did he go out with Cecilia Ludwig.

On this Monday night, Jean and Cecilia chatted with Young on the sidewalk outside the boardinghouse, as close together as three people could stand and talk.

At some point, a half-brick was thrown between two buildings, striking Cecilia, who was standing closest to the street on the sidewalk, on the hip. Young heard the brick strike her but didn't see who threw it. Cecilia complained of pain, but she was able to walk home without a limp. Later, when confronted, Ludwig denied he had thrown the brick.

Young stepped back inside his boardinghouse to get his hat, and the three—Cecilia, Jean, and Fred, two married women and an unmarried man—started walking back north in the fading light toward the Ludwig home. Ackerman, whom Albin later would refer to as the "bridgeman," already had gone on his way.

Albin, angry and jealous, was there when they arrived. "I started off [toward home] before they quit talking," he would remember later. More anger, more jealousy would surface as the evening wore on.

Back on East Marion Street, Jean, Fred, and Cecilia went looking for Jean's children, Lucy and Charles, who, left unattended, were not in the Ludwig yard. Albin followed behind. They found the children playing down the street in a neighbor's yard. The youngsters were gathered up and sent home.

The heated conversation that ensued when they went inside was reconstructed from testimony later given by Ludwig and Young:

"Where have you been?" Ludwig said accusingly to the women, but mostly to Cecilia.

"Over to town," Cecilia responded, which was where she said she was going, to the drugstore.

Albin accused her of going farther than the drugstore, that the sisters had gone across the river to Second Street. "Who was the man you were talking to at the corner of Second and Main?" Albin demanded.

Cecilia denied talking to anyone.

Albin repeated his accusation. "You may as well be honest and tell, and I won't think nothing about it."

"You are a damned liar!" Cecilia said, her voice raised. Albin would remember later that Jean uttered the same profanity. Perhaps they said it simultaneously. Cecilia continued to deny she had talked to any man.

"Well, I have got plenty of proofs. Lots of men on the corner saw you. Mr. Anderson [the patrolman] saw you."

Perhaps because it had been growing dark on Second Street—Anderson had to cross the street to identify the women—but more likely because Albin didn't want to reveal what he already knew, he seemed less upset that his wife and her sister had been chatting with Young than he did about them talking to Ackerman, the man who helped notify Young of their presence at his boardinghouse.

Albin's greeting to Young was cordial when the frequent visitor of late entered the house—"Hello, Fred!"—and Young wasn't dragged into the quarrel, which lasted off and on the rest of the evening, at least until after 11:00 P.M. Most of that time the four adults sat in the sitting room, Albin and Cecilia verbally sparring with each other.

Cecilia's behavior was on trial, and Albin was judge and jury. Jean was an accessory, and Fred was a witness who largely kept his mouth shut.

"You're not going to run around with a bridgeman!" Albin scolded Cecilia, as Young remembered. Ludwig was referring to Ackerman. Young said later that Ackerman, around twenty-two or twenty-three, worked at the Mishawaka bridge over the St. Joseph River. Ludwig suspected that Ackerman had been out "a number of afternoons" with Cecilia while he was at work. Young didn't think so.

"I don't know that he met Mrs. Ludwig before," Young recalled, "but apparently from what I heard afterwards that was the first time he had met her. He had met Mrs. Ellsworth before."

Cecilia accused Albin of throwing the brick that struck her that evening.

"He said it was not him; he did not know anything about it," Young recalled.

At some point that evening, Albin went outside to talk to neighbor Fred Metzler, who lived next door to the east. Albin told him that Cecilia had accused him and Metzler of being "over town"—a common term for going to the business district—together the previous night, a Sunday. Albin fetched Cecilia to hear Metzler's denial. The argument was so loud that Emma Reifsneider, living southeast across the street, could hear much of it.

"Was I over town with you, Fred, last night?" Albin asked Metzler.

"No," Metzler replied.

"You are a God-damned liar," Cecilia said to Metzler.[9]

During another break between quarreling, around 9:00 P.M., Albin visited other neighbors, Marcellus and Veronica Gaze, entering the back door to the kitchen, where they both were. "We talked about nothing else except his trouble with his wife," Marcellus would say later. "He spoke something about a man being with his wife the night before. That would have been Sunday night. . . . I said to him if I were in his place I would pick up and leave. I said that because I knew they had had so much trouble before. I knew what the trouble was about. He said something to the effect that he loved his wife and could not pick up and leave. He said something to the effect that he would put an end to it, or would stop it."

Albin returned home. After an hour and a half of off-and-on arguing, with cursing by both, there was talk of separation.

Young recalled: "Mrs. Ludwig said that he just became so mean to her and accused her of so many things, that she would not try—that tomorrow she would pack her bags and leave, that she could not comb her hair and change her clothes unless he accused her of expecting someone."

Albin replied that she should not take a thing out of the house until the court allowed her. "He said before she would leave he would burn them up; and he said she could go first," Young recalled.

Divorce wasn't mentioned, but it was obvious from the comment that Albin intended to separate from Cecilia. And it was obvious that Cecilia and Jean both intended to leave the next day—Jean and the children back to either a rooming house in South Bend or her parents' farm near Kingsbury. "Mrs. Ludwig did not say where she was going," Young said.

"Well, if we cannot make it, that will be the best way," Albin recalled replying.

It was an uncomfortable yet enthralling evening for Young, who obviously was attracted to Jean and thus wasn't a party to the Ludwigs' marital squabble. He tried to leave two or three times, but Albin said it wasn't necessary. "Mr. Ludwig assured me he had nothing against me."

Sometime between 11:00 P.M. and midnight, Young finally got away. Albin went to bed "as quick as he left the room." Neighbor Metzler, getting up to give his little boy a drink, heard Cecilia's and Jean's voices as late as midnight.

As for the dog that Albin claimed he had been looking for, Fred Metzler found him on East Lawrence Street, three blocks south.

The next spring, while testifying at Albin's trial, Young remembered Ludwig stating that night that "everything would be settled on the morrow."

Did he mean that tomorrow, Tuesday, September 25, 1906, the Ludwigs would separate—or that tomorrow Cecilia would die?

CHAPTER 2

The Families

THE SISTERS WHO PROVOKED Albin Ludwig by walking to downtown Mishawaka and meeting up with men that Monday night had come a long way from their birthplace of Scotland.

Cecilia and Jean were two of four daughters and a son born to James and Christina Henderson. Cecilia Bettie Johnson Henderson, nicknamed Celia, was the second oldest, born July 31, 1876, less than two years after older sister Maggie. Jean was the youngest daughter, born November 25, 1880, two years after sister Jessie. Son Thomas was born in 1883 after the Hendersons arrived in America.[1]

Before marrying James, Christina Henderson had given birth to a daughter in 1863 or 1864, also named Christina. The father, a man named Shaw, died shortly before the baby's birth.[2] Although older than the other children, daughter Christina would settle near the family in Indiana and be known to her nephews and nieces as "Aunt Tina."[3]

Life was difficult in mid-nineteenth-century Scotland. Life for James Henderson and his growing family probably was no exception. A potato blight struck the Scottish Highlands in the 1840s, then spread to the Lowlands. The rapid growth of urban areas caused ill health, including repeated cholera epidemics.[4] Poverty was widespread.

Forty-year-old James Henderson, like many of his countrymen, sought a better life for his family in America. He left Scotland in 1881, arriving in the port of Boston around April 13.[5]

"The father came first," one of his great-granddaughters said in 2017. "The mother came a year later with the children."[6]

In 1964, daughter Jessie gave an account of the voyage to her grandson, Kent A. Berridge, who retold the story in 2017:

> She said her father came from royalty, and was blessed with some money, so he invested in property in Chicago. Well, when they arrived in Chicago he found that he had been duped, as the legal description was somewhere out in Lake Michigan. They then hired a flat boat to carry their belongings to Kingsbury, Indiana. That trip took them down the Illinois River to its confluence with the Kankakee River, then up the Kankakee to Kingsbury. She said she was only five years old and had very little recollection [of the] ocean voyage and the river voyage.[7]

The family lived long enough in Chicago for James Henderson to get a job. His grandson Roy Wheeler told his own daughter, Paula Steiner, the story of a lifelong injury Grandpa Henderson suffered driving a beer wagon. "One day the horse bolted, his leg was caught in the spoke and was injured pretty badly," Steiner wrote. "Dad said he walked with a limp and had an open wound from that time until just a few weeks before he died, when the wound suddenly healed."[8]

Except for its proximity to Chicago, why James Henderson chose to settle in rural Kingsbury, in La Porte County, Indiana, is unknown. However, one story repeated by the family is that after his injury, James was hired as a groundskeeper for a wealthy man in Indiana, prompting the move.[9]

The Hendersons initially located south of Kingsbury in Union Township. In the first decade of the 1900s, the family moved to a farm halfway between Kingsbury and La Porte. Census records list James as a farm laborer. If the Hendersons owned their own farm, it wasn't big enough to show up on plat maps of the era.[10]

The children enjoyed their new lives in Indiana. Cecilia may have enjoyed herself too much.

Because at age fifteen, she was unwed and pregnant.

THE FATHER WAS twenty-year-old Charles "Charley" Henry Hornburg, who married Cecilia on June 9, 1892.[11] The pregnant bride was seven weeks and three days shy of her sixteenth birthday on her wedding day. Two and a half months later, on August 21, her first child, William Charles "Willie" Hornburg, the author's grandfather, was born. It is assumed that Charley was the father since he took custody of the boy after the divorce. A second child, Lyle Ellen, was born November 20, 1894.

It's not known how Charley and Cecilia met, but both lived in La Porte County. Obviously they became acquainted somehow, somewhere in that county at least nine months before Willie's birth.

The marriage broke up seven months after their daughter's birth, according to Cecilia's court filing. The complaint said Cecilia moved out of the house around July 12, 1895, "refusing to longer cohabit with him as his wife, for the reason that the defendant has been guilty of cruel and inhuman treatment of the plaintiff."[12]

Cecilia asked for custody of her young daughter, Lyle Ellen, "being the youngest child, and of such tender years that it is necessary it should receive such attention as the defendant would be unable to provide." She also asked for "the privilege from time to time of visiting the other child, William Charles." The three-year-old already was living with his father.[13]

No record of testimony survives, but a trial was held February 27, 1896. We don't know if Charley attempted to justify his behavior; we don't know if Cecilia had prompted Charley's behavior, as wrong as it was, by actions of her own. But after hearing the evidence, the judge declared Cecilia's allegations to be true and dissolved the marriage. Cecilia was awarded "the care, custody, education and maintenance of Lyle Ellen Hornburg, infant child of said parties."[14]

At best, Cecilia would be a part-time mother to Lyle. The 1900 census shows five-year-old Lyle living with her grandparents and the Hendersons' youngest son, seventeen-year-old Thomas, Lyle's uncle, in Union Township, Indiana. Lyle lived only occasionally with her mother and stepfather during Cecilia's short, tragic marriage to Albin Ludwig.

"My great-grandmother would not talk about any of her family," one of Lyle's descendants recalled. "On occasion I got a little information. When asked about her father she just said he [Charley Hornburg] was a bad apple."[15]

By November 12, 1896, Charley was remarried to Eva D. Wickering in Grand Rapids, Michigan. Willie Hornburg lived with them.[16]

LIKE HER FIRST HUSBAND, Cecilia's second husband was German. Unlike Charley Hornburg, who was born in Indiana to parents born in Germany, Albin Richard Ludwig was born in Germany and lived there the first fifteen years of his life.

Albin was born on August 14, 1869, to Heinrich Wilhelm Jacob Ludwig and the former Eva Ida Schuman.[17] (The father had a brother named Heinrich Christoph, so he used Wilhelm as his first name.) The family lived in Tottelstadt, now in the German state of Thüringen but then in the duchy of Sachsen-Coburg und Gotha.[18]

The Ludwigs were Lutherans. And they were poor.[19]

Albin was educated for seven years in German schools before the family, including his brother Gustave, one year and five months older, boarded the German steamship *Moravia*, departing Hamburg for New York on September 17, 1884.[20]

It was the time of the "second major wave of German-speaking people entering the country," as described by historian Giles R. Hoyt. More than 1.4 million German-speaking immigrants came to the United States between 1880 and 1889, Hoyt wrote, representing 27.5 percent of all immigrants in that decade.[21]

The specific reasons the Ludwig family left their homeland are unknown, but an essay by Keith J. Bell indicates that "the Industrial Revolution began transforming the economies of the many German states from agricultural to manufacturing bases, making it more difficult for farmers to prosper. The lure of apparently unlimited farmland in North America, coupled with news from successful immigrants to provide a powerful lure to emigrate."[22] Wilhelm Ludwig would farm in America.

The passenger steamer *Moravia*, part of the Hamburg America Line, arrived in New York on September 30, thirteen days after departure, and the Ludwig family headed to Indiana, where Germans were the largest immigrant group.[23]

They settled in Elkhart, a natural decision. Brother Louis Ludwig had arrived in northern Indiana from Germany in 1858, settling in Mishawaka, and, in an example of chain migration, four brothers would follow.[24] One of them, Karl Christoph "Charles" Ludwig, already lived in Elkhart. The *Elkhart Daily Review* reported on Monday, October 6, 1884, that "Mr. Ludwig, brother of Chas. Ludwig, a well-known former [*sic*, probably farmer] living north of the city, arrived here from Germany Saturday, and will locate." Although no first name is given, it's likely that Wilhelm Ludwig arrived in Elkhart by train on Saturday, October 4, four days after the family landed in New York City.

Elkhart is about 110 miles southeast of Chicago and eleven miles due east of Mishawaka. Elkhart County is in the upper tier of Indiana counties, hugging the Michigan state line along with St. Joseph County to the west and La Porte County farther west. In the years ahead, the three counties would link the Ludwig and Henderson families in happiness and sorrow.

Wilhelm, a rugged man, quickly Americanized his first name to William, but his life in America would last only thirteen years. The family lived in town on Harrison Street at the corner of Oakland Avenue, in a home the *Elkhart Daily Review* later would describe as "a peculiar-looking residence" because of its unfinished state.[25]

Though he farmed for a livelihood, it wasn't on his own land. Around noon on July 9, 1897, on a day when the temperature would reach a scorching 100°F, fifty-eight-year-old Wilhelm was found dead in the center of a cornfield on the farm of John Anderson, a mile south of Elkhart. "He left home early Friday morning in his usual health and had no complaint except of the excessive heat," the *Goshen Democrat* reported. "When found the man's back was literally cooked by the sun and the work of decomposition had begun."[26]

Coroner M. K. Kreider determined that death resulted from sunstroke.[27]

Son Albin was mentioned occasionally in the Elkhart newspapers years before his wife's murder.

"Ticket No. 87 was held by Albin Ludwig, of North Indiana street, who received the ten dollar prize given by J. L. Wolf, last Monday evening," the *Daily Review* reported among its "Local Brevities" on November 15, 1889. J. L. Wolf, who advertised that he had "the largest stock of boots and shoes in the county," would promote the twenty-year-old Ludwig's prize for several days in his ads.

Like his father, Albin farmed when young. Later, he worked as a teamster, managing the team of horses that hauled a wagon of cargo for the city of Elkhart.[28]

Ludwig began appearing more regularly in the newspapers after he was granted a liquor license in November 1900, a year before his marriage to Cecilia.[29]

Albin became the owner of the Monument Saloon, prominently located downtown at 21 South Main Street.[30] The saloon was named after a Civil War monument in the middle of the intersection of Main and Tyler Streets, almost six blocks south of Ludwig's business.

Elkhart had twenty-seven churches and fewer than twenty-five saloons in a population of seventeen thousand, a ratio that the 1904–5 *Elkhart City Directory* considered respectable and proudly credited to "good average morals." Still, twenty-five saloons were a lot of competition for a thirty-one-year-old immigrant who never had operated a business before.

By the time Albin Ludwig became a saloonkeeper, all of Main Street downtown was paved with bricks, a project undertaken in 1898. Streetcar tracks ran in the middle of the street, as Elkhart in 1889 had been the second city in the world to have an electric streetcar system. Photos from the era show a bustling downtown with pedestrians, horse-drawn buggies, streetcars, and the earliest horseless carriages. Most carriages, buggies, wagons, and harnesses probably came from the Elkhart Carriage & Harness Manufacturing Company.[31]

Life as a saloonkeeper changed Albin's personality, at least according to the *Elkhart Daily Review,* which reported the day after his wife's murder that embarking in the saloon business was when "his troubles began—both with his relatives and his creditors. He was arrested several times for violations of the liquor law. His quiet, more or less amiable disposition underwent a change, and he was not slow to make unkind accusations against his people and his former friends."[32]

A 1901 incident was recounted a hundred years later in the *Elkhart Truth:* "A disturbance in the Monument saloon was investigated Saturday evening by Sgt. Robbles, who discovered that one of the proprietors had an altercation with a customer, but no damage had been done."[33]

In a 1903 incident: "Albin Ludwig, the saloonman, on Thursday filed an affidavit charging Louis ['King'] Pate with embezzling $50, alleging that he gave Pate a fifty-dollar bill to get changed and [Pate] never returned with it. It is understood that Pate really got the bill changed at the Bank saloon and that he has gone to Toledo. Ludwig was himself arrested this forenoon on mandate, having failed to pay an assessment of $34 for selling liquor to a minor."[34]

How he met his future bride while living the life of a "saloonman" is a matter of conjecture. The 1900 federal census lists twenty-three-year-old Cecilia Henderson, using her maiden name, as a boarder in the home of Frank Leroy, a widower, two counties west of Elkhart in Coolspring Township, La Porte County. Her twenty-one-year-old sister, Jessie, was a servant for the farm family. But the *Daily Review* said the divorced Cecilia Henderson Hornburg was working as a domestic for Rev. H. B. Townsend in Elkhart at the time of the 1901 marriage.[35]

Perhaps Cecilia answered an ad that appeared in the January 3, 1900, *Elkhart Daily Review:* "The Rev. H. B. Townsend desires to rent his modern and furnished house for a time during his absence to Europe to a desirable party. Apply at house."

Perhaps Cecilia, bored with living in rural La Porte County where she grew up, and hoping to find a new husband, rented the Townsend home on Pigeon Street (now Lexington Avenue). Although it's unlikely a young woman of that era would hang out at the Monument Saloon, which was within walking distance, perhaps she met Albin on the sidewalk or while both were at a more "proper" location for women. Maybe even at church, since Albin considered himself "a good church worker."[36]

"I became acquainted with my wife in February 1901," Albin would write six years later, without explaining the circumstances. "It was real love with me. My wife [had] been married before, being married two years to her first husband [and when] she left him she had 2 children. She [had] been 15 years old when she married her first husband and 25 when she married me. [At the time of our marriage] she dit [*sic*] not have any money or many clothes. I did not care about it. I married her only for love. I loved her until her death."[37]

Physically, they were a mismatched couple. Cecilia was tall like her father, who was six feet seven. She was more than three inches taller than Albin, who was five feet six and five-eighths inches tall when he entered prison.[38]

The marriage took place November 1, 1901, twenty-five miles north of Elkhart in Cassopolis, Michigan.[39]

It would end less than five years later with Cecilia's murder.

CHAPTER 3

Marriage and Mishawaka

THE NEWLYWEDS MOVED in with Albin's mother, Eva, his brother, Gustave—Gus to his family—and Gus's wife, Minnie, in a house Eva Ludwig owned at 1105 Harrison in Elkhart. The arrangement would last only one year.[1]

"At the end of the year I was coming home from church one Sunday, my mother told me my wife had struck her," Albin recalled in 1907. "I spoke to her about it and she laft [laughed it off]. About ten days after it my wife send for me to come home at once. When I got home she told me she had struck my brother's wife with a stone. The next day my mother told me to get a house for myself."[2]

Albin's recollection in 1907 was that at the point Eva Ludwig kicked Albin and Cecilia out of her house, they moved immediately to Mishawaka. But Albin still owned the Monument Saloon, so he couldn't leave town.

The 1903 *Elkhart City Directory* lists the couple living at 1015 South Second in Elkhart. The lot was vacant in 2016. A neighbor described the home that had sat there as a big, two-story house that was torn down about twenty years earlier.[3]

By late 1902, after only two years, Albin was tiring of the saloon business. The December 6 *Elkhart Truth* reported that Ludwig was negotiating to sell the saloon to Noah Yoder, who had resigned recently from the police force. But the deal apparently fell through. Soon, instead of running a tavern, Yoder was a motorman for the local streetcar company.[4]

Two months later Ludwig had a bigger problem. A big barn he owned on Oakland Avenue, just around the corner from his mother's house on Harrison, burned in a suspicious post-midnight fire. The nearest fire hydrant was more than two blocks away, which meant firefighters had to use so much hose that only one stream of water could be directed on the blaze. Firefighters devoted most of their efforts to saving the old English Lutheran Church, across the alley to the south, then owned by Albin's brother Gus.[5]

Sylvester Hartman, who lived east of Oakland on Harrison, rented the barn. That afternoon's *Elkhart Daily Review* reported that Hartman "lost a horse, a cow, a calf, a rubber tired and steel tired buggy, harness, hay, feed and other articles." The newspaper said the barn was worth between $50 and $100 and was partially insured. The contents were valued at about $350 and were not insured. The horse was a Hambletonian, worth $150; the buggy was valued at $65. The cow and calf had been nearly sold for $35 to a man "who was to come this morning to complete the deal."

The newspaper continued: "Mr. Hartman says he was at the barn at 6 P.M. to feed the stock, but can throw no light on the origin of the fire. Some who were early on the scene say they smelled oil, and the police are investigating, especially as threats to burn the building had been made."

The insurance settlement was quick. The March 4 *Elkhart Weekly Review* reported that an adjustor was in town on February 27 "and paid in full the $200 policy which Albin Ludwig carried on his recently destroyed barn. A carpenter's estimate of the cost of restoring the barn was $271."

Meanwhile, tension was brewing between brothers Albin and Gus. After Cecilia's murder three years in the future, the *Elkhart Daily Review* reported that Albin "frequently displayed a vicious temperament in the past few years, and that when he was angry with his brother over the division of the estate of their father, he would tramp around the brother's residence night after night, flourishing a revolver and threatening dire crimes."[6] In a separate story after the murder, the *Daily Review* reported that Albin's share of his father's estate "and what he had acquired as a hard-working teamster was 'cleaned up' in his venture in the saloon business here," the implication being that Albin had gone broke as a saloonkeeper.[7]

Tension also was brewing in the Ludwigs' marriage. While still living in Elkhart, Cecilia retained the Hile and Baker law firm to file for divorce. After her death, attorney W. B. Hile revealed the grounds for her case: Albin "had a ferocious disposition. If angered he would become almost insane." The case was prepared but not filed after Cecilia consulted with her mother about the advisability of divorce, which would have been her second.[8]

Sometime during the spring or summer of 1903, with the saloon either sold or shuttered, Albin and Cecilia moved eleven miles west to fast-growing Mishawaka, distancing themselves from Albin's family in Elkhart and hoping for a fresh start.

The Ludwigs bought a home on the north side of East Marion Street at the north edge of Mishawaka. Today, it's a quiet neighborhood of well-kept single-family homes, even quieter since direct access from Main Street was cut off with completion of a railroad underpass in 2009.[9] And it likely was a quiet neighborhood when the Ludwigs moved into their home in 1903. The house was one of only five built at that point on the north side of the street in their block. None had been built yet on the south side of the street.[10] As late as 1923, the railroad tracks behind the homes on Marion Street were the northern edge of Mishawaka's development.[11]

The Ludwig home, like most on Marion Street, had seven small rooms, most of which would become well known to newspaper readers and trial jurors following Cecilia's death. There was a porch in front and a summer kitchen with a gasoline stove at the rear. The street door opened into a narrow hall. At the outward or east side of this hall was a stairway leading upstairs. The lower step was far enough from the street door to permit the door to miss it about six inches when swung wide. On the left side going up was a stair rail of pine, with natural finish.[12]

At the left of the hall was a door opening into the downstairs front room. At the rear—the north end—of the hall was a door opening into the dining room. West of the dining room and north of the front room was a small sitting room. There was an open way between the dining and sitting rooms. The sitting room was furnished with a lounge and chairs.

The front room upstairs—the second-story bedroom in the front of the house also was referred to as the front room—was directly over the downstairs front room. The door to this room opened into a small hall at the head of the stairs. There was a windowless closet, about five feet wide, north and south, by about seven feet long, directly over the front part of the hall, with a door opening into the upstairs front room. There was a double window in the south end of this room, just over the porch roof looking onto the street. There also was a single window in this room looking to the west. This was the Ludwigs' bedroom. They furnished it with a bed, two or three chairs, and a dresser.

The closet off the upstairs bedroom would be the scene of Cecilia's murder three years later.

For those families on East Marion Street with children, the three-story Battell Elementary School on the next street south opened in 1900.[13] Cecilia's daughter Lyle Hornburg had a short walk to school during the times she lived in Mishawaka with the Ludwigs.

The Ludwigs had a short walk or bicycle ride to shop for necessities— a seven-minute walk to Milton Robbins's grocery store, nine minutes to A. B. Graham's north-of-the-river drugstore. When they crossed the St. Joseph River on Bridge Street (today's Main Street), a fifteen-minute walk, they found Mishawaka's main business district.[14]

Albin bought and furnished the house on the installment plan, paying $10 a month to John F. Gaylor, a local real estate broker who would repossess it after Cecilia's death.[15]

Mishawaka was booming, and Albin quickly found a job as a shoemaker with a leading employer, the Mishawaka Woolen Manufacturing Company, which had prospered after inventing the all-knit boot in 1886. By the time Ludwig joined the company, the product line had expanded to heavy-duty work boots, called "Lumbermens," and Ball-Band brand rubber shoes.[16]

Albin was not popular on the job. The *La Porte Daily Herald* reported after Cecilia's murder that Albin's "fellow employees declare he appeared to hate everyone—perhaps also himself."[17]

Part of the problem may have been financial. Albin likely had stopped making payments on a house in Elkhart. At a sheriff's sale on July 29, 1905, "Dr. I. W. Short bought Elkhart residence property to satisfy a judgment for $829.03 in the case of John Enders vs. Alvin R. Ludwig for $901." The defendant's first name was listed by the Americanized "Alvin," rather than the German "Albin," but that was common in the newspapers before and after Cecilia's murder.[18]

The Ludwigs' financial situation was dire enough that occasionally they had a boarder[19] to help pay the bills. That contributed to the growing strife in their marriage. Cecilia apparently had been seeing other men—including in their own home—and Albin was furious about it.

"Mr. Ludwig, it appears, was of a very jealous disposition and has been suspicious of his wife for some time," the *South Bend Tribune* reported shortly after the murder. "A week ago he paid a visit to The Tribune and desired an article written announcing that his wife had been out walking with two traveling men. He said the report was substantiated by neighbors. Mr. Ludwig seemed in a frenzy at the time."[20]

Albin wrote his own account of his deteriorating marriage in 1907, the year after the murder. The language in the written account is his—the language of a man raised in Germany, a man who learned English as a second language after arriving in America twenty-three years earlier:

I got work at the Rubber Works, and we got along well until the 15th of August 1903. My wife stayed in bed that morning. I went to work. About 7:15 I went home for my clock. I went to the bedroom and my wife was not there, but her clothes were there. I looked every place but she was not in sight. I looked everywhere for her and could not find her. So I went into the boarder's room and there she was. I got the boarder out in a hurry and told my wife I would see her at supper time and went back to work. When I got home for supper she was crying.

After supper I ask her upstairs, her little girl was there and I did not want her to get on to it. After we got upstairs she asked me to forgive her and I did. She was real good for about one year. Six months after it my neighbor told me the coffee and tea man was stopping at my house from 40 to 50 minutes each week. One night at supper I told her about it. She called me G.D. S of B. Struck me on the hand with the water pitcher and ran out. After [a] little she came back and told me she was sorry for it and she kiss me.

After this she went to South Bend three times a week and at [the] last every afternoon and if I say anything she call me all the low names that she could think of. In February 1906 a neighbor woman wrote to my wife's mother and told her to take the little girl home. The girl had to be on the street after school until about six o'clock. I would be at work and she be at South Bend, I told her she must give up going so much. One day she went and stayed two weeks at a friend of hers at South Bend. At the end of 2 weeks she came home sick and I took first class care of her. She was sick for 10 weeks. I worked every day and stayed up every night until 4 o'clock, then I would sleep from 4 to 5. I got a girl she stay with her while I was at work. I prayed night and day God should help her to get well and I called the Dr. at 1 and 2 in the night. Her mother came to see her and this is what she told her about me. "My husband is so good to me. No other man would do what he has done for me, it will take all my lifetime to make it right. I [would have] never got well if it hadn't been for him. I shall never go to South Bend [any more] unless he go with me" and she told the neighbors the same thing.[21]

But Albin was no saint, despite the saintly picture he painted in his own account of the marriage. Years later, Cecilia's daughter Lyle told a great-granddaughter of an occasion when Albin was beating Cecilia. Lyle, then only a child, grabbed a cast-iron pan and warned her stepfather, "Motherfucker, if you don't leave my mother alone, I will kill you." Albin stopped the beating.[22]

In his 1907 account, Albin brought up the arrival of Cecilia's sister Jean, who, in his eyes, became her accomplice.[23]

The first day of July 1906, her sister with two children came to my house to stay, her husband being out West which being their home. My wife told her they could stay for 10 Dollars a month, but she never paid anything. They stayed till the 25th of September. They would be going every day. I been getting my own breakfasts for the last year. She would stay in bed until 9 o'clock. September 22nd being Saturday I got home from work at one o'clock and found a note in the house saying I should come to South Bend and would find her at some of the stores. I went to South Bend but could not see her. About 5 o'clock I went home. She came about 6. She meet me at the back door and she called G-d-s- of a B- for about 10 minutes.

Sunday morning she told me a man was going to be there for dinner. I told her I don't think it is right for this man to come to see your sister. He had been coming 4 times a week. My wife had hold of a butcher knife and she said to me, "I'll cut your G-D head off if you don't get out." I went out. My neighbor was standing at the back door at the time. About an hour or so she called me in the house. She asked me to help her wash dishes.[24]

The relationship between Albin and Cecilia was nearing a boiling point.

CHAPTER 4

Murder

INDIAN SUMMER HAD COME to Mishawaka, Indiana. Tuesday, September 25, would be hot and dry, the temperature peaking in the mid-80s. The weather the previous week had been almost unbearably hot for an era without air-conditioning, but the weekend was considerably cooler. Now, warm weather was returning.[1]

Peter Young, who manned the Mishawaka office of the *South Bend Daily Times* at the corner of Main and Second Streets, filed his daily report midday for the newspaper's late-afternoon edition. Ironically, his office was at the same busy intersection where Albin Ludwig had stealthily watched his wife Cecilia and her sister Jean talk to a man named Ackerman the evening before.

It was a competitive newspaper market with the *Times,* the daily *South Bend Tribune,* and two weekly newspapers, Edward Jernegan's *Mishawaka Enterprise* and William P. O'Neill's *Mishawaka Democrat,* all vying for the town's news, ads, and readers.[2] Thanks to Young's hustle, the *Times* had enough "copy"—news—to fill its Mishawaka Department column, usually on page 2, every afternoon. Some days the Mishawaka Department filled most of a page.

Young's report that Tuesday included, from the night before, "the sad story of the death of little Lura, the four-year-old daughter of Mr. and Mrs. Samuel Wiess. The child's parents had been out of town and the girl was playing on the porch at the home of her grandparents, having a pair of scissors [with] which she had been cutting out pictures. She fell from the veranda and the points of the shears entered her tender throat, the jugular vein being severed and death ensuing within 15 minutes."[3]

Young also described an "amusing incident" involving a prominent citizen: "Some boys playing near the residence of Joseph de Lorenzi this morning tore a hole into the wire netting surrounding the cage in which Mr. de Lorenzi's fine squirrels are housed and one of the pretty fellows made his escape. It was for Joseph to take to the trail and seek the recapture of the agile animal with the bushy tail. . . . The chase finally led from Main to Fourth street and there some fellow placed his hat over the squirrel just as the latter was ascending a shade tree."

The Mishawaka Department that day included a report that "two gentlemen" from Wilmington, Pennsylvania, "have been in the city several days using their best efforts to induce Mishawaka industries to pull up stakes here and move to Wilmington. . . . It is known that one particularly flattering offer was made to one of the largest industries in this city, but the proposition was turned down because the officials and the stockholders of that company realize that when it comes to advantages for the manufacturer, freedom from strikes, ample power, etc., Mishawaka is 'there with the goods' as well as Wilmington or any other city in any other state."

Chief of Police Benjamin F. Jarrett announced in a notice: "All saloon-keepers are hereby given fair warning to keep their places of business closed all day Sunday and to close at night at 11 and not to open until 5 o'clock in the morning. Unless this warning is heeded the law will be strictly enforced."[4]

The Kirkwood market advertised a three-day sale, starting Thursday, including dill pickles for ten cents per dozen, sauerkraut for eight cents per quart, roast beef for eight cents a pound, boiling beef for five cents per pound, and young chicken for eighteen cents a pound.

As customary in a world without television, radio, or the internet, the *South Bend Daily Times* devoted its front page almost entirely to national news. The big national story on page 1 that Tuesday reported on what would become known as the Atlanta Race Riot of 1906, then in its fourth day:

Following the assassination of a county policeman and the fatal shooting of other white persons, 600 troops today surrounded a negro[5] settlement and arrested every negro carrying arms or who had arms in their person or in their homes. In all 300 were sent to jail. One negro who sought to break through the cordon of troopers was literally riddled with bullets.... Nearly every woman in this city has been provided with a revolver by her husband or relatives, and they will protect themselves.

The *South Bend Daily Times* would make room for another page 1 story, also about violence but much closer to home, before going to press late that afternoon.

TEMPERS WERE AS HOT as the temperature that day at the home of Albin and Cecilia Ludwig on East Marion Street in nearby Mishawaka. The long, late evening of quarreling between the couple, in the presence of Cecilia's sister Jean and childhood friend Fred Young, was fresh in everyone's minds. Would Cecilia still move out, as she had threatened the night before, signaling an end to the five-year-old marriage? If she tried to leave, how would Albin react? With words? With violence?

Albin usually arose for work sometime after 3:00 A.M., leaving for his job at the rubber plant. He arrived at the factory between 4:00 and 5:00 and stayed until noon. On this tense Tuesday morning, after what likely was a restless night for all, he stayed home from work, remaining in bed until about 9:00 A.M. Cecilia was sleeping in a separate bedroom with her sister; they had risen earlier. Cecilia's daughter Lyle, then eleven years old, had gone to school. She would be spared the horrific events of that afternoon. Jean's two children, younger than Lyle and not in school, would not.[6]

Cecilia and Jean made breakfast for themselves "but not for me," Albin recalled with sarcasm a year later; though, in a different account, Albin admitted that he usually got his own breakfast. He continued: "They did not speak to me. After I found out there was no breakfast for me I went in the front room and read the paper."

Jean went upstairs to pack her clothes. Regardless of what Cecilia did, she and her two children were leaving the hostile atmosphere of the Ludwig home. Downstairs, Cecilia told Albin that she would leave that day, too, if she had a trunk for her clothes. Albin replied, "I will give you mine if you want one, but you are welcome to stay if you want to." But Cecilia's mind was made up. She was leaving—but not without what she thought was due her.

"After I gave her the trunk, she wanted all the property," Albin recalled at his trial. "She said she would have it all or none. I told her then that I wanted to talk in peace to her—that if she wanted to go like she had been doing for two weeks," referring to the time she stayed in South Bend for two weeks, "that I would keep up the property and she was welcome to come back. If not, I would give up the property, that is, not make any more payments."

Cecilia told her husband she was leaving for good. "Very well, I will give up the property," Albin replied, knowing that he would lose the house and its furnishings if he stopped the monthly payments.

(Albin gave a different, less cordial account of that morning's property discussion in a statement he wrote upon entering prison. In that statement, he said, "my wife told me she was going to have everything we had. I told her I [would] give her one-half of everything. She said she would burn them before she took half.")

Albin resumed reading the newspaper. Cecilia joined Jean upstairs to pack.

"After a while they came down and started to get dinner," the noon meal, Albin said. "They had a long talk in the summer kitchen and were talking real low."

Cecilia asked Albin to fetch gasoline for the stove so she could boil meat for the meal. Though the risk of explosion always was present, gasoline cookstoves were fairly common in the late nineteenth and early twentieth centuries. "The stoves burned 'stove gasoline,' a 'heavy' or crude form of the fuel," historian Laura Bien explained. "Gasoline stoves offered a quicker cooking time and, unlike wood or coal stoves, didn't make the kitchen unbearably hot in the summer. They also weren't sooty, like coal stoves. They were a blessing to homemakers who were tired of sweltering at every summer meal and who weren't connected to a city natural gas system."[7]

Albin left on his errand shortly after 11:00 A.M. His first stop was at the grocery operated by Milton E. Robbins at 607 North Bridge Street.

"He purchased two gallons of gasoline and took it away with him," Robbins would say later.

   * After leaving the grocery, he met Charles R. Patterson, who lived three houses west on East Marion Street.[8] They stood on the sidewalk talking for about ten minutes. Albin still was rankled about Cecilia's conversation with the "bridgeman," Ackerman. "I asked him if he knew who the man was that my wife was out with the night before," Albin recalled later, "and he said he did not."

Then Ludwig walked to the North Side Drug Store, the same store Cecilia had stopped at for medicine the night before. He bought a half-pint of brandy from druggist Lester Gitre, ostensibly to make cough medicine for himself. Brandy and gasoline in hand, Albin walked the six and a half blocks home.

"When I got home I put a little gasoline in the gasoline stove. I did not fill the tank in the stove, as my wife wanted to finish the dinner," he recalled later.

Ludwig then left the house again, this time with the intent of selling his dog, the hound he claimed to be searching for the night before. "I wanted to sell him because we were going to break up and I wanted to find a place for the dog. He was too valuable to throw away or to give away." Albin first walked to the home of Anna Burkhart on North Bridge Street. Her husband had expressed an interest in the dog previously, but that was news to Burkhart's wife.

"I had never spoken to Ludwig before," Mrs. Burkhart recalled at the trial. "I didn't even know who he was."

Albin priced the dog at three dollars. "He said he was going away rather unexpectedly and wanted to know if my husband would buy his dog," Mrs. Burkhart said. Her husband wasn't home, but she told Albin that he didn't want a dog now.

On his walk home, Albin paid a brief visit to next-door neighbor Fred Metzler. Metzler had taken Albin's side in an argument between Cecilia and her husband the previous night. When Ludwig dropped by this time, Metzler was eating dinner.

"Fred, I am going to kill myself," Albin confessed.

"Don't get such a scary notion in your head, Ludwig," Metzler replied.

"I have got to—she is driving me crazy."

"Never mind, you don't have to do that."

Albin told his neighbor that if he left Cecilia, she would make him support her financially, that she had said that to him.

"We will just go and see some lawyer," Metzler said, suggesting local attorney Charlie Metzger. They agreed to go together that evening after Metzler quit work for the day.

Before he left, Albin pulled out the newly purchased bottle of brandy and, in the spirit of friendship, offered a drink to Metzler, who finished about half the bottle. "He and I had been good friends," Metzler explained. "I and his wife were not on speaking terms."

Meanwhile, Jean had finished packing her trunk and left the house to arrange for transportation of both her trunk and Cecilia's to South Bend. Her children remained behind for now. Patterson saw Jean on the sidewalk five minutes after he and Albin had talked.

The dinner—what many call lunch today—of potatoes and boiled meat was waiting when Albin arrived home. Boiled meat was popular with thrifty immigrant families. Broth from boiled meat could be used later for soup or to add nutrition when boiling rice or oats.[9]

The table was set in the dining room, the usual place. Albin, Cecilia, and Jean's two children, Charles and Lucy, sat down to eat. Cecilia and the children ate well. Albin, stressed, not wanting his marriage to end but not wanting it to continue as it was, ate little.

What followed is a matter of conjecture, even more than a century later. This was Albin's version:

Cecilia went to the summer kitchen to fetch a cup of coffee for her husband. He drank it. "I noticed a peculiar taste about the coffee," he remembered later. "It was a kind of sour, bitter taste."

Cecilia left the table first and lay down on a couch in the sitting room off the dining room, to the west. The children, minding their manners, remained at the table until Albin finished, then went outside to play on the front porch.

Within ten minutes after leaving the table, Albin began feeling ill. "I was in misery—wanted to vomit," he recalled. Fearing he would throw up, Albin went out to the backyard to get the "slop jar," an earthen crock with a handle. (Slop jars, also known as "chamber pots," were used as toilets in the days before plumbing, or when plumbing in a multistory house was limited to the ground floor.) Catherine Brand, living at the house next door to the west, was hanging laundry at the time. "He bowed to me and I bowed to him," she would testify, explaining that it was a friendly ritual between the two.

Albin set the slop jar in the hallway at the foot of the stairs, then went out to the porch and sat on the front steps, hoping the fresh air would do some good. A painter working at a nearby cottage saw a man, presumably Ludwig, sitting on the floor, his feet on the step, his elbows on his knees, his head in his hands. Albin remembered briefly being interrupted by Jean's son and daughter, who asked him for money for candy. Cecilia, still resting on the couch inside, overheard their request and told Albin not to be stingy, to give some money to the children.

The fresh air didn't help Albin feel better. "I sat there a few minutes, then went back in the house." He locked the front door. "I took up the slop jar and went upstairs." He put the slop jar in the closet, where it often was, and lay across the bed in the front room. It's likely his mind raced as he thought: Why was he so nauseous? Was it just nerves? The coffee didn't taste right; had Cecilia poisoned him? She had threatened poison more than once before. What would happen if he died? He had insurance . . . Insurance! Where was the policy?

Only ten minutes had passed, and he still felt bad—"felt like throwing up"—but he got up to search for his insurance policy, issued by the Knights and Ladies of Columbia, $1,000 payable to Cecilia upon Albin's death. If Cecilia was leaving him, he thought, he would change the beneficiary to his mother. "I did not intend for my wife to have the policy and me to pay for it if she left me," he would recall.

First, he checked the dresser, where the policy normally was kept. It wasn't there. Then he entered the closet just off the front bedroom, where, before dinner, Cecilia had been packing her clothes in the trunk Albin had provided that morning. It was dark in the closet; it had no window, and when the door swung open, the light from the south window in the bedroom was cut off. So Albin went back to the dresser, took a kerosene lamp off the top, lit it, and went back to the closet to see if Cecilia had put the policy in her trunk.

"I held the lamp in one hand and was down on my knees or my heels and had just commenced to look in the trunk when my wife came as far as to the dresser," Albin would testify.

"Have you made up your mind to give me all the stuff?" Cecilia said.

"I am willing to give you half," Albin replied.

"I will have it all."

"If you get it all you will get it by law." He meant that a judge would have to make such a declaration.

Cecilia was angry. "You son-of-a-bitch, I will swear out a warrant that you tried to kill me and I will get it all anyhow."

"Go right ahead," Albin dared.

Then Cecilia noticed that Albin was looking in her trunk.

"What are you doing in there?" she demanded.

"I am hunting for my policy," Albin replied.

"You son-of-a-bitch, I will fix you anyhow."

Assuming Albin's version of the dialogue was correct—no witnesses were present—those may have been Cecilia's last words.

Cecilia Henderson Hornburg Ludwig did not leave the room alive.

CHAPTER 5

❧

A "Grewsome" Sight

THE FIRST SIGN THAT something was wrong at the Ludwig home came sometime between 1:30 and 2:30 P.M.—everyone remembered the time differently—when smoke was seen coming from an upstairs window.

Alice McNabb saw the smoke first from her home on the next street south. "I was on my back porch and heard screaming and then saw smoke coming out of the Ludwig house," she told the jury a year later. "I went on my back porch because a little girl called me. I took the screaming for that of a woman." The girl may have been nine-year-old Lucy Ellsworth, who minutes earlier had been given money for candy from Albin Ludwig. The girl would remain on McNabb's back porch for half an hour.[1]

McNabb ran to a cottage under construction on Sarah Street, about 250 to 300 feet from the Ludwig home, to alert the workers of the fire.

One of those workers was David Hull, a painter and paperhanger, who saw the smoke for himself after McNabb "called in at the kitchen window of the house on which I was working, saying that she believed the [Ludwig] house was on fire."[2]

Hull rushed to the scene, along with carpenters James France and Milton Carter, but found the front door locked. "I ran back to the house where I was at work and got a ladder and carried it over and a Mr. Schellenberg took it and put it on the west side of the house and I spoke to have it brought around to the porch roof. A man, a stranger to me, went up first." The identity of that stranger wouldn't be known until after Albin's trial.

Robert F. Schellenberg was the fourth man on the scene after hearing the alarm from his house three and a half blocks away. Schellenberg saw the first man—"a perfect stranger to me"—go up the ladder, so he went around to the back of the house and entered through the kitchen door on the east side. Neighbors were arriving on the scene quickly. "The house was pretty well filled up when I got there—that is, when I got in the back room. There were quite a number in the back room." For some reason, Schellenberg went down to the cellar, where, he would testify, he saw some smoldering paper on a cement ledge. That paper—what it was and whether it really existed—would become a critical part of Ludwig's trial.[3]

By now, someone had activated fire alarm call box No. 43, six blocks southwest at the corner of Ann and Grove Streets, notifying the Mishawaka Fire Department. Fire Chief Albert Buysse would testify that, as near as he could tell, the alarm came in at five minutes to two. The department ledger shows firemen on the scene at 2:30 P.M. It was the department's first fire in two days and would be its last for almost a month.[4]

Buysse wasn't the first fireman in the house (after he kicked in the front door), but, in court the next year, he gave the most thorough description of the scene inside:

> I went up the stairway and found the fire in the closet. This is the closet off the front room on the east side. I had the water turned on and put the nozzle into the roof because the fire was burning a hole in the roof.
>
> Then I noticed a person in the closet. A woman lay inside, right across the front of the door. She was all up in a cramped position. Her head was lying against the corner—the northwest corner of the closet. The closet door is at the west end of the closet. Her legs were drawn up and her arms—they were in about the same position. The clothing had all been burned off, except for the corset stays. Her flesh looked just about like a real hard-baked chicken. . . . No clothes. The woman was dead.[5]

Meanwhile, three men who entered through the window had found Albin unconscious and bloodied in the room off the closet. One of them, Alvia J. Bruce, who owned a meat market a block and a half away, told the story at Albin's trial:

He was just in front of the window with his feet to the south, within about a foot and a half of the closet door, with his head to the north or slightly to the northwest. . . . A dresser was immediately at the side of the closet door against the wall and north of the closet door. Ludwig's body was almost against the dresser. The other man and I lifted Ludwig up and took him out of the window off the porch down in the yard and laid him on the ground. I got a couch and helped him on the couch. We got the couch from the house. I found Ludwig bleeding quite freely from his wounds, and thinking it would probably—the loss of blood—would may be the loss of life, I bound his wounds.[6]

Bruce had served in the US Army for six years, four of them in the hospital corps, so he had dealt with injured men before. "I pulled his trousers up above the wounds. Then I went into the house and got some towels and a sheet and tore those up and put them around his legs and tied them tight and also bandaged his arms."[7]

The fire had been contained, so Bruce and the other men carried the still-unconscious Ludwig back into the house to seclude him from the rapidly growing crowd. "He would twitch his legs or move them and move his arm in a way. There was nothing else about him to indicate consciousness."[8]

Ludwig, who had been nauseous after lunch, finally vomited, once outdoors and once after he had been carried back inside. Bruce remained by his side until the ambulance came.[9]

Estimates later were that as many as five hundred people had gathered at the scene, many of them women. Some of the women became hysterical when Ludwig was carried out of the house and when they learned that a woman remained inside.[10]

Newspapers of the day generally agreed on what happened next, but the *South Bend Daily Times* had the story first, squeezed onto page 1 below the fold in the edition printed that same afternoon. Though not credited to Young—newspaper bylines weren't common in 1906—it's likely that he was the first reporter on the scene.

"Mishawaka was the scene of a horrible wife murder and attempted suicide this afternoon," Young wrote.[11]

In the rush to meet his deadline, he identified the "perpetrator" as "Alvin" rather than Albin Ludwig, and he was two numerals off on the address of the East Marion Street house where the crime occurred. Both mistakes would be repeated by some of the newspapers covering the story. While no doubt exists that Albin's name was properly spelled with a *b,* more than a century later confusion remains about where the Ludwigs actually lived, even among descendants of the family. John F. Gaylor, to whom Albin made installment payments on the house, testified at the trial that the house number had changed two digits since the murder, which explains why the exterior of the house at the original address today does not match the description of the crime scene. It's also unknown if the City of Mishawaka renumbered houses subsequently over the past century. For those reasons, and because the houses on that street are standing and occupied today, the author has chosen to identify the house only as being on East Marion Street.[12]

Young continued his story in the *Times:*

The fire department this afternoon responded to a call from box No. 43, which brought the fire men face to face with the most horrible spectacle any fireman in St. Joseph county has ever witnessed. The fire was located in the southeast corner of the second floor of the Ludwig home. Several streams of water were quickly turned on. Chief Buysee [*sic*] with several assistants hurried up the stairs to locate the blaze.

In a bedroom to the south on the floor lay Ludwig, his throat cut, his wrists slashed, blood gushing from the wounds forming crimson pools on the carpet and staining the white bedspread and pillows. It appears that Ludwig was dying and there were evidences in the room of a struggle. Ludwig, who is still a young man, was carred [*sic*] down stairs and physicians took charge of him.

The firemen, however, were destined to face a still more grewsome sight. Upon opening the door leading to a small closet off the bed room, in the smoke and cinders lay the nude body of Mrs. Ludwig, her flesh burned to a crisp, the only thing recognizable about her being a band ring on the right hand. It is presumed that Ludwig and his wife had quarreled and that he killed her and threw her body into the closet, then set fire to it and slashed his own throat.

Ludwig occasionally drank to excess, it is alleged, and today had not been at work. At 3:30 o'clock he was still alive with three physicians working over him. In addition to the wounds in his throat and arms are several slashes on both legs. His pulse was quite strong and as the jugular vein is not severed, it is thought the murderer and attempted suicide will recover. He was brought to a South Bend hospital.

Note that "alleged"—the adjective journalists use to qualify that the person is accused but not convicted of something—is used only in describing that Ludwig "occasionally drank to excess." There is no doubt in the reporter's writing that Ludwig, as the subhead states, "Commits Horrible Murder and Attempts Suicide."

The competing *South Bend Tribune*—"Monday's Circulation, 7,364" boasted a box on page 1—also reported on the crime the same afternoon with the story prominently displayed at the upper-right corner of page 1. The article was topped by four headlines, signifying that the story was important. The largest read, "MAN KILLS HIS WIFE." The *Tribune* also had a bureau in Mishawaka, at 119 South Main Street, so it, too, may have had a reporter on the scene.

As was common in that era, the *Tribune*'s story lacks a byline and attribution. The readers didn't know who wrote it or provided the information.

A. R. Ludwig . . . this afternoon about 2:30 o'clock murdered his wife, threw her body into a closet on the second floor, and set fire to the house. He then cut his throat and both wrists and severed the arteries in one leg.

The fire department was called to the scene and after extinguishing the blaze beheld a most grewsome sight. The body of Mrs. Ludwig was found in one corner of the closet. All the clothing had been burned from the body and it was badly charred. Just how she was murdered has not been determined. Mr. Ludwig was found in a pool of blood on the floor and was in a dying condition. A doctor was hastily summoned and gave prompt attention. At 3:15 o'clock this afternoon he was still alive but unconscious. The attending physician reported that there is a chance of Mr. Ludwig's recovery. The murdered woman is about 36 years old and the man about 37.

Mr. Ludwig, it appears, was of a very jealous disposition and has been suspicious of his wife for some time. A week ago he paid a visit to The Tribune and desired an article written announcing that his wife had been out walking with two traveling men. He said the report was substantiated by neighbors. Mr. Ludwig seemed in a frenzy at the time. Nothing further was heard of the affair until the terrible tragedy of to-day. The case is in the hands of the coroner.

Ludwig was rushed to Epworth Hospital, a five-year-old, fifty-bed, $87,500 facility at the northeast corner of Main and Navarre Streets in South Bend. Cecilia's charred body was taken to the F. J. Finch mortuary in Mishawaka.[13]

As the citizens of Mishawaka and South Bend read the sensational newspaper reports of Cecilia Ludwig's death that evening, Dr. Henry C. Holtzendorf, coroner of St. Joseph County, was at the mortuary supervising an autopsy conducted by Dr. Charles Stroup and Dr. Edgar Doane.[14]

Dr. Holtzendorf had arrived at the Ludwig home shortly after the body had been discovered. "I found the house in confusion," he would relate at Albin's trial. After sending Cecilia's remains to the mortuary, he examined the closet where it was found. "I found a trunk and also a can in the closet, and a great deal of clothing, more or less burned, and a potato masher. . . . To my best belief the can had recently contained kerosene." He also saw a police officer pick up a straight razor, which Holtzendorf found had dirt and blood on it.[15]

As for the postmortem, "we determined that the cause of death was shock—shock from burning," Holtzendorf continued. "The body was very much charred. We found a scalp wound, a ragged or jagged small scalp wound on the left side of the head."[16]

James G. Bostwick, a physician and Mishawaka city health officer, filed the Indiana State Board of Health Certificate of Death on September 26, 1906. Dr. Holtzendorf entered the immediate cause of death: "Suffocated by smoke. Shock from burning. Murdered." Her name was listed as Celia (her nickname) Bettie J. Ludwig. Her husband's name was misspelled as "Alvin." Personal information was filled out and signed by "Mrs. Jas Henderson, Kingsbury, Ind.," who had arrived in town for a visit that afternoon unaware that her daughter had been murdered.[17]

"My great-grandmother took the train from Kingsbury and got off at Cecilia's house," Judy A. Myer, granddaughter of Cecilia's younger sister Jessie, recounted in 2017, noting that the railroad tracks ran behind the Ludwig home. "She didn't know what happened. When she got off the train, she saw all the police at the house."[18]

The *Mishawaka Enterprise,* in its first edition after the tragedy, described the "affecting" scene at the mortuary: "The mother of the dead woman, Mrs. James Henderson, arrived from Kingsbury, Ind., and with the sister here desired to see Mrs. Ludwig. As they viewed the charred remains they broke down with grief."[19]

Cecilia's body arrived in her hometown of Kingsbury the next afternoon. "Undertakers Weir & Sievert took charge of the funeral and with the holding of brief services the body was committed to a grave in the Kingsbury cemetery," that evening's *La Porte Argus-Bulletin* reported.[20] At the funeral, Christina Henderson told the minister "that she bore no hard feeling toward him [Ludwig], and would go to see him whenever he should send for her."[21]

Cecilia was buried in Section 3, Block 26 of Kingsbury Cemetery, which wraps around the First Baptist Church of Kingsbury (the oldest Baptist church in La Porte County, founded in 1834), though the cemetery isn't affiliated with the church.[22] Two stones mark her grave. A small stone reads "MOTHER" on the top line, "CECILIA H. HORNBURG," not Ludwig, on the middle line, and "1876–1906" on the bottom line. Separately, Cecilia is memorialized on a vertical stone that also honors her parents. Cecilia's death date is listed incorrectly as September 22, 1906, three days before the fact.[23]

The days surely ran together for the grieving family.

On October 3, Christina Henderson filed probate papers on behalf of Cecilia. Christina estimated her daughter's estate at $500. The court approved Christina as administratrix.[24]

CHAPTER 6

❧

Horrors and Shocking Features

THANKS TO NEWSPAPERS, the only mass media of the day, the murder of Cecilia Ludwig was the talk of the town. Actually, the tragedy was the talk of four towns: Mishawaka, where it occurred; nearby South Bend, the county seat, where Albin Ludwig was battling for his life in Epworth Hospital; Elkhart, where Albin grew up after arriving in America, where he had owned a saloon, and where his mother and brother still lived; and La Porte, the county seat closest to where Cecilia grew up and her parents still lived. All four cities had newspapers, most had competing newspapers, and all but Mishawaka had daily newspapers.

Every newspaper in each of those cities latched onto the Ludwig murder like a dog with a bone. Sometimes the stories were based on fact. Sometimes they were pure speculation. The troubled marriage of Albin and Cecilia was dissected, with blame assessed to each, some of it scandalous, and most of the scandal based on anonymous sources. Rumors were printed one day, dismissed the next. Many of the newspapers, especially those farther from the scene, reprinted the stories from those closest to the scene, sometimes with attribution, often without.

A common denominator was the use of the word *grewsome,* spelled archaically, in describing the scene.

Day by day, the newspapers revealed what police thought happened in that upstairs closet after Cecilia caught Albin snooping through her packed trunk—assuming Albin's version of that confrontation was true. It took only twenty-four hours for the newspapers to reveal that the murder weapon may have been a potato masher, which in those days was a long-handled wooden tool with a thick, cylindrical bottom, like a healthy slice from the knob end of a baseball bat. Swung like a bat or a mallet, a potato masher of that era could be a deadly weapon.

Peter Young, who was inside the house shortly after the murder, wrote extensively and emotionally about "TRAGEDY DETAILS" in his Mishawaka Department column in the *South Bend Daily Times* of Wednesday, September 26. The second of four headlines on the story reads, "Make Fiendish Work of Alvin [*sic*] R. Ludwig Seem All More Fiendish."

His article began:

Because of its horrors and its shocking features which have never before been witnessed in Mishawaka, the tragedy of Tuesday afternoon at . . . East Marion street is the topic of conversation in Mishawaka. Mystery surrounds the affair to some extent and it is not likely that the fiend who perpetrated the crime, should he recover finally, will ever describe the course he pursued in ushering into another world the spirit of the woman who had sworn to be his wife. As he lay in the room of heat and blood and within a few feet of the nude and charred body of the woman Tuesday afternoon, it seemed that he must die; then he was removed to the open air through a window and by the aid of the men in the hook and ladder truck and one was almost impelled to stay the hands of the surgeons who were seeking to save his life as he rested upon the cot on the lawn, surrounded by scores of men and women, not one of whom probably had any sympathy for the man who committed murder and then, in a most cowardly manner, sought to hide all evidences of his crime by cremating his victim and in final despair, slashing his own throat.

The case is without a parallel in Mishawaka. The woman had been once married and had two children from her first husband. Then she became the wife of Ludwig. That their life has been a not too happy one seems reflected in the repeated expressions of the husband. He was employed as a shoemaker in the plant of the Mishawaka Woolen Manufacturing Co. and fellow-employees declare he appeared to hate everyone— perhaps also himself. Just what led to the development of this peculiar personal characteristic cannot be definitely stated, yet it is alleged that the woman was in a measure responsible. Men who have known Ludwig assert that he sometimes referred to actions on the part of his wife which were not altogether within range of the public searchlight and it may be that his domestic life has been like that of many others, an unhappy one. It is known that the man who committed the terrible deed of Tuesday afternoon is possessed of an almost ungovernable temper, that he was insanely jealous of his wife, that he watched her one night less than a week ago and even pointed her out to a local policeman. It is said the woman did not give sufficient attention to her home affairs and that he was of a very disagreeable disposition whenever he entered the house. Judgment need not be passed, but no matter who was to blame in the case, Ludwig will find no sympathy from the public and no approval from the state on his cruel, murderous act of Tuesday.

Young wrote that Ludwig had owned a saloon, that he was known to drink liquor "but not often to excess," and that he had been employed for two years at the local rubber-shoe company, where "his high temper and his unpleasant disposition were sometimes brought to the surface. He was not demented, unless it was temporarily Tuesday. In the morning he declined to go to work and a child, related to the couple, is said to have ran [sic] out of the house just after dinner and asked . . . neighbors to protect Mrs. Ludwig because he was abusing her. Soon after the flames were seen in the house."[1] The story continues:

The trouble must have occurred at the dinner table, for few of the dishes had been moved and none washed. It seems that he struck his wife while she was still in the dining room, then followed her up stairs and there used a potato masher with which he beat her into insensibility. This kitchen utensil was not found in the customary place after the fearful tragedy. The supposition is that Ludwig, after placing the limp form of his wife into the closet off the bedroom, slashed his wrists in the hope of severing the arteries. Failing in this he probably went down stairs to get kerosene, not gasoline, for the walls show the marks of bloody fingers and drops of blood are found upon the steps. This would indicate that Ludwig became faint and sought support by placing the hand of the murderer against the walls, these marks to bear silent testimony to the work of the enraged man in his insane course of

Tuesday afternoon. A tin can capable of holding a pint or more of kerosene was found in the room with the charred remains of the unfortunate victim of the frenzied Ludwig and after a Times reporter had been in the blood-stained bedroom a razor was found near one of the bed posts. The sight was a revolting one and only indicated to what low a level man will sink. Ludwig, after being taken out of the room, vomited freely and this led doctors to believe that he had been drinking to excess previously. It is believed that he regained consciousness in the yard and that he did some shamming by failing to open his eyes and feigning unconsciousness. On the way to the hospital he likewise gave indications that he was altogether "dead to this world."[2]

Young continued with details of Cecilia's postmortem, a brief sketch of her life, and an update on Albin's improved condition that morning:

Reports from the South Bend hospital this forenoon were to the effect that Ludwig had passed a fairly good night and that he had slept at intervals. This morning at 8 o'clock he was considered stronger and the attending physician says the man will undoubtedly recover to meet trial for his horrible crime. Under direction of the coroner a warrant has been issued and Ludwig has been placed under arrest on the charge of murder in the first degree.[3]

One of the Henderson family's two home-county newspapers, the *La Porte Daily Herald* of September 26, the day after Cecilia's death, placed the story at the top-right of page 1, the most prominent position, with the headline, "KINGSBURY GIRL MEETS AWFUL DEATH." The secondary headline read: "Mrs. Cecilia Henderson-Ludwig Murdered in Horrible Manner by Husband, Who Then Attempts to Commit Suicide." The *Herald* outdid itself with its graphic description of the crime, with descriptions obviously lifted from the South Bend newspapers, including speculation that Ludwig had cut his wife's throat:

A call for the fire department disclosed the horrible murder and attempted suicide, for when the firemen hurried into the house they found Ludwig stretched out on the floor in a bedroom on the second floor. Blood was gushing from his throat, which was cut almost from ear to ear, and from the wrists, which also had been slashed. Pools of blood were forming on the carpet, while the white bedspread and pillows were stained with the crimson fluid. . . .

Evidences of a struggle in the room led the firemen to continue their search, with the result that upon opening a closet door off the bedroom they faced a most grewsome scene. In the smoke and cinders of the room lay the nude body of Mrs. Ludwig, her flesh burned to a crisp, the only thing recognizable about her being a band ring on the right hand. Every indication pointed to the fact that Ludwig had killed his wife with a potato masher, then cut her throat and after stuffing the body in the closet had poured gasoline over her and applied a match. . . . After disposing of his wife Ludwig had attacked himself, but had made a poor job of it.[4]

Note the confusion over which fuel—kerosene or gasoline—was used to accelerate the burning of Cecilia's body, confusion that would continue through the trial.

The most thorough coverage of the murder was in the local *Mishawaka Enterprise,* edited and published by sixty-year-old Edward Allen Jernegan, who had owned the weekly newspaper—"Published Every Friday"—since 1872.[5] As a weekly, the *Enterprise,* despite a smaller staff, had the benefit of three extra days to assemble the story, as well as to filter through the material published by the dailies for inclusion in the *Enterprise's* coverage. That first week's story, on Friday, September 28, covered a column and a half of the upper-left corner of page 1. The biggest of the three headlines atop the story read, "A BLOODY TRAGEDY."

The story contained slightly differences from the daily papers' coverage, such as where the bloodied Albin Ludwig was found. It began:

A more horrible and bloody tragedy has never been enacted in Mishawaka than on Tuesday afternoon, when Alvin [sic] R. Ludwig, residing at . . . East Marion street, in a fit of insane rage and jealousy, murdered his wife, pouring gasoline over the body, thrust it in a closet after setting fire to the inflamable [sic] liquid and then attempted suicide by cutting his throat and veins in arms and legs.

About 2:30 o'clock Tuesday afternoon an alarm from box 43 called the fire department to . . . East Marion street, where flames had been discovered in the dwelling occupied by Alvin [sic] R. Ludwig. After extinguishing the blaze an inspection of the interior disclosed a most grew-some sight. Ludwig was discovered on a bed in a pool of blood, bleeding from wounds on throat, arms and legs, and nearly unconscious from the smoke. He was dragged through a second story window to a veranda and revived. Further search discovered a still more sickening sight. In a closet from which the fire had originated was found the nude form of Mrs. Ludwig, charred almost beyond recognition, all the clothing but remnants of the corset having been burned off.

After the remains had been viewed by Coroner H. C. Holtzendorf they were conveyed to the Finch morgue. Local surgeons gave the husband's wounds attention, after which he was conveyed by ambulance to Epworth hospital, where he is likely to recover from his unsuccessful suicidal attempt—unfortunately for the county which will now be at the expense of a big murder trial.

The direct cause of the bloody tragedy is obvious, although the details of the crime are yet obscure. Insane jealousy on the part of the husband was undoubtedly the motive.

It is well known that the couple had long lived unhappily and that terrible quarrels between them were frequent. Over a year ago Ludwig was arrested and fined for a display of his insane rage, on which he scattered the headgear of the members of a local fraternal society which his wife was attending, and tore up the hat of a young man who he supposed had accompanied his wife. Frequent altercations were heard at home and on the street, and it is even claimed that the night previous to the murder Ludwig threw a brick at the woman on the street, following up the attack with a particularly noisy row at home, which kept the neighbors awake for hours.

The day of the tragedy Ludwig did not go to his work at the Woolen Co. plant, remaining around brooding over his troubles. It is stated that he intimated to friends that he intended putting an end to the scandal and all his troubles. According to the story, about noon he purchased some gasoline at a north side grocery and went home to dinner. Mr. and Mrs. Ludwig and the latter's sister and her son sat down to eat. A quarrel started and the sister got up from the table and went to get a dray to convey her trunks to the depot, as Mrs. Ludwig had packed her trunk and expected to leave her husband and go with her sister to Kingsbury, Ind. According to the story told by the sister's young son the quarrel increased in fury and finally Ludwig chased his wife around the table and upstairs to the front room. He had given the boy five cents to go and buy some candy, but the lad had remained long enough to hear screams.

The terrible scene enacted in the upstairs room can only be surmised unless Ludwig speaks. It is believed that he struck his wife in the back of the head with a potato masher found later in the closet, rendering her unconscious. Believing her dead he pushed her into a closet to the east and went down and sat on the porch to study his next move. It is said he was seen on the porch by neighbors after screams had been heard. Suddenly he got up and rushed into the house and from indications and the blood found all over the part of the house, stood up in front of a mirror, cut his throat, wrists and legs, hid the razor in some dirt from a plant which had toppled over and then went down stairs and secured either gasoline or kerosene from a can and pouring it in a smaller can threw it over the fornt [sic] of his wife, fired it and lay down to die, expecting the fire to burn all traces of the murder and suicide.[6]

The *Enterprise*'s story concluded with a description of the disintegrating Ludwig marriage, attributing blame to both:

Stories of all sorts are in circulation regarding the relations existing between Ludwig and his wife, showing the strained relations existing between them. A week previous to the tragedy the husband endeavored to have his wife written up in the papers charging that she had been gallivanting around with two traveling men, and that she was neglecting her home. That the dead woman was not above reproach in regard to her conduct is alleged to be true. Ludwig is said to have an ungovernable temper and was not an agreeable companion among his fellow workmen. A brother from Elkhart, who came here at once on learning of the tragedy, also corroborated this statement, but also remarked that he had good reasons for his jealous complaints about his wife's conduct.[7]

CHAPTER 7

Mishawaka Grows—and Gossips

As THE WEEK WORE ON, the murder of Cecilia Ludwig remained, in the words of Peter Young, "the topic of conversation in Mishawaka."[1]

Young wrote in the *South Bend Daily Times* that the "newspapers have not sufficient columns in which to give publicity to the many stories which are told and to the various theories which are advanced. Many of the former are unreliable, no doubt, and it could benefit no one to tell them in print."[2] In the days ahead, as readers yearned for more news about the ghastly murder, the newspaper coverage wasn't always as reliable.

Not all the news in Mishawaka that week was bad. Both the *Mishawaka Enterprise* and the *South Bend Daily Times* reported on Friday about efforts to secure land for three factory sites. "BIG DEAL ON FOOT," headlined the *Enterprise*. A mass meeting was held the night before at City Hall with more than fifty "leading gentlemen" in attendance, the *Daily Times* reported.[3] No mention if any women were invited.

From page 1 of the *Enterprise:*

> For several weeks interested manufacturers, property owners and prominent citizens have quietly been at work perfecting a scheme which will mean the location of three flourishing and growing manufacturing industries, if the public spirited citizens of Mishawaka show their enterprise by backing up the preliminary good work already accomplished.

The story told that the American Simplex Motor Co., the Mishawaka Folding Go-Kart Co., and the South Bend Iron Bed Co. all would
erect new factories on fifty-six lots of donated land, with the necessary
capital being raised by selling an adjacent fifty-six lots for homes at
$275 each.[4]

Albin Ludwig, charged with first-degree murder and under twenty-
four-hour guard at Epworth Hospital in South Bend, remained in the
spotlight, especially when the *Daily Times'* Mishawaka Department
carried the sensational report on Thursday that Ludwig had attempted
suicide the night before, taking advantage of a change in guards to head
for the window "with the intention of leaping to the ground below."
The headline at the top of reporter Young's column screamed, "SEEKS
DEATH LEAP." Ludwig "was thwarted in this design," Young wrote.[5]

But the competing *South Bend Tribune* reported the same day that the
incident never happened: "A report this morning that Ludwig attempted
to jump from the hospital window was found to be untrue."[6] Still, the
Times' story about the suicide attempt at the hospital was repeated almost verbatim in the Elkhart and La Porte dailies in the days to follow.

Despite his trepidation at repeating unfound theories about the
murder, Young speculated that Thursday "as to whether Mrs. Ludwig
was conscious or in an insensible condition when placed in the little
room off the bed chamber. The generally accepted theory is that she
was unconscious at the time the match was applied, but there is some
foundation for the belief that Ludwig may have forced her into the
closet, threw the oil upon her and then the match, closing the door and
matching his strength against that of the woman in holding it closed."[7]

A new theory advanced by Police Chief Benjamin F. Jarrett, Young
wrote, was that Cecilia "may have been stooping over her trunk, into
which she is said to have been packing her clothing preparatory to leaving Ludwig, when the fiend started the fire and that she sank in a few sec-
onds and was unable to make any kind of fight for her life." That theory
would counter future statements by Ludwig that he was the one looking
in the trunk for the insurance policy when Cecilia approached the room.[8]

Another theory espoused by Young that day, but not attributed to a
public official, was that Cecilia might have been responsible for her own
death:

Is it not possible that the woman, after her quarrel with Ludwig, in a state of mental frenzy and in the moment of total depression and bitterness of spirit committed suicide? Could she not have herself carried the kerosene into that room and, while almost insane after her terrible quarrel, sought the end of her own existence? Doubtless these points, originating in the minds of the reporter, will be raised by the attorneys when it comes to trying Ludwig on the murder charge.[9]

Any speculation about Ludwig's culpability and whether he would be put to death for the crime would be moot if he didn't survive his own injuries.

The *South Bend Tribune* reported that Thursday that Ludwig "is still alive and improving." The *Tribune* correspondent also talked to Jarrett, who said Ludwig recognized him when he visited his room the night before. Jarrett assigned patrolman L. A. Foust to watch Ludwig that night.[10]

"When is my wife coming to see me? She should have been here before this," Ludwig asked Foust, according to the *Tribune*. He told the policeman that he felt used up and that he had been in a terrible fight. But despite Foust's prodding, Ludwig did not confess to killing his wife.

The *Tribune* reporter speculated that Ludwig was trying "to play the insane act."[11]

Ludwig also talked to a Mishawaka clergyman who visited one afternoon. The minister "told Ludwig that he would die and that it was time for him to make his peace with the Supreme Being," the *Daily Times* reported later in the week.[12]

Ludwig, it is alleged, admitted that he was a sinner, and declared he desired to get well and that he would explain matters. He asserts that he has been misrepresented by the press and others, and that the charges are not altogether justified. He refused to make a confession to the minister . . .

It is said that he has a completely changed front, and now is willing to live. It seems that something has flashed through his mind which carries with it new courage, and he now seems willing to recover from his injuries and face trial.[13]

At first, justice moved quickly. A preliminary hearing on the murder charge was scheduled for Saturday, only four days after the murder. Thursday's *Elkhart Truth* said Ludwig probably would enter a plea of insanity. "An attorney has not been engaged for the defense but from the accused's peculiar actions the police believe such will be the grounds of his defense if any is made."[14]

The next day, the *Elkhart Daily Review* wrote that Ludwig would receive no help from his Elkhart relatives, referring to his mother and brother, in hiring a lawyer "as he had thoroughly estranged his people during the last few years."[15]

Saturday's hearing would not be held as Ludwig's seesaw condition worsened one day, improved the next. "MURDERER IN WORSE CONDITION," read the headline on Friday's Mishawaka Department column in the *South Bend Daily Times*.[16]

According to information given out by the physician who is attending Albin R. Ludwig, the alleged uxorcide[17] who is at Epworth hospital in South Bend, the latter is worse. It is said that he will have lung fever [pneumonia] and the officers who have been standing guard over him declare that he has continually complained of pains in his chest.

It is also said that gangrene may develop from the knife wound in his leg. Ludwig, after all, may save the county the big expense of prosecuting him for the alleged murder of his wife in this city last Tuesday afternoon.[18]

By Saturday, Ludwig was "somewhat better," the *Daily Times* said. "His temperature is encouraging, and this forenoon he ate more than he has since entering the hospital Tuesday." The newspaper said Ludwig "had been threatening to starve himself, taking nothing of nourishment, except a cup of tea."[19]

Also on Saturday, Ludwig sent word that he wanted to see his estranged brother, Gustave.[20]

The newspapers took Sunday off, giving readers a break from the lurid tale of Albin and Cecilia. The weather in Mishawaka had cooled from the day of the murder but still was pleasant, although a bit windy, with the temperature hitting a high in the mid-70s.[21]

Monday brought a new month and, six days after Cecilia's murder, a new revelation in the investigation. It already was known that the evening before her murder, Cecilia and sister Jean stopped at the North Side Drug Store for a refill of iodine and glycerine, the medicine she applied to her feet but which is toxic if ingested. The bottle was found in the house after Cecilia's death, leading to speculation that Albin's alleged suicide attempt included drinking a portion of that mixture. However, in the trial, Albin would infer that Cecilia poisoned his coffee at their final lunch together.

"Did He Take Poison, Too?" asked the headline of Peter Young's column on Monday, October 1:

> The fact that a vial containing a quantity of iodine mixed with glycering [*sic*] leads to the belief that Ludwig also sought the end of life's road by drinking a portion of the contents of that bottle last Tuesday. Some credence is given the theory because Ludwig vomited profusely and the matter discharged from his stomach was dark in color, showing that iodine might have been taken by the alleged murderer. As the case is investigated further by the officers it seems that he really is a fiend and that he was insane or at least in a state of mental desperation a week ago when the horror occurred.[22]

The next day, Young wrote that "Ludwig continues to complain about his throat burning and of a pain in the passages to the lungs and stomach," which seemed to confirm the poison theory.[23]

In the Henderson family's home county, the *La Porte Argus-Bulletin* reported on Tuesday, October 2, that Albin Ludwig's "little nephew . . . was in all probability a witness to the tragedy." Charles Ellsworth, not quite seven years old, wasn't identified by name, and neither was the source of the report. But it's possible that Charles's mother, Cecilia's sister Jean, and her children were back in La Porte County talking about what happened. The story continued: "Neighbors now recall that when the house was entered the little one was found in the kitchen. He was asked if he had not known the house was on fire, but answered only to the effect that 'Uncle was bleeding.'"[24]

Brother Gustave and wife Minnie Ludwig became the first family members to visit Ludwig in the hospital, though the newspapers disagreed whether the visit occurred on that Monday or Tuesday. "They were advised to ask as few questions as possible," the *La Porte Argus-Bulletin* reported. "They say that Ludwig apparently has little hope of getting well, although his physicians believe to the contrary. There has been bitterness between the brothers, and in sending for Gustav [*sic*] and his wife the object was to ask for their forgiveness."[25]

Ludwig's hometown *Elkhart Daily Review* differed on what the doctors told Gustave, which was that the brother was "is in a very critical condition. . . . The doctor said he had small hope of saving the patient, adding that his danger was due to the poison, the taking of which was at first not suspected. The doctor said he did not think the patient would live longer than a few days."[26]

On the evening of Wednesday, October 3, Ludwig had a surprise visitor, Christina Henderson, Cecilia's seventy-one-year-old mother, who had ridden the train from Kingsbury. One newspaper reported that a "little child" accompanied her.[27] The child could have been Cecilia's daughter, Lyle, homeless since the murder.

Christina "was allowed to speak to him a few minutes and she asked him how the house caught on fire," the *South Bend Tribune* wrote. "He did not give her much satisfaction. She treated him kindly and did not irritate him. Ludwig may yet die without making a confession."[28]

The *Elkhart Daily Review* gave more details about her visit: "Her chief purpose was to ascertain if he would permit her to be appointed administrator of her daughter's estate, but he talked but little, because of his serious condition, and she left with the intention of repeating the visit today in the hope that he would be stronger."[29] It continues:

> Mrs. Henderson had come to Mishawaka to look after the household furniture owned by the mismated pair. She was accompanied to the hospital by the Mishawaka marshal. Mrs. Gustav [*sic*] Ludwig of Elkhart, sister-in-law of the patient, was present when Mrs. Henderson was announced to him, and he looked surprised and asked Mrs. Ludwig what Mrs. Henderson could want with him. Mrs. Ludwig explained that she desired to see him about the estate, and he gave assent to her admittance.[30]

By the end of the week, his second in the hospital, Albin was showing few signs of recovery.

Peter Young's Mishawaka Department in the Monday, October 8, *South Bend Daily Times* led with a bold headline: "LUDWIG MAY NOT LIVE." Young wrote:

From reports supplied The Times it would appear that the condition of
Albin R. Ludwig, the alleged wife-murderer, is serious. He is no longer in
danger from death from any of the self-inflicted wounds, but his throat
is still sore from the effects of the iodine and glycerine which he took on
the day of the tragedy. The symptoms of pneumonia also have passed
away, but the danger now lies in the fact that gangrene is developing to a
serious degree in the man's left leg and if blood poisoning develops there
will be no hope. Some of the flesh already has been putrefied.[31]

As Albin Ludwig lay in his hospital bed, his survival still uncertain,
public interest began to fade. He no longer was a daily story in the newspapers. Life went on in Mishawaka. The October 12 edition of the *Mishawaka Enterprise* carried more news of progress in the growing city:

A majority of the property owners on Main street between the river and
the Lake Shore railway have already signed a petition for the paving of
that thoroughfare with asphalt, and at next Monday night's meeting of
the common council the petition will be introduced and a resolution
will doubtless pass ordering the improvement made. It is too late this
season to begin the work, but early next spring the work will probably
be undertaken and then Mishawaka can boast of two of her principal
thoroughfares being well paved.[32]

The story also noted that a petition was circulating to pave Bridge
Street—the major north-south street just over a block west of the Ludwig home—from the river to the Grand Trunk Western Railway tracks,
which ran behind the Ludwig residence. In conjunction with the paving project, the name of Bridge Street was expected to change to Main
Street "to correspond with the south side connecting thoroughfare," the
Enterprise wrote, adding, "it is hoped to include that street also in the
much needed improvement project."[33] The likely change of the street
name explains the interchangeable use of *Bridge Street* and *Main Street*
during the eventual trial.

If Cecilia had been alive, she might have been enticed by a big ad from
Robertson Brothers, "Mishawaka's Largest Dry Goods Store," in that
week's *Enterprise.* Cooler weather was coming, and the ad touted Black
Broadcloth Coats, satin lined throughout, for $19.75 and $15; Black

Kersey Cloth Coats for $12.50; and Black Cheviot Cloth Coats, with satin-lined yoke, for only $10. The "Complete Line of Ladies' and Misses' Skirts" ranged from $1.98 to $10.[34]

But Cecilia Ludwig, murdered two and a half weeks earlier, would not participate in the sale.

CHAPTER 8

Charges Filed, Attorneys Hired

By Wednesday, October 17, Albin Ludwig's twenty-third day of hospitalization, the accused murderer was "gaining rapidly" and "his wounds are about healed up," the *South Bend Daily Times* reported. "There is no longer any danger from the gangrenous conditions which manifested themselves on one leg, and the attending physician states that within a week or ten days the alleged uxoricide can be taken from the hospital and placed behind the bars in the county jail to await trial for the terrible crime with which he will be charged."[1]

Two days later, with Ludwig's recovery a near certainty, George A. Kurtz, St. Joseph County state's attorney, finally filed formal murder charges. As expected, the charge was murder in the first degree. "Owing to the nature of the crime an effort will be made to secure the death penalty, although the greater bulk of the evidence is circumstantial," the *Mishawaka Enterprise* wrote.[2]

Though improving, Ludwig remained in Epworth Hospital despite a quickly debunked report in the *Elkhart Daily Review* that Ludwig was transferred to the St. Joseph County Jail by police ambulance on Saturday, October 20. It took eight days for the *Daily Review* to correct its error, admitting that the reporting wasn't its own. On Monday, October 29, Ludwig finally went to jail.[3]

The St. Joseph County Jail was the third in the county's history, built in 1897 for $40,000. "The building is a substantial structure, three stories in height, and has cell arrangements for the accommodation of ninety six prisoners," according to a 1901 city history book. The jail included a hospital ward, where Ludwig's treatment would continue.[4]

Meanwhile in Mishawaka, a crime other than the murder of Cecilia Ludwig was making news. The November 2 *Enterprise* reported "A DASTARDLY DEED," that the mayor's windows were smashed "By Cowardly Hoodlums Evidently in the Interests of a Wide-Open Town."[5]

Perhaps in response to the mayor's promised crackdown on violations of city ordinances, on November 11 police tricked one hotel that dared to sell liquor illegally on a Sunday. As reported in the November 16 *Enterprise:*

> By a clever ruse last Sunday morning, Chief of Police Ben Jarrett, followed a crowd of men into the Milburn House through the rear door, while Officer L. A. Foust guarded the main entrance. Chief Jarrett discovered about a score of men being served liquor in a back room, and there was great consternation upon his unexpected appearance. The names of many present were secured and the following morning the proprietor of the hotel Bert Philion was arrested. The case came up for trial before Justice E. E. Long, and as the evidence was so convincing the defendant's attorney, Joseph Talbot, advised him to plead guilty, which he did, and a fine of $25 and costs was assessed against the hotel man.[6]

Ludwig finally appeared in court on November 19, according to the next day's *Daily Review.* Ludwig "was carried on a cot into court at South Bend Monday, and his counsel, Attorney Crabill, waived arraignment and entered a plea of not guilty." The story said he has been in the "hospital ward of the county jail."[7]

Will G. Crabill, who went by W. G., and Samuel Parker of the South Bend law firm of Anderson, Parker & Crabill had been hired by Gustave Ludwig only days before the court appearance—nearly two months after Cecilia's death—to defend his brother against the murder charge. All they knew about the case was what they had read in the newspapers and what Gustave told them when they were retained. Either because Gustave didn't have the money, or, considering his own financial feud with Albin, he didn't want to invest too much in his brother's weak defense, the initial agreement was that Crabill and Parker did not have to search for witnesses and determine who knew what. Instead, Gustave and a Mishawaka attorney, Clinton N. Crabill, would be responsible for finding witnesses for the defense.[8] W. G. Crabill, then thirty-seven, and twenty-five-year-old Clinton N. Crabill, known as C. N., both were natives of Wabash, Indiana, and likely related, but not closely enough for the connection to be mentioned in their separate biographies in a 1907 county history book.[9]

With the defense needing time to research the case, it was no surprise when the *Elkhart Weekly Review* reported briefly on December 1 that the Ludwig trial and the unrelated murder trial of William Eugene Cook, also with Elkhart ties, "are postponed for a time."[10]

For Cook, who claimed to have committed crimes in every state in the Union, the delay was brief. His trial for murdering a hermit began the next Monday, he stabbed himself in an unsuccessful suicide attempt on Thursday, and on Friday he was sentenced to life in prison.[11]

For Ludwig, justice would come slower.

CHAPTER 9

Grand Jury Indicts

THE FEBRUARY TERM of the St. Joseph County Circuit Court opened at 9:00 A.M. on Monday, February 4, 1907, only two days after the previous term had adjourned. "The bar docket is by far the largest in the history of St. Joseph county and it is certain that the session will extend right up to the May term," that week's *Mishawaka Enterprise* reported.[1]

In describing the court's "very full docket," the *Elkhart Daily Review* cited as "among the most important cases . . . that of the state versus Albin Ludwig, the former Elkhartan who murdered his wife in their home in Mishawaka on Sept. 25, 1906, and then attempted suicide with poison. Another murderer to be tried is Day Armstrong . . . who killed a wanton woman in a South Bend hotel, and then attempted suicide."[2]

The *Review* wrote that Ludwig and Armstrong both were being held in the hospital ward of the St. Joseph County Jail, "although both of them are convalescent and the former is nearly fit to be moved to the regular criminal department of the jail. Ludwig has difficulty in moving around and is forced to use crutches. Both prisoners were extremely reticent when called upon Saturday afternoon. They refused to say anything concerning the charges against them and are evidently under the advice of attorneys not to talk."[3]

The Ludwig and Armstrong cases had similarities, including that both suspects allegedly stabbed themselves after murdering a woman and initially were not expected to recover. Albin's victim was his wife. Day's victim was a woman who checked into South Bend's Grandview Hotel with him after "a day of carousal" that included considerable drinking.[4]

The grand jury in the case of *State v. Albin R. Ludwig* convened Thursday, February 7. The *Mishawaka Enterprise* identified the grand jurors as Walter Place, Charles Druliner, and Frederick Tascher of Portage Township; Phillip Horeio of Madison; Byron Christian of Clay; and Etsel Snyder of Lincoln Township.[5]

Examination of witnesses in the Ludwig case began the first day, with Prosecutor Joseph E. Talbot, newly elected and barely one month into the job, and Deputy Prosecutor C. L. Metzger presenting the case. (Probably unknown to Metzger at the time was that shortly before the murder, Ludwig and neighbor Fred Metzler had discussed seeking advice from him that evening.) The prosecution initially hoped that testimony in the Ludwig case and a manslaughter case against another defendant would be concluded by the next day, but the grand jury continued to meet through the next week. Besides the Ludwig and Armstrong murder cases and the manslaughter case, the grand jury was hearing evidence on an incest and rape case and cases against three local saloonkeepers for having gaming devices in their places of business.[6]

On Friday, February 15, twenty-two indictments were returned, including a five-count indictment charging "Alvin" R. Ludwig with the alleged murder of his wife, Cecilia. Twenty-six witnesses had testified before the grand jury. Most would testify at the trial.[7] The erroneous use of *Alvin* as Ludwig's first name was an issue his defense attorneys would raise later.

Regardless of the spelling, with the five counts the grand jury took no chances as to how Ludwig killed her, with one count for each possibility.

The first count charged that Ludwig, "in some way and by some means unknown to the grand jury," murdered Cecilia. The second count charged that Ludwig murdered Cecilia "by striking her with a certain deadly weapon, to the grand jury unknown." The third count charged that Ludwig murdered Cecilia "by making an assault upon her in some manner and by weapons to the grand jury unknown and that she died from this assault." The fourth count charged that Ludwig murdered Cecilia "by striking her with a potato masher, the same being a deadly weapon." The fifth count charged that Ludwig murdered his wife "by feloniously setting fire to and burning the dwelling house owned by a person named John Gaylord [*sic*], in and in which she then was, whereby she was mortally burned."[8]

Ludwig would plead not guilty to all counts.

With the trial expected to begin in about two weeks, the attorneys stepped up their search for evidence. Both Elkhart daily newspapers reported on February 27 that South Bend attorney Isaac Kane Parks was in town that day in connection with the case.

"It is understood [Ludwig's] defense will be a plea of insanity," the *Truth* wrote.[9]

CHAPTER 10

Trial Begins

ALMOST SIX MONTHS to the day of Cecilia Henderson Hornburg Ludwig's fiery death, her alleged killer—her second husband—would stand trial.

The people of Mishawaka and South Bend and Elkhart and Kingsbury and everyone in Indiana who had read the sensational newspaper reports about the case hoped to learn what really happened that hot Tuesday afternoon in the closet off the upstairs front bedroom in the Ludwig home on Mishawaka's East Marion Street.

They would hear different versions of those events—the prosecution's theory and the defense's theory—laying the blame for the tragedy on each of the participants. No living witnesses existed except for the defendant, Albin Ludwig, and possibly the two children of the deceased's sister, Jean Ellsworth. The children, nine and seven years old when the trial began, were too young to testify.

The people also would learn about the deeply flawed characters of both Albin and Cecilia Ludwig.

But would they learn the truth?

The trial was to be held in what's still known as the Third Courthouse of St. Joseph County. Constructed between 1896 and 1898 at a cost of $184,246, the courthouse barely had been broken in by 1907. The courthouse style, Academic Classicism, with Bedford Stone and granite walls, was patterned after the architecture of the 1893 Columbian Exposition in Chicago.[1]

Before a jury could be seated, Ludwig's lawyers tried to negotiate a plea bargain. Ludwig would plead guilty to a reduced charge of manslaughter. "The state is inclined to look with disfavor upon this proposal and is confident that a conviction for murder in the first degree can be secured against Ludwig," the *Elkhart Weekly Review* reported.[2]

Next, because of the extensive newspaper coverage of the case, the defense considered asking for a change of venue to Marshall County, due south of St. Joseph County.[3] It's not known if that request actually was filed as a motion, but the trial remained in St. Joseph County.

Ludwig's attorneys filed two other motions in early April. The first was to quash the indictment because of the misspelling of Ludwig's first name. They argued the indictment was issued against *Alvin* Ludwig, not *Albin*. The court overruled, prompting the *Elkhart Daily Review* to claim its own innocence: "The Review has persistently referred to Ludwig as Albin, contrary to the general opinion, and 'careful' readers have pointed to its 'typographical error.' But Judge Funk evidently thinks there's not much in a name."[4]

A second motion, the *Daily Review* reported, was to "dismiss on the ground that none of the counts of the indictment charged the defendant with an offense against the public." The court also overruled.

On April 3, Ludwig waived arraignment and entered a plea of not guilty.[5]

The newspapers were anxious for the trial to begin, especially the *Daily Review,* which prematurely announced on April 9 and again on April 18 that the trial would start on those days. It didn't. The competing *Elkhart Truth* said the attorneys weren't ready on April 18.[6]

The next day, the *Truth* published a five-paragraph story stating that the trial would begin that day and recounting the crime in case anyone had forgotten the grisly details. The first paragraph predicted that Ludwig "will go to his doom in the death chamber of the prison north or be immured behind penitentiary walls for the natural period of his life. This is the conclusion of the attorneys who today in the circuit court will enter upon the trial of the man. Ludwig is apparently indifferent to his fate."[7]

The trial didn't start that day either.

Finally, on Monday, April 22, jury selection began, with Ludwig sitting in the defendant's chair. It did not go quickly. As the *South Bend Daily Times* reported, "it was with the greatest difficulty that a panel was finally secured, this not being accomplished until 5 o'clock." Eleven men were accepted by noon—it would be 1920 before women could serve on Indiana juries—but the state and defense couldn't agree on the twelfth man. "In securing this juryman the defense used eleven peremptory challenges and the state five."[8]

It was important to the prosecution that the jury be favorable to capital punishment. "The answers were such as to impress the state that a verdict imposing the death penalty would be returned," the *Daily Times* said.[9]

The twelve finally selected to serve were Charles H. Finch, Edward H. Casey, Joseph R. Ullery, E. W. Evans, Simon Cullar, J. H. Flynn, John S. Steele, Clark Sutherland, F. X. Koontz, John Layton, George Kopf, and William Rosenberry.[10] All likely were common men—shopkeepers, factory workers, tradesmen, and farmers—as not one was included in one of the era's books profiling local men of status.

Over the course of trying *State of Indiana vs. Albin R. Ludwig,* the jurors would hear from three attorneys representing the prosecution: State's Attorney Joseph E. Talbot and Deputies Burrell J. Cramer and Isaac Kane Parks.[11] Talbot and Parks would share the examination of the state's witnesses, but Talbot would cross-examine all the defense witnesses.

Samuel Parker and Will G. Crabill represented Ludwig in his defense.[12] The two would share direct examination of defense witnesses, but Parker would handle almost all cross-examination of the state's witnesses.

This would be a crucial trial for the boyish-looking Talbot, thirty-three years old, who had taken office at the start of the year. Six years earlier, a county history book described him as "a rising young attorney of ability and intellect."[13]

Talbot started making a name for himself as a crime-busting prosecutor as soon as he took office. He was praised in a brief profile that appeared in the *Indianapolis Star,* in the state capital, on January 25, 1907:

> Prosecuting Attorney Joseph E. Talbot, one of the youngest men who has held the office during the last quarter of a century, is the man who really put the lid on South Bend after the city had been known throughout the West as the most wide-open town in the State. On the day that Talbot went into office he announced that the laws must be obeyed. Violators of the code winked and kept on as usual. Finally Talbot sent his

constables through the city with orders to rake in the slot machines. It was then that the city administration backed water [reversed direction] and today the lid is as tight as it will ever be. All laws, especially those in reference to saloons, are being vigorously enforced.[14]

An Elkhart newspaper reporter in 1909 described Talbot as "a small, wiry-looking man, regular featured, smooth-shaven and not unpleasant to look at."[15]

Talbot's sterling reputation, his career as a prosecutor, and even his life would be shortened by scandal. But that would come later. On April 22, 1907, his mind was on sending Albin Ludwig to prison—or death.

Parker was one of the best-known attorneys in northern Indiana and a former state senator. The same Elkhart reporter, covering a 1909 trial, would write that Parker "does not seem to be over-particular about his dress" and "is well enough along in years to have gray in his hair and a little bald spot on the top of his head. He is smooth-shaven, blue-eyed and very emphatic in all of his declarations, and seems to have a faculty of saying a good deal in a few words and when he is through, stops—a rare accomplishment. He has a good deal of caustic humor which he uses as occasion permits during the progress of a trial. According to local attorneys he is one of the ablest attorneys practicing at the bar of St. Joseph county."[16]

Circuit Judge Walter A. Funk, forty-nine years old, whose thin face was distinguished by a stylish bushy mustache, would hear the case. Born to a farm family in Elkhart County, Funk "had none of those advantages which served to advance the sons of wealthy parents," a 1901 history book said. He began his own law practice in South Bend in 1886 and entered politics in 1892, losing a state-senate race as a Republican. Eight years later, he was elected circuit judge.[17] He was reelected in 1906.

Any opening statements made at the start of the trial have been lost to history, but Talbot's theory of the case was, in part, that Albin and Cecilia had quarreled downstairs and that the defendant "seized the potato masher and the deceased ran from him and up stairs and that he followed her and struck her on the head with the potato masher, making the jagged wound found after death and rendering her insensible, and that he then dragged her into the closet and then cut his wrists and throat with the razor and got blood upon his hands, and had then gone down stairs to get oil to throw into the closet and upon his wife's body with a view to starting a fire there and destroying the evidences of his crime."[18]

The scenario painted in the defense theory was that Cecilia found Albin searching for an insurance policy in a trunk she had packed, they quarreled, Cecilia said, "she would fix him anyway and struck at him with the potato masher, which she had brought from below in anticipation of trouble; that he warded off the blow and set the lamp down or let it fall and got upon his feet and caught her by the throat and, in his rage, jammed her head against one of the hooks and made the scalp wound found later and choked her until she collapsed and sank down in death." Ludwig's legal team believed him guilty "of no higher degree of homicide than manslaughter."

Testimony began Tuesday morning.[19] Talbot's first witness was Fred Young, the childhood friend of Cecilia Ludwig and sister Jean Ellsworth, who met the two women outside his boardinghouse the evening before the murder. Young then accompanied them to the Ludwig home, where he had been a frequent visitor, and witnessed the arguments that night between Cecilia and her husband. Talbot's obvious intention in calling Young first was to establish for the jury that the Ludwigs' marriage was seriously troubled. He would get into a time line of the murder afterward.

Young explained how he was called down from his boardinghouse sometime after 8:00 that evening to meet the sisters on the sidewalk.[20]

"While you were standing there, what if anything happened?" Talbot asked.

"There was about half a brick thrown, between the other buildings, and hit Mrs. Ludwig," Young responded.

"Do you know where it hit her?"

"Struck her on the hip."

But Talbot's attempt to tie the thrown brick to Albin was thwarted when he next asked Young, "And what if anything happened to a dog?"

"Why, heard a dog bark—and she said it was their dog."

Ludwig's attorney Parker objected. Judge Funk agreed, striking the statement that one of the women, presumably Cecilia, had said the bark came from their dog. Albin would testify later that he was looking for their dog that evening, and accepting that statement as truth could have placed Ludwig—and his dog—at the scene when the brick was thrown. Curiously, Talbot never asked Young if he saw Albin there.

Talbot's questions led Young to describe what happened when the three—Young and the sisters—arrived at the Ludwig home afterward.

"He asked where she had been," Young said.

"Go on, relate the conversation."

"She said that she had been round town—where she said she was going—and he accused her of going further than she said she was going."

Cecilia finally admitted, Young testified, that she and Jean had been across the river to Second Street.

"What did he say then?" Talbot asked.

"He said she talked to a bridgeman over there," Young replied.

"And what did she say?"

"She said—'what of that?'"

"Then what did he say?"

"He said she was not going to run around with a bridgeman."

Young said that Albin and Cecilia "quarreled along quite a while" and that Albin used profanity. "He swore and cursed her," Young said, though he didn't remember the exact words.

Later, after Young, Jean Ellsworth, and the Ludwigs left the home to hunt for Jean's two children, the quarrel resumed, Young said.

"Do you remember anything particular was said there?" Talbot asked.

"Well, along later in the quarrel," Young replied, "she said that he just became so mean to her, and all that, that she could not comb her hair or change her clothes, and he accused her of gossiping, and she would get her clothes and leave."

Young said Albin's response was that "she could not take a thing until the court allowed her."

"What did he say?"

"He said before she would leave he would burn them up; and he said she could go first."

In response to Talbot's next question, about whether Ludwig used the word *rinse,* as in "cleaning up the place," Young said: "He said everything would be settled on the morrow."

Later in Talbot's direct examination, Young was asked again about the brick that had hit Cecilia.

"She accused him of throwing the brick and striking her," Young stated.

"What did he say?"

"He said it was not him; he did not know anything about it."

Under cross-examination from Parker, Young filled in the blanks about his background. He had been a widower for three years, he had two children who were not living with him in Mishawaka, and he had worked as a machinist for several companies since moving to Mishawaka in March 1906.

Young testified that he first met Albin Ludwig when Albin, Cecilia, Jean, and Jean's children strolled by his boardinghouse one Sunday. He was sitting outside at the time.

"They recognized me—Mrs. Ludwig and her sister did," he said. Young visited the Ludwig home for the first time about a week later.

Parker tried to pin down Young on how many times he visited the Ludwig home. "You called quite frequently?"

"I called several times."

"You called as many as a dozen times, did you not?"

"No, sir, I did not." Young said he probably visited a half-dozen times.

Parker wanted to know the purpose of Young's visits, which woman he wanted to see. Young answered several times that it was "Mrs. Ellsworth"—Jean—and her children, emphasizing that he was visiting the children too. He knew Jean was a married woman and had known her husband, too, while growing up in Kingsbury.

"You did not call to see Mrs. Ludwig?"

"No, I did not."

"Though you knew her just as well as you knew Mrs. Ellsworth?"

"Although I knew her—yes, sir."

"Well, it is a fact, Mr. Young, that you frequently went out upon the streets with these women?"

Young responded that he went out only with Jean and sometimes with her children. Some of the walks were in the evening, after dark.

"Well, isn't it a fact that you occasionally went out with Mrs. Ludwig in the evening?" Parker asked.

"No, sir."

"Never did?"

"Never did."

Parker wanted to know about the evening before Cecilia's death, when she and Jean asked a friend of his—the so-called "bridgeman"—to call him out of his boardinghouse. Ludwig's attorney asked fifteen questions about the brick-throwing incident, but nothing new was revealed other than how the three were standing on the sidewalk and that Mrs. Ludwig was hurt slightly.

"Had you expected to meet the women that evening?" Parker asked, again trying to show that the rendezvous had been planned.

"No, sir," Young said.

Parker asked about the quarreling when all arrived back at the Ludwig home that night. First, he wanted to know how strong the language was.

"Both swear?"

"Both swore some," Young said.

"Mrs. Ludwig called him some harsh names, didn't she?"

"Not that I remember of."

Parker again tried to show that Cecilia and Young had an improper relationship considering that Cecilia was married. But Young denied that he sat alone on the porch at night with either Cecilia or Jean, though he might have stood on the porch with Jean as he was leaving. Young always referred to Jean as "Mrs. Ellsworth."

Again, Parker asked about the quarrel. Young repeatedly denied participating.

"Well, didn't Mr. Ludwig say to his wife in your presence that her behavior was not such as it should be?"

"No, he did not say that."

Parker asked about Ackerman, the friend who fetched Young out of his boardinghouse that evening when the sisters came by.

"He called him the bridgeman?"

"Yes, sir," Young said, adding that Ackerman worked on the new bridge at Mishawaka.

"He knew Mrs. Ludwig?"

"He had met her before? Not that I know of. I don't know that he met Mrs. Ludwig before; but apparently from what I heard afterwards that was the first time he had met her; he had met Mrs. Ellsworth before."

Parker again led Young, in detail, through that night's discussion about Albin and Cecilia separating. Young's story did not change from what he said in Talbot's direct examination.

"Mrs. Ludwig said that he just became so mean to her and accused her of so many things, that she would not try—that tomorrow she would pack her things and leave—that she could not comb her hair, and change her clothes, unless he accused her of expecting someone," Young said.

"What did he say to that?"

"He said she should not take a thing out of the house until the court allowed her."

"That is, in answer to her statement that she would pack her things and leave?"

"Yes, sir."

But Young said only separation was discussed, not divorce. And he confirmed that Cecilia planned to leave the next day. "Mrs. Ludwig did not say where she was going," he responded to one question.

"What did Mr. Ludwig say about her leaving?" Parker asked.

"Said she should not leave," Young responded.

Parker again got Young to confirm that Albin said "everything would be settled tomorrow." Young also confirmed that he saw Jean Ellsworth from a distance early the next afternoon, before the murder, as she walked past the shop where he was running a lathe.

Young surely was exhausted by now from the repetitive questions from both attorneys. His testimony would take up thirty-six pages of the official transcript. But he wasn't done yet, as Talbot returned to question him on redirect. Young, whose testimony had been succinct thus far, showed fatigue as the queries continued.

"Here is a matter I probably should have brought out on direct [testimony]," Talbot said, "Do you remember the evening at the house there of anything being said about support?"

"About what?" Young replied.

"About support?"

"At which house?" Young asked, still confused by the question.

"At the Ludwig house during this controversy that evening between Mr. and Mrs. Ludwig, was anything said by Mrs. Ludwig about support?"

"I don't think there was—not that I know of."

"Or about the court?"

"Only when Mr. Ludwig mentioned the court settling their differences in regard to her taking the things away," Young said.

"Do you remember before the grand jury of making this statement— that the night before the tragedy—the night before this murder, she said she would compel him to support her, and he said, 'Not unless the court would allow her?'"

Defense counsel Parker objected to the question, pointing out that Young was a witness for the state, that he hadn't shown any hostility, "and therefore it is not competent to call his attention to what he stated before the grand jury."

Judge Funk overruled the objection, but it didn't matter. Young said he didn't think he had made that statement to the grand jury.

The *South Bend Daily Times* commented on that exchange in its trial coverage in that afternoon's newspaper:

> The state is having considerable trouble to have its witnesses relate the facts of the case, and is frequently compelled to call their attention to statements made by them before the grand jury. It is not thought that the witnesses are attempting to hold any of the facts back, but have forgotten the details of their evidence.[21]

Talbot's final question to Young asked what he saw on the bed in the Ludwig home when he visited the murder scene the day after the crime.[22]

"Well, the bed-clothing was all torn around—upside down, and bunches of Mrs. Ludwig's hair tangled up in the covers and around the room."

Talbot's question and Young's graphic answer—the first description of the murder scene in the trial—brought the defense attorney back to the witness stand for more questions.

"What did you go over to the house for—just out of curiosity?" Parker asked.

"No sir, I did not. I went with Mrs. Ellsworth and the police, to help Mrs. Ellsworth get her trunk—with the police," Young said.

He repeated that he noticed the bed but, when asked, did not see blood.

"There was hair in the bed clothes, or on the bed, and one or two small bunches of hair on the floor."

Responding to Parker's questions, Young admitted that water had been sprayed into the room by firemen, that people had been in and out of the house looking around, including "one or two strangers." Parker's point was that his client, Albin Ludwig, had not necessarily been responsible for Cecilia's hair being where Young saw it more than twenty-four hours after the incident.

Talbot then returned to question Young a third time, getting Young to clarify that despite having known the women since childhood, he had known Albin for only six weeks to two months.

Parker returned for his third round of questions, concentrating on the brick-throwing incident the night before Cecilia's death—and the accusation that Albin had thrown it.

"Now somebody said to Ludwig that he had thrown the brick?" Parker asked.

"She did—Mrs. Ludwig," Young said.

"And he said he had done no such thing?"

"Yes, sir."

"Did he say that he had not been over there?"

"Yes, sir."

Talbot was frustrated. Young was his witness—the state's witness—a witness who had spent the better part of an hour giving answers that showed the jury that Albin Ludwig was a jealous man with a temper. But Young's testimony hadn't shown that Ludwig's temper and jealousy had prompted the defendant to act physically against Cecilia. Young hadn't seen who threw the brick at Cecilia the night before, and he had testified repeatedly that Ludwig denied his wife's accusation that he had been in the vicinity of the incident, across the river.

Talbot couldn't help but rise to ask Young, one more time, the same question the defense attorney just had asked him:

"He said he had not been over there to that side of the river?"

"Yes, sir."

His testimony finished, Young stepped down from the witness stand. Talbot stepped back, probably wishing he could call Jean Ellsworth as his next witness. Cecilia's younger sister could be a corroborating witness to virtually everything Young, Jean's suspected suitor, had testified. She had spent much of the summer in the Ludwig home witnessing the tension between the man and wife, though Parker probably would blame her for some of that tension on cross-examination. She was with Cecilia the evening before when they walked to Young's boardinghouse with Ackerman, whom Albin scornfully called the "bridgeman." She was present later that night when Cecilia and Albin quarreled. She was in the house the morning of the murder, leaving shortly before the noon meal to find a livery to transport their trunks. Her children were present during the meal and may have witnessed whatever happened afterward. Jean was loyal to Cecilia and hostile to Albin. She would be the perfect prosecution witness.

But Jean was nowhere to be found. Maybe she was hiding out at her parents' farm in Kingsbury. Maybe she was back in Nevada with her husband.

"The sister was not at my trial and no one knew where she was," Albin would write when he entered prison. In fact, the Henderson family, possibly because of distance, more likely because the testimony would make them relive the tragedy, stayed clear of the courtroom most of the week. "My wife has four sisters, one brother, father and mother and they were not at the trial," Albin wrote. "The mother was there the last day."[23]

Representing his family, Albin's mother and brother were present the entire trial. As described by the *Daily Times,* the case had taken a toll on Eva Ludwig:

> Most pathetic is the appearance of the accused's mother, Mrs. Eva Ida Ludwig, who with her son, G. H. Ludwig, both of Elkhart, are in attendance at the trial. Mrs. Ludwig is 69 years old, but appears much older. This is easily explained by the worry and nervous strain caused by the trouble her son is in.
>
> When the accused was brought into court this afternoon, the aged lady broke down and wept bitterly. During the recital of the evidence, which bids fair to convict her son of the awful crime of murder, Mrs. Ludwig paid the strictest attention to every word spoken by the witnesses.[24]

Those who knew Albin Ludwig before the murder might not have recognized him at the trial.

"Since his incarceration Ludwig has grown a full beard and mustache and presents a much changed appearance than at the time of the murder," the *Daily Times* reported. "He listens with considerable interest to the statements of the witnesses and frequently consults with his attorneys."[25]

Testimony moved faster after Young stepped down. Talbot called John F. Gaylor to the stand to state that he owned the Ludwigs' house on East Marion Street, although Albin was buying it from Gaylor on installments. A portion of the upstairs was "very badly damaged" by the fire. He estimated the damage at about $50, roughly $1,400 in 2019 dollars.[26]

The state's next witness was James Anderson, who told the jury what Talbot was unable to elicit from Young: that Albin indeed had been south of the river the night before the murder.

Anderson, a Mishawaka police officer, said he spoke to Ludwig at the corner of Main and Second Streets that evening. Talbot asked him to describe the encounter.

"Well, I stood on the corner—it was on the southeast corner of Main and Second Street—and I stood leaning up against a telegraph pole. Felt somebody tap me on the shoulder, and I turned around and said to him, 'What's your trouble?' And he says, 'Do you see those two women across the street?' They was [sic] opposite to me, standing on the northwest corner. I says, 'Yes, sir, what about them?' He says, 'Do you know who they are?' I says, 'No, sir.' He says, 'I would like to have you find out.' So I walked over that way, to see the women—who they were—and he says, 'Do you know them?' I say, 'Yes, sir, I do. What about it?' He told me they left the house and wanted him to stay with the children, and he made up his mind to follow them, and he came over there and saw them talking to a man. He wanted me to see the same as he did. And he says, 'I am going to put a stop to that, and if anything happens, I want you to remember it.'"

"What then occurred?" Talbot asked.

Anderson said the women started north on the west side of the street. "The man was with them, in between the women." Ludwig went north on the east side of the street.

Talbot failed to ask Anderson whom the women were, a point rectified when Anderson was cross-examined by Parker's deputy, Will G. Crabill. Anderson said they were Ludwig's wife and her sister.

"You know them from seeing them on the street together?" Crabill asked.

"Yes, sir." Anderson added that he also knew the sisters because "they lived on the same street that I lived on."

Anderson didn't know the identity of the man but said he was about five feet seven or eight inches tall, weighed about 150 pounds, "real dark complected," and "in the neighborhood of twenty-five years."

Crabill asked if he overheard anything that was said.

"No, sir, it was none of my business, and I did not."[27]

The next witness, Marcellus Gaze, was Albin and Cecilia Ludwig's neighbor, living two houses west of their home on East Marion Street, a distance Gaze estimated at only about forty feet. With Isaac Kane Parks conducting direct examination for the prosecution, Gaze recounted how Ludwig had dropped by their home around 9:00 the night before his wife's death. "He spoke something about seeing some man with his wife the night before. I don't remember what he did say, but we talked quite a bit. I said to him if I was in his place I would pack up and leave. He said he couldn't do that."

Under cross-examination from Parker, Gaze said Ludwig had visited with him and his wife for about five minutes while they were in the kitchen. "We talked about nothing else except his trouble with his wife." Gaze recalled that Albin didn't sit down. "He seemed to be in trouble and spoke right away about a man being with his wife the night before."

Parker asked Gaze why he made the comment about picking up and leaving if he had been in Ludwig's place.

"I said that because I knew they had had so much trouble before. I knew what the trouble was about."

Gaze said Ludwig told him he loved his wife and could not pick up and leave.

"As he went out he said something to the effect that he would put an end to it, or would stop it."[28]

Gaze's wife, Veronica, then gave a similar account to Talbot about how Albin had come to their home around 9:00 the night before his wife's death. "He said something to the effect that he had seen his wife out with another man," Mrs. Gaze said. "My husband said to him that if he were in his place he would pick up and get out." Ludwig didn't know what to do, she said. "He always said that he thought everything of his wife and that he could not leave her."

Mrs. Gaze said that in leaving, Ludwig "made a threat of some kind, but I don't think it was on his wife, if I remember right."

When Talbot asked how Ludwig responded when her husband said he would pick up and leave in Ludwig's situation, she said, "I think Ludwig said he could not do that because she could make him support her. He also said that he thought everything of her. He had made that same remark to me before."[29]

Talbot was rolling now. He had thirty-five witnesses to present, and, except for Fred Young, he and Deputy Prosecutor Parks were moving through that list quickly. Talbot didn't want to overwhelm the jury, but he also didn't want the jurors to get bogged down in minutiae and forget his main points. He was working through the case chronologically. He had presented the events of Monday night, September 24, and was ready to move on to the events of Tuesday, September 25, the day Cecilia Ludwig died.

Lester Gitre's testimony was quick and to the point. With Parks asking the questions, Gitre, the druggist for the North Side Drug Store, recalled Albin Ludwig buying a bottle of brandy between 11:00 A.M. and noon the day Cecilia died. "I don't remember how much—six or eight ounces," he said.[30]

Next, Milton E. Robbins, a grocer at 607 North Bridge Street, only a seven-minute walk from the Ludwig home,[31] testified that he saw Ludwig in his store around noon on the same day. "He purchased two gallons of gasoline and took it away with him," Robbins told Deputy Prosecutor Parks.

Parker asked in cross-examination how Ludwig paid for the gasoline.

"Ludwig was running a bill at my store at the time," Robbins replied. "He was a regular customer and paid once a week."[32]

The last witness to describe Ludwig's whereabouts that Tuesday morning was Anna Burkhart, who lived at 1022 North Bridge Street, a short walk west of the Ludwig home. She related to Talbot how Ludwig had talked to her in her yard around 11:30 that morning. "He said he was going away rather unexpectedly and wanted to know if my husband would buy his dog." She told him no.

In cross-examination, Mrs. Burkhart told Parker that she never had spoken to Ludwig before. "I didn't even know who he was," she said. "I asked him if he was Mr. Ludwig, and he said, 'Yes.'" Ludwig told her that the dog was a black-and-tan hound. "He made the price $3."[33]

Now it was time for the prosecution to call to the stand the neighbors who were at home, and the craftsmen who were working at neighborhood homes, when fire broke out at the Ludwig address that Tuesday afternoon.

David Hull, a painter and paperhanger working on a house—he called it a "cottage"—250 to 300 feet away, was the first of those witnesses. The *South Bend Daily Times* would describe Hull's testimony as "probably the most interesting evidence submitted" that morning.[34]

Questioned by Parks, Hull remembered walking by the Ludwig home early that afternoon to get a pail of water. "I saw a man sitting on Ludwig's porch, but I couldn't swear it was Ludwig," he said, adding that the man was "sitting flat on the floor with his feet on the step." Hull then saw the man get up, go into the house and close the door.

Hull returned to the house where he was working. Within five minutes, a woman called to him through the kitchen window that the Ludwig house was on fire. Hull went outside and saw smoke coming from the upstairs window.

He raced to the burning house and found the front door locked. "I ran back to the house where I was at work and got a ladder and carried it over and a Mr. Schellenberg took it and put it on the west side of the house and I spoke to have it brought around to the porch roof," Hull said.

A man Hull didn't know went up the ladder first and entered the house through the upstairs window above the porch roof. Hull said he went up the ladder but initially didn't go into the house. "I saw Mr. Ludwig when they brought him out on the roof through the window," he said. Hull then helped get Ludwig to the ground, after which he went around to the kitchen door, which was open, and entered the house.

"There was some smoke below—it was coming downstairs," he said. Hull then went up the stairs, checking all the rooms except the front room, which Fire Chief Albert Buysse stopped him from entering. "I saw into the front room," he said. "I saw blood on the floor near the window."

Hull gave more details in Samuel Parker's cross-examination. He told how it had been around 2:00 P.M. when he went to a water pump to fill a bucket of water, seeing a man, presumably Albin Ludwig, on the Ludwig porch as he did so. "He had his elbows on his knees, resting his head in his hands," Hull recalled.

"It was just as I stepped on the side porch to go into the house after I got the water that I saw the man get up and go into the Ludwig house," he told Parker. "I had just commenced work when I heard the woman speak about the fire. Immediately after that I ran over to the Ludwig house." Two coworkers went with him.

Hull clarified that smoke was coming out of the upstairs window on the west side of the house as well as the double window above the porch roof on the south side. He repeated that he didn't follow the "stranger" into the house through the upstairs window, but when he entered through the kitchen, "a good many folks were around when I went into the house and upstairs."

With Parker asking the questions, Hull detailed what he saw through the door of the upstairs front room, the bedroom, after the fire chief stopped him from entering: "I noticed some dirt in the front room near the window; also a flowerpot. The dirt and the flowerpot were close to the blood that I saw in the front room." The blood, he testified, was splattered over the walls and in pools on the floor. "I did not notice the bed— couldn't say whether there was blood on it or not."

When Hull stepped down from the witness stand, the jury might have assumed that the blood belonged to Cecilia, the alleged victim of the man on trial. The wounds to that man, Albin Ludwig, and how they may have occurred would be a point of contention as the trial moved forward.[35]

Continuing to call witnesses who could tell the story in chronological order, Talbot asked another neighbor, Catherine Brand, to come to the stand. Mrs. Brand lived in the home of her daughter and son-in-law, Mr. and Mrs. John Wilson, the first house west of the Ludwig home.

"I saw Mr. Ludwig shortly after dinner on that day," she testified. "I was hanging clothes and saw Mr. Ludwig come out of the house and get the slop jar and come back in." As had become a ritual between the two neighbors, "he bowed to me and I bowed to him. I did not hear him say anything."

Mrs. Brand said she saw Jean Ellsworth "going across the field"— not every lot on East Marion Street had a house on it yet—about fifteen minutes before she saw Albin.

Later, when she saw smoke coming from a window, Mrs. Brand went to the back door of the Ludwig home, where she saw Charles Ellsworth, Jean's son, "who was eight or nine years old," she said. But she did not enter the house, instead returning home.[36]

When Talbot finished the direct examination of Mrs. Brand, Judge Funk ordered a recess for the noon meal. Court was adjourned until 1:30.

CHAPTER 11

"She Certainly Was Dead"

CATHERINE BRAND WAS BACK on the stand after dinner to answer defense attorney Samuel Parker's questions, starting with how well she knew her neighbors, the Ludwigs.

"I was on talking and friendly terms with Mr. Ludwig and also with his wife, but was not intimate with her," she replied. Mrs. Brand wasn't sure exactly what time she saw Albin go outside to get the slop jar, but it was after her dinner at noon and not later than 1:00. She described the slop jar as "an earthen crock with a handle to it."

Mrs. Brand said she "first smelled the smoke and then looked and saw it coming out of the windows. There was just enough smoke so that I could notice, when I first saw it." The windows of the house were opened, not a surprise considering the midday heat. She told her daughter, Mrs. John Wilson, who rushed to the home of another neighbor, Mrs. Charles Patterson, to report the fire on the Pattersons' telephone.

After picking up her daughter's baby, who had been with another neighbor, Mrs. Brand, carrying her grandchild, went to the Ludwig home to "tell Mr. Ludwig that his house was on fire."

"Did you see anyone there?" Parker asked.

"Only the little boy," Mrs. Brand answered, referring to little Charles Ellsworth. "He came right to the back door."[1]

Milton Carter was the next witness called by the state. He had been a carpenter working on the same nearby house as David Hull and James

74

France; France would follow him to the stand. On direct examination by Isaac Kane Parks, Carter said he had seen Ludwig during the morning of the fire but had not noticed him that afternoon. On cross-examination, he contradicted Hull's statement that Hull had called his attention to the fire. Instead, Carter claimed he had learned about it from the woman who also alerted Hull. He said Hull "called my attention to somebody sitting on the porch of the Ludwig house, but when I looked, I didn't see anybody."[2]

France, also questioned by Parks, explained that the house where the men were working was about half a block west and half a block south of Ludwig's home. France also went to the fire scene but didn't remember how long he remained nor whether he saw Albin. "I saw a man brought down the ladder, but I was not acquainted with Mr. Ludwig."[3]

Now the stage was set for the prosecution's key witness of the afternoon, Albert Buysse, Mishawaka's fire chief at the time of Cecilia's death. Joseph Talbot would handle this witness personally.

Buysse said the fire alarm was received about five minutes to two. He rode to the fire on the hook-and-ladder truck, arriving after the hose wagon. He kicked in the locked front door and went upstairs to the front room, which two of his men already had entered through the window. Those firemen already had applied the chemical fire extinguisher and laid the hose by the window. Buysse called out the window to the men below to turn on the water.

Buysse told Talbot he realized the fire wasn't in the front room but in the closet on the east side.

"And what did you do then, after you hollered to turn the water on?" Talbot asked.

"Took the nozzle and put it into the roof, because it was burning a hole in the roof, put a little water—enough to put it out—and pulled the hose back out," Buysse replied.

"What did you do then?"

"Then, of course, I discovered there was a person in there, and me being chief of the fire department, I thought it was my duty to keep everybody out of the house."

Talbot asked Buysse to describe for the jury where he saw the person.

"She lay right inside—right across the front of the door—almost in front of the door. She was all up in a cramped-up position."

Talbot asked a series of questions attempting to get Buysse to explain, in words, the exact position of the body—her head, legs, arms, and hands—when he found it. Twice Parker objected when the fire chief attempted to demonstrate the position. Funk sustained the objection both times.

"Did you notice as to her clothing?" the prosecutor asked.

"She did not have any on."

"Did you notice any remnants of clothing?"

"All that I saw that she had on was a partly consumed corset. Stays."

Talbot asked whether the stays were iron or cloth. Buysse said they were iron. Talbot asked about jewelry. Buysse saw none.

"And what was the condition of her flesh?"

"Well, sir, as near as I could tell you, her flesh looked just about like a real hard-baked chicken."[4]

The trial transcript and the newspaper reports don't relate whether Buysse's last statement elicited a gasp in the courtroom, but it seems likely. The *South Bend Daily Times* softened Buysse's response, quoting him indirectly as saying, "the body was burned almost to a crisp." The competing *South Bend Tribune* wrote "the body had the appearance of having been 'baked.'"[5] Those descriptions probably were more than enough for those reading the trial coverage with full stomachs that evening, even considering the colorful journalism of the day.

Talbot briefly changed the subject to whether Buysse had extinguished the fire—he had—and the dimensions of the closet, which the fire chief estimated as five by eight feet, with no window.

"What was her condition as to being alive or dead when you found her?" the prosecutor asked.

"She certainly was dead."

Talbot shifted gears. He asked Buysse if he found a can in the closet.

"Well, I found a baking-powder can in there," Buysse replied, estimating its size as a quarter of a pound.

Talbot asked what he did with the can.

"I picked it up and brought it out, and says, 'Here is a can.' And I looked at it, and it had an oily appearance, if I am not mistaken. I handed it to Mr. Jarrett, the chief of police."

Parker objected to the description of the oily appearance and wanted it stricken from the record. He knew where Talbot was heading, that the prosecutor would attempt to show that Albin Ludwig used a can to carry gasoline or kerosene upstairs to burn his wife's body. If it were gasoline, it could have come from the two gallons Ludwig bought that morning. But Judge Funk sided with Talbot.

"Did you make any investigation as to what it contained?" Talbot continued.

"No, I did not," Buysse said. "Some of the other people spoke about that."

"Not what they said, but did you smell it, or feel of it?"

"Yes, I was satisfied there had been oil in it," Buysse said.

Parker objected again, and this time the judge agreed to strike everything but "yes" from Buysse's answer.

Talbot tried again, and Buysse was allowed to say that it smelled of kerosene.

The questions continued. Buysse said he saw a razor on the floor. He saw that the flowerpots in the front room "had been kicked or thrown over and the dirt spilled on the floor." He saw blood about two feet from a flowerpot.

Buysse testified he saw Albin Ludwig both outside and inside the house, after he had been carried down the ladder. He saw vomit in both locations, both examples "a dark reddish color."

Talbot asked if he saw blood upstairs. Yes, Buysse said, he had seen blood on the bed. "Both pillows had blood on [them] and so did the spread."

And what about Albin?

"I noticed that Ludwig's throat was cut and also his wrists."

More details emerged when Parker cross-examined Buysse. The fire chief repeated that he had kicked open the front door, which was locked, to enter the house. "When I got upstairs into the front room there were two firemen there," he said. "They had come through the window. These firemen had got to the building while I was on my way there." The fact that others had been in the front room before Buysse wasn't news to the jury, but the more people Parker could place in the room before the chief found the can—the can that smelled as if it had contained a flammable liquid—the more doubt the jury might have that Albin was responsible for it.

Buysse repeated how he had ordered the water turned on because of fire in the roof above the closet. "I noticed the woman in the closet before we got the fire out," he said.

Asked what else he saw in the closet, Buysse mentioned the trunk in the east end of the closet, a foot or two from the wall. That trunk would be an important part of Albin's defense.

He told how some men carried Ludwig and his cot back inside the house after the fire was extinguished, placing him in the downstairs room west of the dining room. He described the blood in the front room in more detail: "I noticed the blood upstairs, that it was about two feet from where the pile of dirt was, near the window. The spot of blood I noticed on the bedspread was about as big as your hand and it was near the middle, and on the pillows the spot of blood on each was about as big as a half a hand. The blood was fresh."[6]

Buysse stepped down. Talbot called Otto N. Goeller, a Mishawaka fireman who had entered the house through the window above the porch roof. Goeller said he discharged a "chemical apparatus"—a fire extinguisher—in an effort to put out the fire in the closet, which "was full of smoke and a kind of flame." He corroborated his chief's testimony that water from a hose finally quenched the fire. "Then I could see the woman in the closet." He agreed with Buysse that the woman was in a cramped-up position on the floor.[7]

William C. Hose, with the perfect surname for a fireman, testified next. Hose was a "call man" for the fire department, which meant he did not sleep at the department like a "bunk man" did. Hose said he arrived at the Ludwig home as Albin was being carried down the ladder. Then he went up the ladder with his colleague Goeller.

Hose told Talbot he started to throw water on the flames when he noticed that the greater part of the fire appeared to be coming through a crack over the closet door. Before he could open this door, he had to move a rocking chair and some other obstacles that apparently had been piled in front of it. (This was the first mention of obstacles blocking the closet door.) When Hose opened the door, "we put out the fire. . . . Then I saw the woman lying in the closet. She was dead." Hose said the body was on the floor in a semisitting position. She later fell completely to the floor.

Hose was the first witness to testify that he had seen blood on the closet door around the knob and on the casing, down at the bottom. Like the previous witnesses, Hose said he noticed blood on the carpet in front of the window and about two feet from the window. "I noticed blood on the bedspread also."

Will G. Crabill, handling his first witness for the defense, asked Hose to describe the double windows on the south side of the front room, over the porch roof. Hose said he climbed in the east window of the two. "Others had been in the front room before we went in," he said.

Hose described the fire as being "all over the closet," even scorching a dresser just north of the closet door.

Crabill asked Hose about the broken flowerpots that others had noticed in the front room. Hose said he saw a single flowerpot by the east side of the double window.[8]

The *South Bend Daily Times* reporter was impressed by Hose's testimony. "No attempt was made to confuse him, and his testimony was given in such a manner as to be exceptionally good."[9]

Judge Funk called a fifteen-minute recess at 3:15 in the afternoon. Six more witnesses would testify before Funk halted proceedings for the day.[10]

James France was first. Parker recalled the carpenter, who had been working on a nearby house at the time of the fire. He clarified that it "must have been a half hour" between the time his coworker Hull had called attention to a man sitting on the front steps at the Ludwig home and when he heard the woman say the house was on fire. Hull's testimony that morning had made the time seem like five minutes.

France's new testimony also cleared up what the flowerpots were doing on the floor. "I saw someone raise one of the windows," he said. "I noticed plants in small jars sitting on the window sill. When the window was raised the plants disappeared. They fell on the inside."[11]

The *Daily Times* reporter explained to his readers that France's testimony "was used in contradicting the impression that a plant had been knocked from a window ledge in a possible struggle which might have taken place between Mr. and Mrs. Ludwig, or that the plant pot had been placed in front of the closet door by Ludwig as an obstruction."[12]

Physician C. A. Dresch of Mishawaka testified next. He had examined Albin Ludwig in the yard after Ludwig had been carried down the ladder. He detailed the injuries in a series of answers to Deputy Prosecutor Parks.

"He was cut across both wrists and also the calves of both legs and the neck," Dr. Dresch said. "The cut in the neck was in front and went through the skin to the cartilage. I don't remember which was the deeper of the cuts on the wrists. They were both cut through. The cuts in the calves of the legs were between the ankle and the knee. One was considerably deeper than the other. I don't think either one was to the bone."

Dresch said he believed Ludwig was conscious despite his closed eyes, that Ludwig resisted when the doctor attempted to open the eyes with his fingers. "An unconscious man would not resist the opening of the lids," he said. Asked if he examined the mouth, Dresch said no, that he couldn't say whether it was blistered. Blistering could have indicated whether Ludwig had ingested poison.

In cross-examination by Parker, Dresch said his examination of Ludwig was "superficial." Parker asked questions about each wound, and Dresch explained which were superficial—"that is, just through the skin"—such as those on the wrists, and which were more serious, such as a cut in one calf that was three inches deep, "very close to the bone." He said the victim could have inflicted the wounds to the calves while in a sitting position.

Dresch testified that Ludwig vomited the food he had eaten at noon. The doctor "did not notice any blood and would have noticed it had there been any." Parker asked if Dresch had not told the grand jury that the vomit smelled as if Ludwig had drunk iodine. But Dresch replied that he didn't remember having made such a statement. If the smell of iodine was there, Dresch said, he hadn't noticed it.[13]

The parade of prosecution witnesses continued. At one point on Tuesday afternoon, Talbot said he had expected the hearing of evidence to take most of the week, but the progress being made that day meant the state would rest its case sooner.[14]

The next witness was Emma Reifsneider, who lived southeast of the Ludwig home on Christyann Street, close enough to hear one woman and two men arguing outside the night before. She testified that she heard a man say, "Was I over town with you, Fred, last night?" She heard a man answer, "No." Then a woman responded, "You are a God-damned liar." Though she didn't recognize the voices, she suspected one of the men was Albin and the other his neighbor to the east, Fred Metzler. The "Fred" also could have been Fred Young, but Mrs. Reifsneider might not have known about Young's recent presence in the Ludwigs' lives.

Mrs. Reifsneider also was asked when she knew about the fire the next afternoon.

"My attention was called to the fire by the fire whistle," she told Deputy Prosecutor Parks. "I went out on the front porch. I heard voices screaming as though it was a lady screaming for help."[15]

Her last comment—the possibility that she heard a lady screaming for help—might have elicited a gasp from those crowded into the courtroom, who wondered if the screaming lady had been Cecilia Ludwig. Surely Talbot and Parks liked the testimony. But Mrs. Reifsneider contradicted herself under cross-examination.

"When the fire alarm sounded I went out and heard a number of voices crying, 'Fire!'" she told Crabill. Did she hear a lady screaming? "I did not hear any other voices except those calling, 'Fire.' I do not mean to say I heard anything else."[16]

Actually, any screaming Mrs. Reifsneider heard could have come from Jean Ellsworth's daughter Lucy. Alice McNabb, who followed Reifsneider to the stand, told how she heard screaming and saw smoke coming from the Ludwig house while on her back porch. Mrs. McNabb lived on Broadway, the next street south. With no houses yet on the south side of Marion Street, her back porch faced the front of the Ludwig home without obstruction.

"I went on my back porch because a little girl called me," she told Talbot. Initially, she thought the screaming came from a woman. The girl, whom Mrs. McNabb didn't identify by name, stayed with her about a half hour. Then the girl went back home but later returned to her.[17]

It's logical to assume that Lucy and her brother Charles ran to neighbors' homes in hysterics after hearing all or part of the final, fatal quarrel between Albin and their Aunt Cecilia. Their mother wasn't there to console them because she had walked downtown to find a livery to carry their packed trunks. But neighbor Catherine Brand already had testified that Charles was in the house when, after seeing smoke, she went to the back door. Lucy, who was older, may have gone for help.

"The screaming that I heard lasted two or three minutes," Mrs. Mc-Nabb told Crabill in cross-examination. She said she was the woman who alerted the carpenters who were working on the cottage on Sarah Street.[18]

The long day continued. By now, the jury surely was growing weary. But the prosecution still had two more witnesses before resting for the day.

Talbot called Alfred Heiney to the stand. Heiney was the painter and paperhanger who repaired the damage to the Ludwig house four to six weeks after the fire. Talbot asked detailed questions about where he had found blood and the size of the stains. Strangely, Heiney found "a spot that looked like blood on the casing of the back door" leading to the summer kitchen. He described the spot as one that "might be made by the base of my thumb." Cecilia certainly didn't go out that door after the deadly fight upstairs, so Heiney's testimony raised the question of where Albin went after murdering Cecilia. Maybe to fill a can or a slop jar with gasoline from what he had bought for the stove?

Upstairs in the front room, Heiney said, the casing to the closet door upstairs was "kind of blistered," but he found no blood on the door casing or the knob. The door itself had been replaced since the fire. But, he added, "I saw what looked like blood on the window sill of the window that goes to the south, one of the double windows."

Today, the crime scene investigation team would have taken samples of the suspected bloodstains within hours of the crime and, in the lab, matched them to the victim, the killer, or a paramedic. But no such technology existed back then. "I could not tell it was blood or not. It looked like blood," Heiney said under cross-examination.[19]

The last witness of the day was Henry C. Holtzendorf, the St. Joseph County coroner and also a physician and surgeon, who described what he saw the afternoon of the murder in clear and concise answers to Talbot's questions.

Holtzendorf said he arrived at the Ludwig house around 2:00 P.M. on the day of the fire. "I found the house in confusion, and I went upstairs, into the front bedroom, and off the front bedroom, in a closet, I found a body supposed to have been Mrs. Ludwig."

"A woman was it?" Talbot asked.

"Yes."

"What was the condition of the clothes on the body?"

"Very much charred from burning."

"What if any clothes do you recollect were left on the body—or do you recollect?" Talbot asked.

"There was not very much of clothing left," the coroner replied. "From the hips to probably the armpits was about all. The rest of the body was entirely nude."

Talbot asked him to describe what else he found in the closet. Holtzendorf mentioned a trunk, a can, and "a great deal of clothing, more or less burned."

And he found a potato masher. "Looked like a potato smasher," he added.

It was the first mention of the alleged weapon by a witness.

"Where did you find that?" Talbot asked.

"Well, it was in the closet. It was a very small closet, and it was there."

"Was that partially burned?"

"Yes, it looked as though it had been burned."

Talbot showed Holtzendorf a partially burned potato masher, calling it State's Exhibit A, and asked if it was the one he found.

"It looks very much like the one that I found up there," the coroner replied.

Talbot also asked if Holtzendorf could tell what had been in the can he found.

"To my best belief the can had recently contained kerosene."

He said he saw Officer Foust pick up a straight razor "out of some dirt right near the closet door and near the front window. . . . I opened the razor there and found blood and dirt on it."

Holtzendorf continued that at the postmortem that evening, Dr. Charles Stroup and Dr. Edgar Doan conducted the examination. "We determined that the cause of death was shock. . . . shock from burning."

Talbot asked the coroner to describe the position of Mrs. Ludwig's body when he saw it in the closet.

"The body was lying on its back, cramped up and drawn up," he said, adding that the legs and arms were drawn up. The skin over the mouth was blue. Asked about the body's condition at the postmortem, Holtzendorf described it as "very much charred."

"Where was the body charred most—in the upper or lower part of the body?" Talbot asked.

"In my opinion it was very much equally distributed over the whole body."

He said the doctors also found a "ragged or jagged small scalp wound" on the left side of Cecilia's head.[20] Left unasked was whether the scalp wound could have been the result of a blow from a potato masher.

But State's Attorney Talbot wasn't done with Holtzendorf. It had been a long day, and Judge Funk adjourned court until 9:00 A.M. Wednesday.

Talbot, with assistance from Parks, had presented twenty witnesses and likely was satisfied that he had woven, as the *Elkhart Daily Review* reported, "a strong case of circumstantial evidence."

The defense would have been pleased that, thus far, nobody had placed Albin Ludwig at the precise scene of the crime prior to the discovery of Cecilia's charred body and Albin's bloodied body. Yes, Albin had been seen entering the house after sitting dejectedly on the porch, but nobody had heard the quarrel the afternoon of the murder; nobody had seen who carried the potato masher, the suspected weapon, up the stairs; and nobody had witnessed what happened in the closet. The absent Jean Ellsworth could have recounted what happened at the dinner table, but she couldn't be found.

As for those watching the trial from the hard wooden benches of the courtroom, the *South Bend Daily Times* wrote that most of the "large number of interested parties" were "acquaintances or neighbors of the Ludwigs" and that an "unusually large number of ladies are present."[21]

After hearing how Cecilia Ludwig died, it's unlikely any of the women would have wanted Albin Ludwig to escape the death penalty.

CHAPTER 12

The State Rests

A FEW MILES EAST IN MISHAWAKA, the trial was being followed closely, as Peter Young noted in his Wednesday column in the *South Bend Daily Times:* "The interest in the proceedings at the trial of Albin Ludwig, at South Bend, grows as the trial proceeds and in consequence great numbers of our citizens have hied[1] themselves away to the county seat to be present and listen to the proceedings."

Young then plugged his newspaper's extensive coverage of the trial in Tuesday's edition, a jab at the unnamed *South Bend Tribune,* which devoted only three paragraphs to the start of the trial and incorrectly referred to the defendant as "Alvin." The *Tribune's* article didn't even rate page 1 placement.

"The Times was highly complimented today on the very complete report of the testimony which it gave in Tuesday's issue," Young wrote. "It was interesting from beginning to end, and moreover truthful. The murderer receives little sympathy and the general concensus [sic] of opinion as near as it can be summed up is that if he gets his just deserts [sic] he will dangle at the end of a rope."[2]

State's Attorney Joseph Talbot was ready to resume his parade of witnesses Wednesday morning, but he would wait until later in the day to finish his direct questioning of Coroner Holtzendorf. He called the Ludwigs' neighbor Fred Metzler to the stand as his first witness of the day.

Metzler told how he had come home from work—he was a mold

maker—for dinner at noon and was eating at the table about twenty minutes after twelve when Albin entered his house.

"Mr. Ludwig came in the house and says, 'Fred, I am going to kill myself.' I says, 'What for? Don't get such a crazy thing in your head, Ludwig.' He says, 'I've got to. She's driving me crazy.' I says, 'Never mind, you don't have to do that.' And he went on to tell me that if he left her that she would make him support her. I told him no such thing could be done. He said she said so. Well, I says, 'We will just go simply to see some lawyer.' He says, 'Who will we go to see?' I named Charlie Metzger, the only lawyer I thought of. He says, 'Well,' he says, 'when can you go?' I says, 'After I quit work this evening.' And he says, 'All right.'

"Well, after then he says, 'Take a drink with me.' He pulled out a small bottle there of whisky or brandy—I don't know which, I should judge it was whisky—and I drank about half the contents of the bottle, and got done eating my dinner. And after that I started out, and we walked out to the well, where he was after a pail of water. Now, he says, 'We will go this evening.' I says, 'Yes, sir.' I says to him, 'Now we will have to make some arrangements so as your wife [Cecilia] won't see us go,' because she would not allow me to say anything or have anything to do with him."

So Metzler said he proposed they leave separately and then meet. Albin agreed. Metzler got on his bicycle and headed back to work. "That was the last I saw him until after the accident."

Talbot asked Metzler if he and Albin had been pretty good friends. "Yes," Metzler replied.

"You and his wife were not, however," Talbot stated.

"His wife and I were not on speaking terms," Metzler said bluntly.[3]

Under cross-examination, Metzler said he had seen Albin, Cecilia, her sister Jean, and Fred Young go into the Ludwig house the night before, but he "had no talk with them."[4] Albin would testify differently about whether they talked that night.

The next witness, Loren A. Foust, a Mishawaka police officer, confirmed Coroner Holtzendorf's statement from the day before that he had found the razor in the upstairs front room. "The blood on the razor was fresh," he told Deputy Prosecutor Parks.[5]

The state continued building its chain of evidence. Parks called George H. Wilklow to the stand. Wilklow, who was in the livery business in Mishawaka, confirmed that he had picked up Cecilia's body and delivered it to Finch's undertaking room.[6]

The next witness, Benjamin F. Jarrett, Mishawaka's police chief when the murder occurred, would take longer on the stand. His testimony would be similar to that of the fire chief and the coroner.

Jarrett testified he arrived at the Ludwig house around 1:30 in the afternoon and first noticed the dining table. "I saw the four plates—looked as though set for four persons—and there was some dinner left on the table," he said. "It was a boiled dinner—boiled beef and potatoes—butter and such as that."

Talbot tried to ask Jarrett whether the dinner had been partially or fully consumed, but Parker objected several times to his wording. Finally, Jarrett was allowed to say that one of the four plates "looked as though it had not been used."

Jarrett continued that he then saw Albin, who, by that point, had been carried back inside the house and placed on a sofa. "His limbs had bandages on." Jarrett also noticed that Ludwig's "hair was singed a little and also his eyebrows"—details that had not been disclosed previously.

He said he went upstairs and saw Officer Foust find the razor. "I found a bottle of iodine and glycerine," Jarrett said. "At least, the bottle had a label on stating that."

Next, Jarrett entered the closet and saw Cecilia's body, describing its position to the jury, which by now probably needed no reminding. He also found a can—he assumed it was a baking-powder can—in the closet.

Jarrett said he returned to the house the next day, Wednesday, for a more thorough look. He found a piece of a slop jar in the closet and a piece of a key outside the closet door. "I found the rest of the door key in the door," he said. "I put the piece of the key into the lock from the inside and it fit on the piece in the lock." Talbot did not pursue the significance of the key, whether it meant Ludwig had locked the closet door with Cecilia, unconscious and afire, inside.

Going downstairs, Jarrett said, he found a two-gallon can of gasoline in the summer kitchen. "Between a pint and a quart had been taken out of the can," he said. "I shook the tank on the gasoline stove and found enough gasoline to rattle."

Jarrett then talked about where he found bloodstains, including on the casing of the door leading to the summer kitchen. "There was a bloodstain of the fingers and the palm of a hand upon the door casing about three feet from the floor." Jarrett also described bloodstains he found upstairs on the closet door and its casing, including a handprint. Once again, it would have been useful to Jarrett and Talbot if fingerprint technology had been available to the Mishawaka Police Department so they could confirm that the stains came from Albin, but the use of fingerprints for personal identification in the United States was in its infancy in 1906.

Also on the day after the fire, after the smoke and steam had cleared, Jarrett said, he found a potato masher on the closet floor. Talbot showed him the potato masher previously introduced as State's Exhibit A, and Jarrett identified it.

"I will ask you if you have made an examination as to whether or not these shiny spots on the edge were on there then?" Talbot asked.

"I did," Jarrett replied. "Yes, sir."

But under cross-examination, Jarrett told Parker: "I found nothing on the potato masher that I'm willing to say was blood."

Also under cross-examination, Jarrett told Parker that he had noticed the trunk in the closet. "I raised the lid of the trunk. It was full of clothing." Jarrett also told of smelling the baking-powder can he had found. "It smelled to me as if it was gasoline," he said. Jarrett added that he did not notice any blood on the can when he examined it. This time, he referred to it as "the oil can."

Jarrett explained that he found the bottle of iodine and glycerine on a small dresser in the northwest room upstairs, where Jean Ellsworth slept, not in the front room. He remembered taking the bottle with him the Sunday after the fire, when he returned to the scene with Albin's brother, Gustave.

"There might have been something said, but I can't remember what, to Mr. [Gustave] Ludwig about the probable cause of the bloodstains," Jarrett testified. "I might have stated to him that there were many persons around there, some of whom had helped to carry the defendant out when he was bloody, and that the stain was put there by some of these people when they had gone down. I did not see the man that put the blood there, and it might have happened either way."[7]

Jarrett stepped down having given a small victory to the defense.

Talbot then recalled Dr. Holtzendorf, the coroner, who had been on the stand when court adjourned the previous day. He presented Holtzendorf with the razor that had been found upstairs in the Ludwig house.

"What is its condition now with reference to the rust or blood on it?" Talbot asked.

"Very similar—only dried," the coroner replied.[8]

It was Parker's turn to question the coroner, asking him how he had accessed upstairs (the stairway), what he did with the potato masher (gave it to the police chief),[9] and the size of the trunk ("a very large Saratoga trunk" with iron or tin corners).

"I opened the lid of the trunk and found wearing apparel in it," Holtzendorf said. "I noticed wearing apparel particularly. It was nicely arranged." He also noticed a hat in the compartment for hats, but he said he didn't look further into the trunk.

Parker asked about the can he saw.

"I think the can that I found was a tomato can or a fruit can," he said. "It would hold a pint and a half. I smelled of it and thought I detected kerosene."

Parker asked if he could have mistaken the "kerosene" smell for those of a fire extinguisher, since the Mishawaka firemen had used one.

"I know the smell of chemicals used in extinguishing fires," Holtzendorf said. "I did not detect any there."

Parker pushed Holtzendorf to give a detailed description of Cecilia's head wound, which he did using medical terms. The coroner said the wound was through all three layers that compose the scalp, but it "was not such a wound as would cause death."

The defense attorney handed Holtzendorf an ordinary wire hook used to screw into a hook rail for hanging clothing.

"I will ask you to examine the front end of that, and state whether or not the wound that you saw was such a one as might have been produced by the head being forced against or chugged against the end of that hook. Is it—was it—such a wound as might have been made by that?"

"It is possible," Holtzendorf said.

Parker wanted more. He wanted the jury to forget the possibility of Albin striking Cecilia in the head with a potato masher. He wanted to show an alternate way that Cecilia could have suffered a head wound, a scenario that would fit with Albin's upcoming testimony.

"That is judging from the wound itself," Parker said, "and from the hook, if the head were to come in contact with the hook with sufficient force, the wound would indicate that it might have been made by that. Not necessarily so, but might have been."

"If that was firmly enough held," Holtzendorf agreed.[10]

After the noon recess, the state recalled James Anderson, the Misha-waka policeman who had testified the day before, to question him more on Ludwig's condition when Anderson arrived at the fire scene. In par-ticular, Parks wanted to know the color of Ludwig's vomit, with the in-tent of convincing the jury that besides cutting himself, Ludwig drank from the bottle of iodine and glycerine that Police Chief Jarrett had seen on a dresser in the next room.

Anderson testified that when Ludwig vomited while being treated on a couch outside the house, "the vomit was a kind of pale red and there was a greasy look about it." After Ludwig and the couch were carried inside, "he vomited there, and the vomit was the same color as that I saw out of doors."

Anderson's description of the vomit changed slightly when questioned by Parker. "There was partly digested food in the vomit and quite a bit of liquid. It was of a greenish cast. I didn't pay much attention to it," he admitted.

In his responses to both attorneys, Anderson said Ludwig opened one eye—"just lifted the eyelid," he told Parker—in the ambulance en route to Epworth Hospital in South Bend. The implication was that Ludwig was more aware of what was going on than he wanted his res-cuers to know.[11]

The prosecution had two more witnesses.

Dr. Charles C. Stroup, a Mishawaka physician who assisted in Ce-cilia's postmortem, was first. Stroup described the puncture wound on her scalp, adding that her skull was not fractured. Cecilia's flesh "was very badly burned and in some places it dropped off," he said.

"The woman died from shock," he told Parks.

"The heat resulting from the fire causes an overstimulation of the nerves in the skin, and this overstimulation causes an irritation of the nerves throughout the body," Stroup explained. "This brings on an overstimulation of the nerves of the heart, which stimulation brings about a paralysis of the heart."

He said Cecilia's fingers were so badly charred the nails were gone. Rings on her fingers showed signs of melting, and the pearls in her ear-rings were blackened.

Parker, in cross-examination, asked him to describe Cecilia's scalp wound in detail.

"A jagged wound is one that is irregular—a wound made by a sharp instrument is not irregular in the sense that I used the word," Stroup explained. "This one was irregular in shape. Its general shape was triangular. It was about the size of a quarter, but not round. By passing my finger around the place where the scalp wound was I could notice a slight depression. The wound was just about large enough to permit me to pass the end of my index finger through it."

Stroup said he thought a blunt instrument made the wound. Parker showed him the same wire hook he had shown Coroner Holtzendorf that morning. If Cecilia's head had been forced against the end of the hook with sufficient force, Parker asked, or if the hook had been fastened such to give a blow to Cecilia's head, could it have caused the wound?

"The head might have struck this point of the hook," Stroup said, indicating the point, "and if for any reason it would have turned on this—swung around it in any way—this might have made that wound."[12]

That was a victory for the defense. As he had done with Holtzendorf, Parker again was trying to show that Cecilia could have fallen against a clothes hook on the closet wall rather than being struck with a potato masher by Albin. Parker scored again when Stroup admitted that Cecilia's heart had been removed in the autopsy, but the doctors "made no such examination of it as would enable us to say that the subject had any heart disease." Another defense supposition—still to be presented—was that a weak heart could have contributed to Cecilia's death.

Talbot would counter with a win of his own. The state's last witness, Robert F. Schellenberg, who lived a few blocks away, dropped a bombshell when he testified that upon entering the Ludwig house on the afternoon of the fire, he checked the cellar first.

"I saw a bunch of papers lying there on a shelf or in the base of the cellar window, not blazing, but just smoldering," Schellenberg testified. He said the papers, "roughly folded into a bunch," were about eighteen inches from the joists.[13]

As reported by the *South Bend Daily Times*: "This information was received with considerable surprise by the defense, as it had not been presented by the state heretofore." The *Elkhart Daily Review* wrote that Schellenberg "presented the most sensational evidence because [it was] wholly unexpected by the defense and very potent in undermining the line of defense that was presumed to have been determined upon."[14]

When it was Parker's turn, the defense attorney asked Schellenberg why he went to the basement when he knew the fire was upstairs.

"I was looking for the woman [Cecilia] at that time," he replied. "I learned that she had disappeared."

Schellenberg said he told another man who was with him in the cellar, a Dahlman or Diehlman, to extinguish the burning papers, which were "about the size of an ordinary hat."

He did not report what he had found to either the police chief or the fire chief.[15]

As the state rested its case, the jury was left wondering what the papers were, who set them on fire two floors below where Cecilia Ludwig burned to death, and whether the bloodstain the police chief found on the casing of the door leading to the summer kitchen had anything to do with it.

CHAPTER 13

"Wife the Aggressor"

THE THURSDAY, APRIL 25, edition of the *South Bend Daily Times* continued the newspaper's in-depth trial coverage with a lengthy article headlined "WIFE THE AGGRESSOR," which discussed the defense's opening statement on Wednesday afternoon. After covering the basics of the Ludwigs' marriage, Samuel Parker brought up the stresses that were gnawing at it:

The defense would show that for some time their married life had not been pleasant and that the reason was because Mrs. Ludwig did not conduct herself as a good woman should and that she persisted in frequenting the company of other men. Also that several times she had threatened his life and at one time said she would poison him. A short time before Sept. 25, a sister, Mrs. Ellsworth, visited their home and brought her two children. The visit was apparently a pleasant one at first, but after two or three weeks Mr. Ludwig claimed that the two women were not conducting themselves as they should. The additional cost of living expenses coupled with their action made him dissatisfied. The evidence, Mr. Parker said, will show that on the day of the tragedy it was arranged that the sister would go away and that Mrs. Ludwig would go also, and that there should be a separation; also that some time before Mr. Ludwig had consulted with an attorney regarding a divorce and had been advised to separate. While there were disagreements and unpleasantness at the same time, Ludwig had a deep regard and affection for his wife.[1]

Parker's first defense witness was Albin Ludwig's older brother, Gustave, a carpenter still living in nearby Elkhart.

Gustave told the courtroom that he learned at 6:00 the evening of September 25 that his brother's wife had died. He started at once for Mishawaka. Then he went to South Bend to see Albin in Epworth Hospital, where he spent an hour and a half. "He did not recognize me," Gustave said. He returned to the hospital on Friday evening. "He was then conscious." If the conscious Albin revealed anything of consequence to his brother that Friday, Gustave didn't say.

On the Sunday following Cecilia's death, Gustave, his wife, Police Chief Jarrett, Jarrett's wife, and possibly Jarrett's brother, John—Gustave wasn't sure—went to Albin's house on East Marion Street. "We examined the dining-room table, the upstairs, the bed clothing, and also the bedroom where Mrs. Ellsworth had slept," Gustave said.

He said he found a bottle in Jean Ellsworth's room and handed it to Jarrett. This was the same bottle of iodine and glycerine that others had described.

Gustave said he did not clean out the closet that day, but he and his wife "took charge of my brother's goods. I gave part of the goods away and sold the other part." He obviously did not expect his brother to return home.

On a later visit after the furniture was out, Gustave cleaned out the closet with a shovel and basket. (It's remarkable to think of police today allowing a suspect's brother to sweep out a closet—and all its trace evidence—where a murder occurred.) "Among the burned stuff I found parts of a lamp. I saved the burner and a few pieces of glass," he said. Parker showed a battered burner of a lamp and a piece of glass to Gustave, and the witness identified them as what he found in the closet.

Besides "lots of small pieces of glass," Gustave said, he found a strip of hook rails, with hooks, along the north side and another along the south side of the closet. "There was a shelf in the closet, and it was pretty well loaded down," he said. "It was covered with different articles. Mostly jelly glasses. There must have been fifteen or twenty of these, and some tin cans."

The defense had just introduced the possibility that the can the state's witnesses found in the closet—the one that smelled like gasoline or kerosene—could have fallen off a shelf instead of being carried upstairs by Albin, containing a flammable liquid, with the intent to burn his wife's body.

In cross-examination, State's Attorney Talbot clarified when Gustave had been in his brother's house. Not surprising considering the strained circumstances that caused Albin and Cecilia to leave Elkhart, Gustave had not been in the house before Cecilia's death. Gustave said the trunk and other items in the closet were destroyed about two weeks after he talked to Albin in the hospital.[2]

The defense then recalled Fred Metzler, Albin's neighbor to the east. Metzler remembered hearing "people talking pretty loud in the Ludwig house" the night before the fire. "I heard the talk as late as twelve o'clock, when I got up and gave my little boy a drink." Metzler also recalled the previous Sunday, during an argument about finding a dog, hearing Cecilia calling her husband "a damn liar." Attorney Crabill made an effort to have Metzler tell of the alleged difficulties between Albin and his wife, but the state objected to each question.[3]

Anna Spies, who lived one block directly south of the Ludwig house, was the last witness of the day. She recalled seeing Albin sitting on his porch close to noon on the day of the fire. "The two Ellsworth children had just started away from him."[4]

Judge Funk then adjourned court until 9:00 Thursday morning. Undoubtedly the courtroom would be packed. For the first time since Cecilia's death, Albin Ludwig would tell his side of the story in public.

CHAPTER 14

Albin Testifies

ALBIN LUDWIG RAISED his right hand and swore to tell the truth, the whole truth, and nothing but the truth. He was the chief witness for his own defense. With his new beard and mustache, he barely was recognizable to anyone in the courtroom who had known him before his wife's death.[1] But members of the audience were more interested in what Ludwig would say than how he looked.

Samuel Parker, Ludwig's lead attorney, covered the basics first: name, age, birth date, where he was born, and so on. Ludwig's answers were brief. Sometimes, one or two words were enough.

"Had your wife been married before?"

"She had."

"Did she have any children?"

"Yes."

"Did they ever live with you?"

"One lived part of the time with me."

On his twenty-eighth question, Parker began asking about Cecilia's sister, Jean Ellsworth, although both he and Albin referred to her only as "Mrs. Ellsworth." Albin explained that he had known Mrs. Ellsworth since shortly after he and Cecilia were married, that in 1906 she had come to their house the first time in June, staying three weeks, then going to La Porte before returning "sometime in July" with her two children. The three remained at the house until the day Cecilia died.

If anyone had not been paying attention to Parker's routine questions and Ludwig's routine answers thus far, surely their interest was piqued with Parker's next question: "Now you may state, Mr. Ludwig, whether or not your wife made any threats against you."

"She had," Ludwig replied.

"About how long before her death, or how long after your marriage, was it that she made the first threats?"

State's Attorney Joseph Talbot objected to the question. "Unless it is shown to be within some reasonably recent time, I will object to this as being too remote," he said.

But the judge sided with Parker and let Ludwig answer.

"Well, I could not remember the first, but I can remember some of the last," he said.

"How long before the twenty-fifth day of September do you remember of her making any threat?"

"Six weeks before."

Ludwig said he complained about Cecilia and Mrs. Ellsworth "going out every day." He said he told his wife that he wouldn't mind if they went out two or three times a week.

"And what did she say then?" Parker asked.

"She said some of these days she would give me something that I would never move again."

Her next threat, he continued, came about two weeks later. Parker asked what prompted it.

"Why, she had been to an excursion, and come home late at night, and wanted to go right away again to La Porte the next day."

Albin told her that he couldn't afford that, he testified.

"And what did she say then?"

"She said she would knock my God-damned head off some of these days."

Cecilia's next threat, Ludwig said, came the Sunday before her death. He thought it would be appropriate for his wife to go out "three times a week, and every night if she wanted to with me, and all day Sunday if she wanted to." He objected to Cecilia "going out every day, and never intending to go out with me."

Parker asked Ludwig to tell the jury about her "going with other persons—other men."

Talbot objected: "It must be shown that he knows himself." The prosecutor didn't want any hearsay.

Ludwig didn't wait for Judge Funk's ruling. "I do know," perhaps sounding testy since this was Talbot's fourth objection since Ludwig took the stand. "Shall I answer?"

Judge Funk overruled Talbot's objection, and Ludwig answered.

"She used to go out to the lake with men, and met men at South Bend. While I would be working."

Talbot was on his feet again, objecting that Ludwig's statement was hearsay. Funk again overruled. Parker explained to his witness that he could tell the jury on what occasion he saw Cecilia with other men.

"As far back as I want to?" Albin asked.

"Yes," Parker replied.

A flustered Talbot objected for the sixth time. "I cannot see the purpose of it," he argued.

Parker argued back "that the point is to show that her conduct in that respect was not transitory, that it was habitual, that it began back some time ago and was continued. And that all of that had, of course, its influence on this tragedy."

The judge agreed. Ludwig could tell his story—and what a story it was!

"I caught her in the closet of the northwest bedroom with one of the boarders," he said. Ludwig did not elaborate on what Cecilia and the boarder were doing in the closet, or their state of dress, or undress, but the implication to the jury was that Cecilia's behavior was not appropriate for a married woman.

"About when was that?"

"That was [the] fifteenth day of August, 1903, half-past seven in the morning, when she thought I was at work."

Talbot objected again, asking that the last part of Ludwig's answer—"when she thought I was at work"—be stricken. This time, Funk agreed, although surely it would not be stricken from the minds of the twelve men on the jury, especially those who were married.

Parker tried another route for Ludwig to testify about the incident with the boarder.

"Had you gone to work that morning?"

"I did," Albin replied.

"About what time?"

"About twenty minutes to seven."

"Was there anybody at the house at the time you went to work?"

Talbot objected again, arguing that Parker already had "in the fact"—
on the record—what he wanted to show. "Now why go into detail?"

Parker and Talbot argued back and forth—respectfully, as lawyers
normally do in a courtroom—about the appropriateness of the question.
Judge Funk eventually agreed with the prosecution. Parker took exception to the ruling and resumed questioning Ludwig.

"At what time did you return to the house that morning?" Parker asked.

Again, Talbot objected to the question "as a mere detail to the fact
that they have already proven by the witness." This time, Funk overruled the objection, to which Talbot took exception.

Now the court reporter, Hugh Noel Seymour Home, repeated Parker's prior question to Ludwig: "Was there anybody at the house at the
time you went to work?"

"There was," Ludwig said.

"Why was that?"

Talbot wouldn't give up, objecting once more. Once more, the young
prosecutor was overruled. Once more, he entered an exception to the
ruling.

Albin was allowed to answer: "A boarder—a man was staying with us."

"Can you give his name, or the name by which he went?" Parker asked.

Talbot interrupted with another objection. "It is immaterial. The main
fact has been proven, and its details are incompetent." By incompetent,
Talbot meant it had no bearing on the case.

Funk disagreed. Again, Talbot put his "exception" in the record.

Ludwig said the boarder was "Meinen," spelling it at Parker's request.

"Did he go by some other name commonly?" Parker asked.

Talbot objected, and Parker withdrew the question. He already had
succeeded in identifying the boarder.

"What time did you return to the house?" Parker asked.

"About half past seven, as near as I can tell," Ludwig replied.

"Did you go upstairs or not?"

"I did."

"And was it then that you saw what you have related?"

"I did."

"Now you may state whether at any other time you yourself saw your wife in company with another man or men."

After another objection, also overruled, Ludwig answered yes, about a year before. Parker asked about the circumstances.

Ludwig said she was with a "Manning's Tea man," a man who sold a brand of household products door-to-door.[2] Ludwig didn't know the salesman's name.

"I came home—he was sitting on my wife's lap as I opened the door," he said. The incident occurred as Ludwig returned from work at 5:00 that afternoon.

Ludwig told Parker that he didn't say anything to Cecilia about it. "I just kept quiet."

In another incident, Ludwig "saw her with a man, coming from the lake, twelve o'clock at night," in South Bend. Parker asked which lake, and Ludwig said "Chain Lake," but the name was stricken from the record after Talbot objected that Ludwig was drawing a conclusion, that the defendant hadn't seen her at the lake.

Ludwig gave a more exact location where he saw Cecilia and the man in South Bend, adding that they were in a buggy. He didn't say anything to her about it that night but did the next day, he testified.

"And what did she say?" Parker asked.

"She says it was another lady along."

"Did you see another lady along?"

"I did not."

Parker asked Ludwig about the size of the buggy (single-seated), what kind of lighting the street had (electric), how close the buggy was to the street light (fifteen feet), and how close Ludwig was to the buggy (twenty feet).

"Now you may state whether when you saw them there was anybody else in the buggy, except this man and your wife?"

"No one else," Ludwig said.

Parker moved on to the next incident. "Now you may state whether at any other time you saw her in company with another man."

"The night before," Ludwig said, meaning the night before Cecilia's death.

Ludwig said he saw his wife and her sister at the corner of Second and Main in downtown Mishawaka that Monday evening. He told how he saw the sisters with a man at the northwest corner, then watched the three of them walk north. Although he knew of the boardinghouse where Fred Young lived, Ludwig denied seeing the sisters and a man in front of it that evening.

Parker asked him if he threw a brick "or some other substance" at the trio.

"I did not," Ludwig replied.

Parker had Ludwig retrace his steps that evening. Ludwig said he left his house "sometime after seven" to search for his dog at the Four Corners of Mishawaka, which he estimated at being about five blocks away. In effect, Ludwig was claiming that his dog might have wandered as far as Mishawaka's main business district, eight-tenths of a mile away on the other side of the St. Joseph River.

"Now where was it that you first—where were the women when you first saw them?" Parker asked.

"At Landis' meat market," Ludwig said.

"Was there a man with them then?"

"No."

Ludwig admitted that he watched Cecilia and Jean at that time, that they stopped at Graham's North Side Drug Store, where he watched them from across the street. He saw Cecilia hand a bottle to a clerk. The clerk walked away, returned, and handed it back to Cecilia.

"Was anything said between you and your wife about what it was they got at the drug store?" Parker asked.

"She asked me for an empty bottle to get some iodine and glycerine." Ludwig confirmed that he had rinsed out a bottle and given it to her. He said he did not ask what she wanted with the iodine and glycerine.

"I will hand you this bottle, which has a label upon it—'Iodine & Glycerine'—with a death's head, and 'Poison' above, and ask you to look at it carefully."

Ludwig examined the bottle and said it looked like the same bottle because of the marks identifying ounces.

Next, Parker had Ludwig detail what he saw from across the street when Cecilia and Jean met the man on the corner of Second and Main.

"My wife called him out to one side," Albin said. "She was talking to him." Parker's intent was to show that Cecilia was more active than her sister in talking to the man.

Parker had Ludwig confirm that he talked to a patrolman while watching the women and the man from across the street, but he didn't ask what was said.

Instead, he concentrated on what happened when everyone got home.

"I asked them who the man was they were talking to on the corner of Second and Main," Ludwig said.

"What was the answer?"

"You are a damned liar."

"Who said that?"

"The two—both of them."

Ludwig went into more detail.

"I says, 'You might as well be honest and tell, and I won't think nothing about it,' and they said that I was a damned liar if I said they was talking to any man. Well, I says, 'I have got plenty of proofs. Lots of men on the corner saw you. Mr. Anderson saw you. And they said, 'You are a God-damned liar, and so is everybody else.'"

Parker asked Ludwig to tell the jury whether his wife was in the habit of swearing, but Talbot objected, arguing that whether Cecilia was in the habit of swearing would not "throw any light in this case." Judge Funk sided with Talbot.

The defense attorney changed the subject, asking about the conversation with neighbor Fred Metzler before Ludwig, Cecilia, and Jean went inside the house. Parker did not remind the jury that Metzler had testified earlier that he didn't talk to them that night.

"I proved to him that I was not over town with him. My wife claimed that I was over town with him," Ludwig said.

Parker asked how Cecilia responded.

"She told him he was a God-damned liar. He was over town with me."

Parker then had Ludwig testify about what happened after they entered the house. Ludwig confirmed there was talk about him and Cecilia separating, "but not very strong that night." He said there also was talk about Jean Ellsworth leaving. "She said that night they"—referring to Jean and the children—"had best pack up and get some rooms at South Bend."

"What did your wife say, if anything?" Parker asked.

"She said maybe she guessed she had better go with her," Ludwig replied.

"What did you say if anything?"

"Well, I says, 'If we cannot make it, that will be the best way.'"

The testimony moved on to the next morning, Tuesday, the day of Cecilia's death. Ludwig said he arose at 9:00 rather than the normal 3:00 to 5:00. Usually he left for his job at the rubber factory around 4:00 or 5:00 and worked until noon. Albin didn't go to work this day; Parker didn't ask why. Cecilia and her sister already were up.

Parker asked whether the subjects of a separation between Ludwig and his wife and of her sister going away were brought up that morning.

"My sister-in-law started to pack up," Ludwig said, "and my wife said she would pack, too, if she had a trunk to pack her clothes in it. I said, 'I will give you mine, if you want one, but you are welcome to stay, if you want to.'

"Well, then, after I give her my trunk, she wanted all the property. She said she would have it all or none."

Parker asked what else was said about her leaving for good and about him not continuing to make payments on the property.

Ludwig said he offered options in the presence of Cecilia's sister. "I says, 'Now, I want to talk in peace to you. If you want to go, and go like you have been doing, for two weeks, I will keep up the property, and you are welcome to come back. If not, I shall give up the property, not make any more payments.'"

"Then what did she say?" Parker asked.

"She says, 'I am going for good.' I says, 'Very well, I will give up the property.'" Ludwig explained that he had "paid a little down" on the property and was making monthly payments.

Ludwig said he sat around and read for a while until Cecilia asked him to buy some gasoline for the cookstove—she said she was out—so they could have a boiled dinner, the noon meal. He left a little after 11:00 for the grocery store, where he bought two gallons of gasoline. Then he stopped at the drugstore for half a pint of brandy, which, Ludwig said, he bought "to make cough medicine for my own use."

When he arrived home, he put "a little" gasoline in the tank of the cookstove, explaining that he couldn't fill the tank because Cecilia wanted to finish preparing dinner. Then he left the house again, this time in an effort to sell his dog.

"What did you want to sell your dog for?" Parker asked.

"Because we intended to break up . . ."

Ludwig couldn't remember the name of the woman he had talked to about the dog other than that she lived at Bridge and Marion Streets, but he agreed that it was the woman who had testified earlier, Anna Burkhart.

When he got home, he said, he talked to his wife a minute. Ludwig was obsessed with the "bridgeman" he had seen Cecilia talking to the night before.

"I told her she might as well tell me who the man was, that young Mr. Patterson told me she talked with a man," Ludwig said, adding that he had talked to Patterson while buying gasoline.

"Was there anything else said?" Parker asked.

"She said, 'He is a son-of-a-bitch of a liar.'"

Ludwig left the house again, this time to see "young Mr. Patterson," whom he just had seen at the store. But he wasn't home. He said he talked to "the old gentleman, Mr. Charles Patterson," then returned home. Charles R. Patterson would testify later for the defense.

When Ludwig got home from the Pattersons', it was time for dinner. The table in the dining room was set for four: Cecilia, Jean's two children, and himself. Jean had left to hire a livery a little after 11:00. Ludwig testified that the others ate their dinners, "and I just ate a little bit."

Now it was time for Parker to suggest to the jury that Cecilia had poisoned Albin with the cup of coffee she served him at dinner.

"Where did your wife get the coffee that you drank?" Parker asked.

"Out of the summer kitchen from the gasoline stove," Ludwig replied.

"Did she bring it all in and pour the coffee, or bring a cup in?"

"She brought the cup in."

"With the coffee in it?"

"Yes."

Ludwig said he drank the coffee.

"Now at the time you drank the coffee, did you notice any peculiarity about the taste?" Parker asked.

"I did."

"What did you notice? How did it seem to you to be?"

"To me, it seemed a kind of a sour, bitter taste."

Ludwig said his wife left the table first and laid down on the "lounge"—in that era, probably a backless sofa with a headrest at one end—in the room opposite the dining room.

Parker asked what became of Jean Ellsworth's children.

"They stayed at the table till I got through, and then they went out playing on the front porch," Ludwig said.

Parker returned to the poisoning theory: "Now you may state how you felt, if you felt any different from ordinary, after you had eaten."

"I did," Ludwig said. "Not right after, but about ten minutes after that."

"How did you feel?"

"Well, I was in misery. I felt like I wanted to throw up and could not, and felt like I ought to do something else and could not." Ludwig answered in the affirmative when asked if he meant that he had the urge to defecate. Both were reasons that he went outside to fetch the slop jar. He also confirmed that he saw his neighbor, Mrs. Brand, outside and greeted her with a bow and a wave of his hand, as he always did.

Ludwig said he reentered the house, placed the slop jar at the foot of the stairs, and went out the front door to sit briefly on the porch. State's witnesses had described seeing Ludwig in a pose of apparent despair, but Parker skipped over that, asking the defendant whether he hooked the screen door when he came back inside (no), and, next, when he went upstairs to the front room—the bedroom—whether he carried the slop jar with him (yes, putting it in the closet, "its regular place").[3]

Up to this point of the trial—the point when Albin Ludwig said he came in from the porch and went upstairs carrying the slop jar—previous witnesses had corroborated virtually every move the defendant made that day and the evening before, except for whether the front door was locked when Ludwig went back inside. Ludwig's testimony had not varied significantly from what neighbors, storekeepers, and even Fred Young, his sister-in-law's apparent suitor, had told the jury. If the twelve men had retired to the jury room at that moment to deliberate whether Ludwig generally had spoken the truth, there would have been no reasonable doubt.

But no living witnesses existed to confirm the events Ludwig described next, events that had been speculated about but not detailed in the newspapers because the defendant hadn't talked to the press. The testimony describing how her daughter died surely would be painful to hear for Ludwig's seventy-two-year-old mother-in-law, Christina Henderson, who arrived in the courtroom for the first time around midday and would be a surprise witness that afternoon.[4]

Parker asked what Ludwig did after placing the slop jar in the closet.

"I laid across the bed," he replied.

But not for long. Ludwig testified that he got up after about ten minutes and went to the dresser, which was "right close" to the closet door. "I looked inside of it for my insurance policy," he said, explaining that his wife was the beneficiary. The policy from the Knights and Ladies of Columbia required monthly payments.

"Did you find it when you looked for it?" Parker asked.

"I did not."

Failing to find the policy in the dresser, Ludwig continued his search in the closet. "I thought it would be in the trunk with her clothes," he explained, adding that Cecilia appeared to have packed all her clothes in preparation for her departure, "except what she was going to wear."

He said the closet was dark, as usual. It lacked a window, and, when the door swung open, it obstructed light from one of the twin windows on the south side of the room. Ludwig said he went out to the dresser to get a kerosene lamp, which he lit, and carried it back into the closet. He held the lamp in one hand as he looked in the trunk.

"Did anybody come there while you were doing that?" Parker asked.

"As far as the dresser?" Ludwig replied.

"Yes, who was that?"

"My wife."

"Did she say anything to you?"

"She did."

"You may tell the jury what is the first thing that you remember she said," Parker continued.

"She says, 'Have you made up your mind to give me all the stuff?'"

Ludwig said he again offered to give Cecilia half their property, and his wife again demanded to have it all.

"I said, 'If you get it all, you will get it by law.'"

To which Ludwig said his wife replied: "You son-of-a-bitch. I will swear out a warrant that you tried to kill me, and I will get it all anyhow."

"What did you say?" Parker asked.

"I says, 'Go right on.'"

He said Cecilia then asked what he was doing in the closet. He told her he was looking for his insurance policy.

"She said, 'You son-of-a-bitch, I will fix you anyhow'—and she hauled off with the potato masher." By "hauled off," Ludwig meant that Cecilia swung the heavy, wooden potato masher at him.

Parker handed Ludwig a potato masher and asked if it was the same one. Ludwig couldn't say for sure, but he offered, "It is one just like it."

Ludwig said he warded off the potato masher's blow by getting to his feet; he had been kneeling while searching the trunk.

"And then what?" Parker asked.

"And got her by the throat."

Parker asked Ludwig to describe what happened.

"She was standing against the wall," Ludwig said. "The north wall. And I knocked off the blow—jumped up, knocked off the blow—and got her by the throat, and held her against the wall. And when I let loose, she kind of clawed me. And when I let loose, she went down."

Ludwig's memory, which up to this point of the trial had been so good, suddenly failed him. Or at least he claimed it failed him.

"Do you know what happened after she went down, as you say?" Parker asked.

"I do not."

"Do you know where you went?"

"I don't think I went anywhere. No, I don't know."

"You may tell the jury what if anything you recollect and what you did after that."

"I don't recollect anything after that. The shock . . ." Ludwig didn't finish the sentence.

Parker asked if he remembered anything about the fire.

"I do not," Ludwig said.

"Now I want to ask you whether or not you took any gasoline or any kerosene up there into that closet?" Parker asked.

"I did not."

After establishing that the kerosene lamp already was upstairs, that Ludwig didn't bring any fuel upstairs for the lamp, Parker asked Ludwig what the next thing he remembered was.

"I don't remember what become of me or where," Ludwig said.

"Well, there was a time when you remember of where you were," Parker continued. "Where was that? When you came to, where were you?"

"At the hospital." Ludwig said he was in Epworth Hospital six weeks, "as near as I can tell."

Now it was time for Parker to tie up the loose ends. He started by asking Ludwig whether he had gone into the cellar that day and set fire to any paper. The prosecution's last witness, Robert F. Schellenberg, had testified that he found smoldering paper in the cellar.

"I did not," Ludwig replied.

Parker asked if Ludwig "had any intention or purpose to kill her" when he took hold of his wife in the closet that day. Parker wisely did not say "by the throat."

"I did not," Ludwig replied.

"Why did you seize hold of her at all?" Parker asked. "What reason?"

Ludwig's reason was self-defense: "I thought it would be my last, and I just wanted to keep her from it. That is all."

Parker asked what became of the potato masher that, according to Ludwig, Cecilia had swung at him.

"She dropped it, but I don't know. I heard it drop, did not see it drop. I heard it drop."

Parker asked if Ludwig had drunk any liquor that day.

"Not a drop." But he confirmed that he handed the bottle of brandy he had bought that morning to his friend Fred Metzler, who drank from it.

State's Attorney Talbot objected when Parker asked Ludwig if he had a habit of drinking. Parker was trying to show that Ludwig did not drink alcohol regularly. But Judge Funk sustained the motion, and Parker changed the subject, remembering a question he had forgotten to ask earlier:

"You may tell the jury whether or not your wife ever talked to you about other men, and her intimacy with them."

Talbot again objected, arguing that Parker was "calling for the declaration of the deceased," which would be hearsay. Parker tried three times to reword the question. He desperately wanted the jury to hear Ludwig say that his wife had admitted her intimacy with other men. Funk wouldn't allow it, but Parker had succeeded in raising the subject in front of the all-male jury.

Parker moved on. His next-to-last series of questions established that Cecilia was physically bigger than her husband, the implication being that Ludwig felt threatened when his wife swung the potato masher at him.

Ludwig said Cecilia weighed 168 pounds and was "about an inch or a little over" taller than the five-foot-eight height he claimed for himself that day. Albin actually was almost an inch and a half shorter than that.

"What kind of a built woman was she?" Parker asked.

"Kind of broad-shouldered and heavy-boned," Ludwig replied.

"Big-boned?"

"Big-boned."

Parker was nearly finished.

"Now you may tell the jury what your feelings towards your wife were," he instructed his client. He planned to end on a positive note.

"I loved her as much as any man could love his wife," Ludwig declared.

"You may state whether or not that was the reason that you did not separate from her."

"It was."[5]

CHAPTER 15

Cross-Examination

FOR MORE THAN AN HOUR, Albin Ludwig had painted a picture of himself as a patient, hardworking husband (though perhaps a little gullible) and a good neighbor. But he was bewildered why the woman he loved seemed to enjoy the company of other men more than his own. His testimony depicted his wife as a foulmouthed gadabout who attacked him with a wooden potato masher when he refused to give her everything they owned in a separation. Fearing for his own life, he grabbed her by the throat until she collapsed. The next thing he remembered, he was in the hospital.

State's Attorney Joseph Talbot planned to destroy the sympathetic image of a spurned husband created during Ludwig's direct examination.

He planned to prove Ludwig was a liar—and a murderer.

First, he established that the potato masher usually was kept downstairs in the summer kitchen. He would get back to that later.

Then he discussed Fred Young's visit to the Ludwig home, not the night before the murder but on the Sunday before, two days before Cecilia's death. Ludwig admitted that he and Young drank "coffee cocktails," an alcoholic beverage, that day, though he denied mixing the drinks. He admitted that he had been a bartender in Elkhart, a reminder to the jury that the defendant wasn't unfamiliar with liquor.

"And you had a talk there with Young that day, and with your wife, and with your sister-in-law—that is, you talked together there—the four of you—you were friendly," Talbot stated, referring to the Sunday.

"Yes," Ludwig agreed.

"And he stayed for dinner, didn't he?" Talbot asked, referring to Young.

"Came there for dinner," Ludwig agreed.

"And the four of you ate together."

"Yes."

"There was no animosity between you and Young, was there?"

Ludwig didn't want to give a yes-no answer. "May I state it in full?" he asked.

"Kindly answer the question."

"You mean no bad feeling?"

"No ill feeling between you and Young," Talbot repeated.

"I did not like to have him come and see a married woman," Ludwig finally answered.

Talbot immediately asked Judge Funk to strike Ludwig's answer "as not responsive to the question." Funk agreed.

The prosecutor changed the subject, asking Ludwig whether his testimony to Defense Attorney Samuel Parker had included everything that occurred after 8:00 the night before the murder.

Ludwig said it did, but Talbot reminded him about visiting neighbor Marcellus Gaze's house that night. Ludwig said that was true.

"And didn't you tell Gaze that you were leaving the house, that you would put an end to it?" Talbot asked.

"Mr. Gaze . . ."

Talbot interrupted. "Did you, or did you not?"

"Not in that way," Ludwig said.

"Not in that way?" Talbot pressed.

"I did not."

Talbot forged ahead, mentally checking off the list of flaws he perceived in Ludwig's direct testimony.

"You say that you came home some time—that was in 1903, was it not?—and found your wife in a compromising position with a Mr. Miner?" Talbot was referring to the boarder previously identified as "Meinen."

"Yes," Ludwig said.

"That is Spot Miner, or Smoke Miner?" Talbot asked.

"Yes, yes."

Talbot stated as fact that shortly after that incident, Ludwig accompanied his wife on the train as far as South Bend while she continued on to her hometown of Kingsbury. Ludwig agreed, saying it was two days after the incident, and that Cecilia "was going home on her own accord."

"And you met Spot Miner here in South Bend, or in Mishawaka, after you left, didn't you?" Talbot asked.

"He met my wife at the train," Ludwig replied.

"Well, did you meet him, sir, that is the question I am asking you?"

"Could not help but meet him."

"And then, sir, you took him back to your home, and you and he lived together three weeks in your house alone, did you not?" Talbot asked.

No, Ludwig said, only one week.

Talbot asked who did the cooking while they lived together. Ludwig said he did.

"That was after you had found him with your wife there in your house at 7:30 in the morning?" Talbot asked incredulously.

"May I answer this . . ."

"You can answer this 'yes' or 'no.'" Talbot interrupted.

"Yes," Ludwig said.

"Sitting on your wife's lap?"

"Oh, no. No."

Talbot did not give Ludwig a chance to explain that he had caught Smoke Miner in a bedroom closet with his wife, not sitting on her lap. It was the Manning's Tea man Ludwig had caught sitting on Cecilia's lap.

The prosecutor then reviewed the time line of the evening before Cecilia's death. Ludwig repeated that he had watched from across the street as his wife bought the bottle of iodine and glycerine at the drugstore, though he denied knowing that it was for her feet.

"Why did you go down to the center of the north side to look for your dog?" Talbot asked.

"I thought he followed them down," Ludwig said, referring to Cecilia and sister Jean.

Talbot asked whether he went over to them after seeing the women.

"I thought they would come to me," he answered.

Ludwig repeated that he followed them across the river.

"You did not let her know that you were following her?" Talbot asked.

"No, I did not. No."

"And when you got over there on the principal corner of the town over there—Main and Second Street—you saw her and her sister talking to a man. Is that right?"

"No," Ludwig said. "Not when I got there."

Ludwig said he first saw his wife from the corner across the street as she and her sister were looking over the curtain into Schellinger's saloon, next to the post office, east of Main Street. Then they walked to the northwest corner, the location of Graham's South Side Drug Store. Ludwig stayed on the southeast corner.

"And while they were standing there, you had a talk with Mr. Anderson, did you not?" Talbot asked, referring to the Mishawaka police officer who had testified earlier.

"A very short talk, two or three words," Ludwig claimed.

"In that conversation to Mr. Anderson," Talbot countered, "did you say, 'I am going to put a stop to it. If anything happens, I want you to remember it'?"

"I did not."

"You did not?"

"I did not. I made some remark . . ."

But Talbot didn't let Ludwig finish, moving the narrative to Ludwig watching the women and a man—later identified as a "bridgeman"— walk north to Fred Young's boardinghouse. But Ludwig denied seeing them stop there, explaining that they crossed the street behind him. He also denied that he stood between two houses and watched them.

"Did you there at that time throw a brick and hit your wife in the hip?" Talbot asked.

"I did not," Ludwig said.

Ludwig said he headed home without waiting for his wife and sister-in-law on the advice of the police officer. "Mr. Anderson told me to go home and see how long they would stay."

At first Ludwig said the women arrived home fifteen minutes after him. He revised his story when Talbot asked if he met them away from the house and the four of them, including Fred Young, arrived at the house together.

"Then when the four of you got home, you asked her who the man was that she was with, is that correct?" Talbot asked, adding that he was referring to the man she talked to in front of Graham's drugstore on the south side of the river. "And she said to you, 'You are a damned liar'?"

There was more to it than that, Ludwig explained. He said he asked her who the man was she was talking to. "She said she was not talking to anybody, and I said she was."

"Then she said, 'You are a damned liar'?" Talbot asked.

"Yes," Ludwig replied.

"And you told her, 'You may as well be honest'?"

"I did."

Talbot continued, mimicking Ludwig asking his wife: "'And tell me, because you were seen'?"

"Yes."

Talbot asked several questions trying to pin down when Ludwig talked to neighbor Fred Metzler that evening. Ludwig wasn't positive when they talked, but he said Metzler found his dog on East Lawrence Street, three blocks south.

Then Talbot shifted his questioning to the events the rest of the evening after Young, Albin, and the sisters went inside the house. Ludwig said it was around midnight when Young left for the night and that he went to bed "as quick as he left the room."

"How late did your quarrel continue that night?" Talbot asked.

"That I could not tell you," Ludwig replied. "It was not a quarrel all the time."

"You probably quarreled ten to fifteen minutes after you saw Metzler?"

"About."

"That would bring it to eight or eight-thirty, is that right?"

"No, it is not."

Talbot and Ludwig sparred several more rounds over when and how long Albin and Cecilia quarreled that night. Ludwig explained that they would argue and then speak "agreeably"—Talbot's term—for a while.

Ludwig said the quarrel broke out again when he brought up the conversation he had seen his wife have with the stranger at Second and Main earlier that evening. He asked, "Celia [her nickname], why don't you tell me who you was talking to?" In response, both Cecilia and sister Jean called him names, he claimed.

The arguing ended around 10:00 P.M., and then they talked about different subjects, including "slightly" about the couple separating, Ludwig said.

"It was not determined that your wife would leave, was it?" Talbot asked.

"No, she guessed maybe it would be the best thing," Ludwig said.

Talbot then brought up Ludwig's visit that evening, "between the two little quarrels," with neighbors Marcellus and Veronica Gaze.

"You had told Mr. and Mrs. Gaze—Mr. Gaze had said to you, hadn't he?—'Why don't you leave her? Why don't you quit?' And then didn't you say to her [Mrs. Gaze], 'I love her too much to leave her.'?"

"Yes," Ludwig replied.

Talbot started to ask Ludwig about what he had said as he was leaving the Gaze house—Marcellus Gaze had testified that Ludwig said "something to the effect that he would put an end to it, or would stop it"—but Talbot withdrew the question before Ludwig could respond. Perhaps he feared an answer contrary to what already was on the record.

The cross-examination moved to the morning of Cecilia's death, starting with the discussion about Jean Ellsworth moving out of the Ludwig house where she and her children had been living much of the time since June.

"Mrs. Ellsworth talked about leaving, and she told my wife, 'You had better go, too,' and she [Cecilia] said she guessed she would, if she had something to pack up."

Jean Ellsworth left the home around 11:00 but without her clothes and children, Ludwig testified. She was expected back before she left for good.

"You and your wife, after [Mrs. Ellsworth] left, talked about this question of separation?" Talbot asked.

"Yes," Ludwig agreed.

"You did not want your wife to leave you?"

"I did then, yes," Ludwig responded in an answer that took Talbot, and probably the courtroom, by surprise, because it was the opposite of anything the defendant had said previously.

"You did then?" Talbot asked, emphasizing the last word.

Ludwig said yes, but asked to repeat his previous answer. It was becoming obvious that Ludwig, the German immigrant to whom English was a second language, was answering Talbot's questions as precisely as he could, perhaps too precisely for his own good.

"I said if she would not have it no other way," Ludwig said.

Talbot wanted more clarification. "Did you yourself actually want her to leave? Were you opposed to her leaving, or were you anxious to have her go?"

"I was not anxious to have her go," Ludwig said.

"And you told her that you would give her the trunk, but that she was welcome to stay?"

"Yes, I did."

"And then you and she had a discussion about who should have the furniture?"

Ludwig repeated that he offered to divide the property but that Cecilia wanted it all.

Talbot moved on to Ludwig's movements the rest of the morning— that the defendant had gone to the grocery store to buy the gasoline for the cookstove, as Cecilia requested, and also bought a bottle of whisky or brandy. After leaving the grocery, he met friend Charles R. Patterson. "I asked him if he knew who the man was that my wife was out with the night before, and he said he did not." Ludwig's answers varied little from what he had said in direct examination or, for that matter, what other witnesses had testified.

Ludwig told Talbot that he went home with the gasoline, then went next door to see friend Fred Metzler.

"And in that talk, when you went over and saw Fred Metzler, you said, you told Fred Metzler, 'I am going to kill myself,' didn't you?"

"I would not swear to it," Ludwig replied. "I might have said it, but I don't remember whether I did or not. I might have said it."

Talbot then asked Ludwig to recount the story of him attempting to sell his dog to Anna Burkhart, who lived in the neighborhood.

"Why did you want to sell that dog, Mr. Ludwig?"

"Why, because we was going to break up, and I wanted to find a place for the dog. He was too valuable to throw away, or give away."

"You had made arrangements to quit your job?" Talbot asked, introducing a new subject to the trial.

"Why, you can make arrangements in five minutes," Ludwig said.

"You had made no arrangements about leaving your house as yet?"

"Was going to sell what little I had."

Talbot asked about the coffee Ludwig drank at the noon meal.

"And you noticed that the coffee was sour, and had a bitter taste, is that true?" Talbot asked.

"Kind of a bitter, sour taste, yes," Ludwig said.

"But you drank the coffee, didn't you?"

"Didn't think anything about it at the time."

Talbot pressed Ludwig on what happened next. The prosecutor wanted to know exactly how much time elapsed before Albin went outside to fetch the slop jar.

"Oh, I could not tell you—about fifteen minutes after dinner," was the best Ludwig could do.

"Where had you been that fifteen minutes?" Talbot asked.

"In the house."

"In what part of the house?"

"Downstairs—in the rooms."

"What were you doing in the rooms?"

"Sitting, reading," Ludwig replied.

"Sitting, reading?"

"Yes."

Talbot had just established that a fifteen-minute window existed during which Ludwig could have killed his wife. He could have accused her of poisoning him with the coffee. He could have grabbed the potato masher and chased her upstairs. He could have knocked her unconscious with the potato masher. Then, realizing he needed to finish the job, Ludwig could have gone outside for the slop jar, figuring it would be a handy container for gasoline to set her body on fire.

Talbot returned to the subject of the dinner. First, he forced Ludwig to pin down that he was seated in the middle of the west side of the table.

"What did you eat for dinner?"

"We had boiled dinner—potatoes and boiled meat."

"That dinner had been prepared by your wife, hadn't it?"

"It had."

"It was about the usual kind of dinner you have?"

"Yes, yes, only later," Ludiwg said. The family normally ate at noon, but it was closer to one on this day.

Ludwig could not remember if he had left partially eaten bread on his plate with gravy on the bread.

"Isn't it a fact that you were eating bread when the quarrel broke out afresh, and you quit then?" Talbot said.

"There was no quarrel," Ludwig insisted.

"There was no quarrel?"

"No quarrel whatever."

Ludwig said the last time he and Cecilia had quarreled was before dinner. "She talked about going away from me," Ludwig related. "I told her if that was the only way she wanted to have it, why, all right, it would have to be that way."

"There was no quarrel?"

"No quarrel. No."

Ludwig recounted how, after dinner, he sat downstairs about fifteen minutes, then retrieved the slop jar and set it down in the hallway near the stairs. He then went out to the front porch to sit on the steps a few minutes. He remembered sitting in a "kind of cramped-up position" before returning to the house, picking up the slop jar, carrying it upstairs, and lying down on the bed.

"While lying there you thought about the insurance policy, didn't you?" Talbot asked.

"Yes."

Despite feeling ready to throw up, Ludwig said, he began searching for the policy. He first went to the dresser near the bed. But Talbot didn't ask him if he found the policy there. Instead, the prosecutor began a series of questions about the slop jar, such as how it got from the closet to the back of the building. Ludwig said Cecilia customarily took it outside about 10:00 in the morning, though he didn't see her do it that day.

"Do you remember when you were in the hospital Mr. Jarrett, the chief of police, coming down there and talking to you?" Talbot asked.

"He was down there once that I know of talking to me."

"And in that conversation at that time, did you say this to Mr. Jarrett: 'I went up and laid down on the bed, face down, and when I came to I was cut, and I don't know how it happened.'"

"I did not," Ludwig said.

Talbot repeated the question. Ludwig repeated his denial.

"Did you tell Mr. Jarrett this, that Mrs. Ludwig was cleaning a black skirt, and that she had some oil in cleaning the black skirt up there at that time?"

Ludwig attempted to reply, but Talbot cut him off. "Did you, or did you not?" the prosecutor insisted.

"I did not—not—not in that way."

"Did you tell him that she had the oil there in a can?"

"I did not."

"Did you tell him the oil was there in a can or dish in that conversation at that time?"

"I did not."

Talbot gave up, unable to prove that Ludwig knew there was a flammable liquid in the room that could have been used to set Cecilia on fire. He tried a different tack.

"The trouble that you are in now is not the first time you were in trouble, is it?" Talbot asked. Parker objected; Talbot recast the question to be more specific: "You have, prior to this, been arrested and convicted of an assault, have you not, in which a man's hat was torn to pieces by you."

Although the incident was reported by the *Mishawaka Enterprise* in its murder coverage, it had gone unmentioned so far in the trial. Parker immediately objected, arguing that the question was "wholly immaterial" and not subject to cross-examination. But Judge Funk overruled, allowing Ludwig to answer.

"I would not know in which way to answer this," a confused Ludwig responded.

Parker, his defense attorney, asked if he understood the question. Ludwig said he did. The question was reread, and Ludwig responded, "I have not been arrested, but I paid a fine."

Talbot resumed questioning: "At that time you had a talk with Mr. Foust about that matter—Mr. Foust, who is now an officer, did you not?"

Ludwig answered no, but the answer was stricken after the judge upheld an objection from Parker.

Talbot tried to establish that Foust had worked closely with Ludwig at the woolen mill, but Ludwig minimized their relationship. "Once in a great while" they talked, he said.

"He prevented you—grabbed your hand one day—while you were starting after a fellow with a knife?" Talbot asked.

Parker objected to the question as being "wholly immaterial," that if the state had intended to bring it up, it should have been in Talbot's direct examination, not in cross-examination. Judge Funk overruled the objection. Ludwig could answer.

"He never did," Ludwig insisted.

"And didn't you at the time that you were fined for trespass, go to him and ask him to swear that you were at another place at the time?"

Parker was on his feet again with an objection. This time he won, though the damage had been done in that the jury had heard the question.

Talbot returned to the subject of the whisky or brandy Ludwig bought the morning of Cecilia's death.

Ludwig said he bought it to make cough medicine, though he admitted to giving "a little drink" to neighbor Fred Metzler later that morning.

"That was at the time you told him you were going to kill yourself," Talbot pressed.

"I told you before I don't recollect whether I tried to kill myself or not," Ludwig replied.

"You say now, do you, that you choked your wife?"

"I did," Ludwig said, probably not realizing that the incriminating word "choke" hadn't been used in testimony yet.

"You remember when you were lying in the house that afternoon and Dr. Holtzendorf spoke to you, don't you?" Talbot continued.

"Dr. Holtzendorf didn't speak to me," Ludwig insisted.

Talbot continued trying to get Ludwig to admit that he had spoken to Holtzendorf, that the doctor had asked Ludwig whether he had hit his wife, to which Ludwig supposedly answered no. But three more times Ludwig denied speaking to the doctor.

"You don't remember anything that happened after you choked her?" Talbot asked, probably in exasperation.

"I do not."

"You did not hear her scream?"

"She did not scream at the time."

"She did not scream?"

"No."

Ludwig was sticking to the story he offered during direct testimony, that after he grabbed his wife by the throat in self-defense, and she collapsed, he remembered nothing until he was in the hospital.

Talbot continued trying to trip him up.

Left: Cecilia Henderson Hornburg Ludwig in a studio photo probably taken between her marriages to Charley Hornburg and Albin Ludwig. (Courtesy of Paula Steiner)

Below: Albin Ludwig, Prisoner 3701, upon reporting to the Indiana State Prison in Michigan City in May 1907. (Indiana Images, Indiana State Archives, Indianapolis)

A wooden potato masher similar to this one was a weapon in the murder of Cecilia Henderson Hornburg Ludwig. (Photo by Helen Sosniecki)

Bridge Street Bridge, which Cecilia Ludwig and sister Jean Ellsworth crossed the night before the murder to reach Mishawaka's main business district and Jean's apparent suitor, Fred Young. Cecilia's husband Albin surreptitiously followed the women. (Photo from a vintage postcard with a 1907 Mishawaka postmark; printer unknown)

Mishawaka Main Street, looking north, just south of its intersection with Second Street, similar to how it looked to Albin Ludwig on the evening of September 24, 1906, when he surreptitiously watched his wife Cecilia and her sister Jean talking to a man on the northwest corner. Albin's viewpoint was in front of the three-story Milburn House, a hotel, the second building south of the intersection on the right. (Courtesy of the St. Joseph County Public Library, South Bend, Indiana)

Mishawaka Main Street today, looking north from the onetime location of the Milburn House, just south of the intersection with Broadway, formerly Second Street. (Photo by author)

Above left: James and Christina Henderson, parents of Cecilia and Jean. (Courtesy of Paula Steiner)

Above right: Henderson Family stone in Kingsbury Cemetery. The death date for daughter Cecilia is incorrect. Cecilia also has her own stone. (Photo by author)

Left: A 1901 photo of Charles Ellsworth, who five years later would witness at least some of the violence that resulted in the death of his Aunt Cecilia. (Courtesy of Chuck Ellsworth)

Facing page: Ora Ellsworth, twenty-seven, with children Lucy, six, and Charles, four, in a 1903 photo taken by his wife, Jean Henderson Ellsworth, in Railroad Flat, California. Three years later, Jean would take the children to Mishawaka, Indiana, where the three would move in with Albin and Cecilia Ludwig, Jean's sister. (Courtesy of Chuck Ellsworth)

A mural today in downtown Elkhart, Indiana, depicts a street scene from the era when Albin Ludwig owned the Monument Saloon. (Photo by author)

A bank now occupies the site of Albin Ludwig's Monument Saloon at 21 South Main Street in downtown Elkhart, Indiana. (Photo by author)

East Marion Street today. Albin and Cecilia Ludwig moved to the quiet neighborhood in 1903, when not every lot had a home on it yet. (Photo by author)

Mishawaka Woolen Manufacturing Company, where Albin Ludwig was hired to do piecework after he and Cecilia moved to town. Albin stayed home from work the day Cecilia was killed. (Vintage postcard postmarked December 26, 1913)

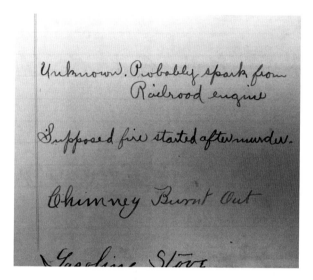

The *Daily Report of Fires in Mishawaka* for September 25, 1906, shows the fire department being on the scene of a residential fire at the residence of Alvin [*sic*] Ludwig on East Marion from 2:30 to 4:00 P.M. "Supposed fire started after murder." (Photo of ledger by author at Heritage Center, Mishawaka-Penn-Harris Public Library)

Epworth Hospital at the northeast corner of Main and Navarre Streets in South Bend, Indiana, where Albin Ludwig was confined under twenty-four-hour guard for more than a month while being treated for his own injuries. (Vintage postcard printed in Germany for the South Bend Post Card Company; postmark unreadable)

St. Joseph County Court House, South Bend, Indiana

9A-H1953

Albin Ludwig's trial was held in what is still known as the Third Courthouse of St. Joseph County, built between 1896 and 1898 and still in use today. (Unmailed vintage postcard printed by City News Agency, South Bend, Indiana; date unknown)

JOSEPH E. TALBOT.

Left: State's Attorney Joseph Talbot, who prosecuted Albin Ludwig. (Photo from *South Bend and the Men Who Have Made It: Historical, Descriptive, Biographical,* published 1901. Courtesy of the St. Joseph County Public Library, South Bend, Indiana.) *Right:* Judge Walter A. Funk presided over the trial of Albin Ludwig. (Photo from *A History of St. Joseph County,* published 1907. Courtesy of the St. Joseph County Public Library, South Bend, Indiana.)

```
State of Indiana
                          ss.        Criminal No. 727
County of St. Joseph

                  In the St. Joseph Circuit Court,
                  February Term, 1907.

State of Indiana

       vs.

Albin R. Ludwig

              V E R D I C T.

       We, the Jury find the defendant, Albin R.
Ludwig, guilty of murder in the second degree; and further
find that he shall be imprisoned in the State's Prison
during life.
              JOHN LAYTON,
                  Foreman."

          * * * * * * * * * * * * * * * * *
```

Verdict finding Albin Ludwig guilty of murder in the second degree, as recorded in the trial transcript. (Photo by author at Indiana State Archives, Indianapolis)

Samuel Parker, Albin Ludwig's defense attorney. (Photo from *South Bend World Famed,* published 1922 by Handelsman & Young; courtesy of the St. Joseph County Public Library, South Bend, Indiana)

Gustave Ludwig, Prisoner 7142, joined his younger brother Albin in the Indiana State Prison in Michigan City in December 1917. (Indiana Images, Indiana State Archives, Indianapolis)

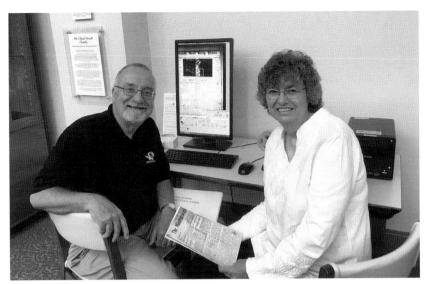

Above: Author Gary Sosniecki and wife Helen examine microfilm of newspaper stories about the Cecilia Henderson Hornburg Ludwig murder in August 2016 at the Heritage Center, Mishawaka-Penn-Harris Public Library, Mishawaka, Indiana. (Courtesy of Mishawaka-Penn-Harris Public Library)

Left: Author Gary Sosniecki examines the trial transcript for the second time in July 2018 at the Indiana State Archives in Indianapolis. (Photo by Helen Sosniecki)

Above: Author Gary Sosniecki (*left*), great-grandson of murder victim Cecilia Henderson Hornburg Ludwig, and Chuck Ellsworth, grandson of Cecilia's sister, Jean Henderson Ellsworth, who was living with the Ludwig family at the time of the crime. Photo taken October 29, 2018, in Lebanon, Missouri. (Photo by Helen Sosniecki)

Right: Author Gary Sosniecki at the grave of his great-grandmother, murder victim Cecilia Henderson Hornburg Ludwig, in July 2018 at Kingsbury Cemetery. (Photo by Helen Sosniecki)

"You don't know how the bloody handprints got on the outside of the closet door?"

"Don't know anything about it."

"You don't know how the handprint got on to the kitchen door leading to the summer kitchen?"

"I do not."

"You don't know about the burning paper in the cellar?"

"I do not."

Talbot asked Ludwig if he knew Arthur Householder, a Mishawaka constable who had guarded him at Epworth Hospital. "Slightly," the defendant answered.

"Did you state to Arthur Householder, at the hospital while he was there, that your wife, this way, 'My wife did the cutting,' or words to that effect?"

"I did not."

Talbot asked him about the day a James Girton and a nurse, Mrs. McElroy, were sitting at his hospital bed, and Mrs. McElroy asked, "Why did you kill your wife?" Talbot said Ludwig answered, "Why did she cut me?"

"I did not."

Surprisingly, Parker did not object to Talbot asking his client about a conversation with Householder and a conversation overheard by Girton when neither witness had testified yet, probably knowing that they were not on the prosecutor's witness list. Mrs. McElroy would not be called as a witness.

Ludwig also couldn't recall—at least in open court—any details of the contracts for his house and its furnishings other than that he made monthly payments.

"How much did you pay down originally?"

"I don't recollect," Ludwig said.

Talbot had another surprise for Ludwig and the jury.

"Do you remember when you lived in Elkhart, do you remember at a dance in Elkhart, in Germania Hall, before you moved to Mishawaka, in which you choked your wife, and had her down on the floor choking her, and Sergeant Whiteman separated you?"

Parker was on his feet again, arguing that the question was wholly immaterial to the inquiry. But Judge Funk overruled the objection.

"I never did," Ludwig proclaimed.

Surely by now Talbot had introduced doubt in Ludwig's veracity. The defendant's memory had been like an elephant's up to the point he testified about grabbing Cecilia by the throat and she collapsed. Now, not only couldn't he remember what happened immediately after the choking, but he also couldn't remember the details of his mortgage or a serious accusation from only a few years earlier.

Talbot forged ahead, taking his witness back to the day of his wife's death, back to Ludwig's search for the insurance policy that would have benefited Cecilia if Albin had died.

Ludwig repeated his earlier testimony that when he couldn't find it in the dresser, he went to the trunk in the closet that Cecilia had packed that morning.

"What did you find? The policy?" Talbot asked.

"I did not," Ludwig said. "I did not."

Responding to Talbot's questions, Ludwig explained in detail how he searched the trunk, how he sorted through his wife's clothing but didn't find the policy.

"Why did you want that policy?"

"I did not intend for her to have the policy and me pay for it if she left me," Ludwig answered.

"You know you had only to quit paying one assessment to invalidate that policy, and that the failure to pay the next month's policy would?"

"I wanted to turn it over to my mother," Ludwig explained.

Talbot asked Ludwig if he remembered Jean's daughter, Lucy Ellsworth, whose name was not used in court, going over to Mrs. McNabb's, another neighbor.

"She went over that way somewheres," Ludwig agreed.

"You had given her five cents before that?"

"Not until she asked me for it."

But Talbot and Ludwig disagreed on the time line. Talbot tried to prove that Lucy left the house just before the fire started in the closet. Ludwig argued that he still was on the front porch when Lucy asked him for money—and when Cecilia, lying on a lounge within hearing distance inside, told him to give it to the girl.

"She heard the children ask me, and she said, 'If you were not so stingy, you would give them some money for candy.'"

Talbot saved his most damning question for last.

"Do you remember when you were fighting your wife with the potato masher downstairs, the little girl coming back and running away?"

It was a shot in the dark considering that not a single piece of evidence had been introduced by either the state or the defense to place the potato masher in Ludwig's hands at any point, either upstairs or downstairs.

Parker knew it and objected before Ludwig could answer, calling it "palpably a catch question, and containing an assumption which counsel for the state has no right to put into it."

Judge Funk sustained the motion, probably no surprise to Talbot. The state's attorney sat down, and Parker approached Ludwig for redirect.[1] It would be Parker's task to undo any damage Talbot's aggressive cross-examination had done to Ludwig's defense. Talbot would get one more shot at the witness afterward.

First, Parker took Ludwig back to his visit with neighbor Marcellus Gaze. Talbot had kept a tight rein on Ludwig's answers, at times demanding yes-or-no responses without allowing explanations. Now, Parker was letting the defendant explain himself.

"Mr. Gaze says, 'If I were you, I would pack up and go,'" Ludwig said. "I says, 'I think that will be the only way to make an end of it.'"

"That is the only way to make an end of it?" Parker asked, wanting the jury to hear it a second time.

"Yes, sir."

Next, Parker gave Ludwig a chance to elaborate on how he and the man he had found in a compromising position with Cecilia had wound up living in the same house for a time.

"Mr. Talbot asked you also if it was not a fact that after your wife went to Kingsbury on the Grand Trunk road, if you and this man Smoke did not keep house together, and you started to make an explanation of that?"

"I would like to explain that and tell the truth," Ludwig replied.

"Tell it now."

"I was informed that he would be at South Bend waiting for her to go along to Kingsbury . . ."

Talbot interrupted Ludwig, as he had when Ludwig tried to explain under direct examination, with a motion to strike the defendant's answer. But Judge Funk overruled him.

Ludwig continued: "and I went along to South Bend, and he was there, and I knew it would be the best way to take him along home." Talbot again was on his feet, this time asking Funk to strike the latter part of Ludwig's answer. This time, Funk agreed.

Parker asked Ludwig if he took Smoke home to Mishawaka with him. Ludwig said he did, that he kept him there.

"For what purpose?" Parker asked.

"To keep him away from Kingsbury." What Ludwig really was saying was he didn't want Smoke near his wife, and his wife was going to her hometown of Kingsbury.

Parker then asked Ludwig to explain what he wasn't allowed to say about his conversation with Anderson, the police officer, at the corner of Second and Main the night before his wife's death, when Cecilia and sister Jean were talking to a man across the street.

"I said, 'Mr. Anderson, you remember this.' I says, 'I may want you.'"

Next, Parker asked Ludwig about a conversation he had with Police Chief Jarrett at the hospital that might explain why a can smelling like gasoline or kerosene was found at the scene of his wife's death.

"Did you state anything to Mr. Jarrett about oil used to clean clothes or a skirt?"

Talbot objected to the question but was overruled. Ludwig was allowed to answer.

"Mr. Jarrett and Mrs. Henderson—she was my wife's mother—made some remark about the oil and fire to me. I says, 'I know nothing about the oil, excepting my wife spoke in the forenoon about taking her black skirts—taking out the spots—which she always did with gasoline.' She said, 'Did she?' I says, 'I don't know.'"

Parker then told his witness that he wanted to bring up "a matter or two that I think I overlooked in the direct examination." He started by asking Ludwig where he had been since he left the hospital, but Parker's intent was to work up to the subject of Cecilia's health before her death. He hoped to build a case that Cecilia might have suffered from a weak heart that caused or hastened her death the day of the final quarrel.

Talbot objected from the outset, calling the first question, about Ludwig's whereabouts, "immaterial," a motion Judge Funk sustained.

Parker asked Ludwig if "Mrs. Ludwig complained at any time of any disease of the heart, or otherwise." Talbot objected on the grounds of hearsay. Funk agreed.

Parker tried again. "You may state, Mr. Ludwig, what the condition of your wife's health was at the time of her death, and prior to that time, for, oh, a matter of a year." Talbot again objected. This time, Funk over-ruled the objection.

Ludwig began to respond, "Complaining of the heart," but his answer was stricken from the record after another objection from the prosecutor.

Parker tried another tack: "You may state, Mr. Ludwig, what the con-dition of your wife's health was at the time of her death, and prior to that time, for, oh, a matter of a year—whether it was robust, or whether she appeared to have any ailment or not."

"Weak heart," Ludwig replied.

"Now you may state what she did along during that period, what she did to show that she had a weak heart?"

Talbot objected again, calling the question immaterial and one that the state "cannot refute because of its being peculiarly within the knowl-edge of this defendant, if it exists at all." Parker argued that if permitted to answer the question, Ludwig would reveal that "frequently within the period of a year prior to her death, she would complain of having smothering spells, and ask him to open the window, and do other acts indicating that she had some affection [an archaic term] of the heart." But Judge Funk sustained Talbot's motion.

Parker tried rewording the question, asking what Ludwig had ob-served during this period "that tended to indicate that there was some-thing the matter with her."

Ludwig's answer was unusually long for him: "On a foggy day, or a cloudy, real close night, I used to have to run and open all the windows, so she could breathe." That answer—which today might have suggested asthma—also was stricken from the record when Talbot objected on the grounds that it wasn't responsive to the question. Funk agreed.

Two more times, Parker reworded the question. Two more times, Talbot objected. Two more times, the judge sustained the objection.

Surely by now the jury understood that a physical ailment could have contributed to Cecilia's death. Surely Parker knew that the jury knew it. There was no need for Parker to try again to word a question that Talbot and Funk would let Ludwig answer. He sat down and let Talbot start his re-cross-examination.[2]

Talbot began by asking Ludwig if he talked about the lamp—its flame was the likely source of the fire—in his conversations with Jarrett or Cecilia's mother at the hospital.

"No, I did not," Ludwig replied.

"You never told that before you took the witness stand, did you?" Talbot asked.

After Parker objected to the question and Funk sustained the objection, Talbot got to his point: "You did not think about this lamp story till after your brother had cleaned out the house and came back with the pieces of the lamp, did you?"

Talbot didn't get an answer to this question, either, but it probably didn't surprise him that Parker objected and Funk had sustained the objection. He had made his point that Albin Ludwig was a liar.[3]

With that, it was time to eat. The judge recessed the trial until 1:30 that afternoon.

That evening's *South Bend Daily Times* would describe Ludwig's morning testimony as a victory for the defense:

> For three hours Albin R. Ludwig was on the witness stand this morning giving testimony in his own behalf during which time he was subjected to the severest kind of crossfire on the part of the prosecution. His evidence did not in any way differ from the line of defense as presented by Hon. Samuel Parker in his opening speech of Wednesday afternoon. Efforts were made by the state to confuse him in his testimony, but with little success. Several impeaching questions were propounded to him, all of which he emphatically denied.[4]

But the writer for the *Mishawaka Enterprise* wasn't as impressed, describing Ludwig's testimony as "a queerly concocted story of the affair."[5]

Ludwig wasn't done. He returned to the stand after dinner to answer more of Talbot's questions. The state's attorney started by asking about Cecilia's mother visiting him in the hospital.

"At that time when she saw you at the hospital, I will ask you if this statement was made by you to her. Did she say to you, 'How did the fire happen?' And did you say, 'I don't know, but I saw Celia . . . take a cup of gasoline upstairs to clean skirts'?"

"The statement was not made in that way," Ludwig said.

Talbot didn't pursue, instead asking one of the most damaging questions of the trial: "I will ask you if on the second Saturday before your wife's death, at a time when Mrs. Henderson was at your house, if you said to her—that is to Mrs. Henderson—at the time when your wife was working in the kitchen, and you and Mrs. Henderson were in the other room, 'If she, Celia, leaves me, I will kill her. She will never live to live with another.'"

"I did not," Ludwig said.[6]

Parker had the last opportunity to question the witness. He immediately returned to Ludwig's claim that his statement to Mrs. Henderson at the hospital about the gasoline was not made in the way Talbot suggested.

"What was said?" Ludwig asked himself. "I said she spoke in the forenoon that she had to clean a black skirt, but I did not know whether she did or did not. She had always used gasoline to do it with."

Talbot moved to strike Ludwig's last sentence. Judge Funk overruled.[7]

Albin Ludwig's long day on the witness stand was over. When court reporter Hugh Noel Seymour Home finished the trial transcript, Ludwig's testimony would consume eighty-four double-spaced, typed pages.

But was it enough to save his life?

CHAPTER 16

Wrapping Up

SAMUEL PARKER STILL PLANNED to call ten more defense witnesses, and State's Attorney Joseph Talbot would call four more in rebuttal. But, for all practical purposes, the trial had climaxed with Albin Ludwig's testimony. All evidence to connect Albin to the crime was circumstantial—no witnesses had seen how Cecilia Ludwig died—but State's Attorney Talbot clearly had proven that her husband had the means, motive, and opportunity to kill her. Somebody set the unconscious Cecilia on fire, probably with the aid of a flammable liquid, and, logically, Albin was the only person who could have done that. Albin's defense that the lit oil lamp fell on his unconscious wife during their altercation was his only hope, and it seemed a weak one.

But in a case built on circumstantial evidence, the defense only had to convince one juror of reasonable doubt.

The *South Bend Daily Times* noted in its coverage of the day's events that Ludwig's defense was hurt when Judge Funk repeatedly ruled against Parker's efforts to show that a bad heart had been a factor in Cecilia's death.

"The evidence which had been intended to be produced by the defense was ruled out by Funk and as a result will somewhat shorten the trial," the *Daily Times* predicted. "In all probability the taking of evidence will be completed this afternoon and it is very probable that the case will go to the jury Friday."[1]

The first defense witness following the conclusion of Ludwig's testimony Thursday afternoon was John Gaylor, who had sold the Marion Street house to Ludwig on installments and repossessed it after Cecilia's death. Gaylor, a real estate broker, explained to Defense Attorney Will Crabill that furniture, clothing, and other items were removed from the house over the next month. The trunk in the closet, where Ludwig said he had been searching for a life-insurance policy, was removed a day or so after the fire. "The debris in the closet was not removed for three or four weeks," Gaylor said.[2]

Gaylor's testimony, according to the *South Bend Daily Times,* "was made with a view to refuting the impression that the particles of the lamp and the lamp burner might possibly have been placed there by Gustav [*sic*] Ludwig as a matter of evidence."[3]

Crabill asked Gaylor about the hooks in the closet wall. Cecilia Ludwig had suffered a nonlethal head wound, and Crabill was hypothesizing, as cocounsel Parker had earlier, that Cecilia collapsed from striking her head on a hook when Ludwig pushed her against the wall, not from being choked, nor from being struck by the potato masher that Ludwig claimed she had used against him.

"There were clothes hooks in the closet wall on three sides," Gaylor recalled. "There were hook strips nailed to the wall and the hooks were screwed into the strips. The hooks were five feet from the floor. The hooks were what we call wire hooks, that is, hooks made out of pieces of wire."

Crabill next called Alvia J. Bruce to the stand. Bruce operated a meat market near the Ludwigs' home and was one of the first on the scene of the fire. He recounted what he and other rescuers found when they climbed the ladder into the upstairs front room. He explained how the unconscious Ludwig was removed from the home and described his condition when he was examined outdoors. By emphasizing that Ludwig was unconscious, the *South Bend Daily Times* reported, Bruce, a former member of the US Hospital Corps, discredited "the theory advanced by the state that the accused was feigning unconsciousness at the time."[4]

But what Crabill really was looking for was for Bruce to debunk the testimony of Talbot's last witness, Robert F. Schellenberg, who said he had found smoldering papers in the Ludwigs' cellar.[5] The prosecution's goal was to show that Ludwig, bleeding from his self-inflicted knife wounds, had gone to the cellar to burn some papers, and that he had left bloodstains along his route. Perhaps the smoldering papers were the insurance policy he accused his wife of packing.

Bruce did what Crabill wanted him to do. "After we placed Ludwig on the couch I went into the cellar," the witness said. "Someone had said there were children and a woman in the house. Another gentleman followed me into the cellar, but I didn't know who he was. There was no smoke in the cellar and no evidence of any fire. I saw no bunch of paper on the shelf smoldering."

Under cross-examination, Bruce admitted that he saw a bloodstain on the banister and on the door casing going into the kitchen from the dining room. "There were the four prints of the four fingers of a man's hand on one side of the casing and a thumb mark on the other side, about three feet from the floor," Bruce said. But with a bleeding man being carried and cared for by multiple men, and with what Bruce called a "pool of blood" on the upstairs floor, local law enforcement couldn't prove whose blood it was.

Bruce also told Talbot that he, too, had smelled the can from the closet that prosecution witnesses had said smelled like gasoline or kerosene, pushing the theory that Ludwig carried a flammable liquid upstairs to set his wife's body on fire. But Bruce didn't give Talbot the answer he wanted. Bruce said, "the only odor that came from it was the odor of smoke. There was no smell of kerosene about it. I told the officer so."[6] As with blood typing, the technology didn't exist yet to prove what had been in the can.

Parker next called a first-time witness to the stand, Nettie May Hess, a former neighbor of the Ludwigs, who said she had heard Cecilia Ludwig "say on one occasion that she would poison her husband if he did not do different . . . I heard her say on one occasion that she would brain him with a chair or the first thing she could get hold of."

In cross-examination, Hess said Albin Ludwig was present when the threat to poison him was made. "He made no threats against her at that time. He said not a word. I never heard Mr. Ludwig make a threat against his wife."[7]

Charles R. Patterson, the next witness, confirmed that he had talked to a "very calm" Ludwig, his neighbor, shortly before the fire. They were only two feet apart, and "I smelled no liquor on him."[8]

Parker recalled another neighbor, Veronica Gaze. "About a month before the fire I heard Mrs. Ludwig, referring to her husband, say that she would fix him. She made that same statement to me at other times." But under Talbot's questioning, Gaze admitted that on one of those times, Cecilia showed her a bruise on the arm.[9]

James Anderson, a Mishawaka police officer, was called to the stand for the third time. He told Parker that he had seen bloody fingerprints "about every other step" on the banister following the fire at the house.[10]

Charles A. Daugherty, a St. Joseph County physician for the past twenty-seven years who had no personal involvement in the case, was called as an expert witness. Crabill began with an extraordinarily long, hypothetical question—312 words—that asked if Ludwig, given the circumstances of his marriage and the events of that day, "would or might have an entire lapse of memory, so that he would not be conscious of pain, or of the events immediately succeeding the homicide."

The state objected to the question. Judge Funk agreed, sustaining the motion.

Crabill tried again. "Doctor, under such circumstances as are detailed in the hypothetical question just put to you, you may state whether after the patient recovered from the condition of unconsciousness, he would remember or recall, or there would come back to his mind, a knowledge of recollection of the facts and circumstances which succeeded the homicide?"

The prosecution objected again, using the same argument. Funk agreed again. The witness was dismissed, and the jury was left to its own conclusions about Ludwig's claimed memory loss.[11]

The next defense witness was Grace Jarrett, wife of the police chief, who accompanied her husband, Albin's brother Gustave, Gustave's wife Minnie, and another man, John Jarrett, to the house on East Marion Street on the Sunday after the Tuesday tragedy. Under questioning by Defense Attorney Parker, she testified that they saw a trunk in the closet and brought it out to the bedroom, where it was opened and emptied.

"You may state whether or not you saw an insurance policy in the trunk," Parker said.

"I saw the insurance policy that was taken out of the trunk," she replied. "It was on the bed in the clothing that had been taken out of the trunk."

So the insurance policy Albin Ludwig had claimed he was looking for existed after all. And somebody had placed it in the trunk, either Cecilia while packing on the day of her death, or somebody else in the five days since her death when the house was not a secured crime scene as it would be today. Nor would it be likely today for the wife of the police chief to be allowed at a crime scene, let alone testifying for the defense after her husband had testified for the prosecution.

Under cross-examination, Mrs. Jarrett told Talbot that the trunk "was neatly packed before we disturbed it. It did not seem to be disturbed at all."[12]

Gustave Ludwig, the defendant's brother, followed Grace Jarrett to the stand and confirmed the circumstances under which the insurance policy was found. Gustave also confirmed that it was the life-insurance policy on his brother "in favor of his wife" issued by the Knights and Ladies of Columbia.

In response to Talbot's questioning, Gustave explained that a fire-insurance policy also was found, this one in a little box in the room, but the life-insurance policy for $1,000 was found in the trunk. Then, in new information, Gustave revealed that somebody else had found a second life-insurance policy. "I don't know where it was found, but it was not in the trunk at the time we opened it," he said. This policy was for $500 on Cecilia's life, with $250 payable to Albin and $250 "to the girl," presumably her daughter Lyle Ellen. Son Willie, still living with his father, Cecilia's first husband, wasn't mentioned in the policy, though the attorneys didn't ask that question.[13]

The last defense witness was policeman James Anderson, who walked to the witness stand for the fourth time. Parker asked Anderson to describe Cecilia physically. "I had seen Mrs. Ludwig a great many times," the officer said. "She was probably five feet, nine or ten inches tall and was a large, raw-boned woman, and would weigh 165 to 170 pounds."[14]

The jury only had to look across the room at Albin Ludwig to see that he was smaller than the woman he was accused of murdering.

Testimony was almost over. State's Attorney Talbot now had the opportunity to call witnesses in rebuttal to anything Parker had presented in defense. Talbot would call four to the stand: Christina Henderson, Cecilia's mother; Police Chief Benjamin F. Jarrett; Arthur Householder, a Mishawaka constable who had guarded Ludwig at Epworth Hospital; and James Edward Girton, also a hospital guard.

Calling Mrs. Henderson to testify deviated from the rules of the court considering that she had been in the courtroom earlier in the day listening to testimony, including that of her son-in-law, the defendant. Judge Funk would have to rule on whether she would be allowed to present evidence. Before he could do so, Talbot asked her whether she was aware of the rule that witnesses could not be in the courtroom before testifying.

"I was not a witness when I came into court," she replied. "I did not come in as a witness. I did not expect to."

As expected, Parker objected to Mrs. Henderson testifying, citing the violation of the rule. Talbot responded that neither he nor his assistants knew that a witness was in the room, that Mrs. Henderson did not know she was to be a witness, and that she was excluded from the room before Ludwig was asked two questions about which the prosecution wanted her response.

Funk overruled the objection, Parker took exception, and testimony began.

Talbot asked about her conversation with Ludwig in the hospital. "Did you ask him, 'How did the fire happen,' and did he say, 'I don't know, but I saw her take a cup of gasoline upstairs to clean a skirt'?"

"Yes, sir."

After Mrs. Henderson confirmed she had been at the Ludwig house the Saturday a week before the fire, and that she had talked to Albin while Cecilia was in the kitchen, Talbot asked if he told her, "If she leaves me, I will kill her, that I will never let her live with any other."

Mrs. Henderson answered "yes," prompting Parker to object on the grounds that the statement should have been introduced as direct evidence, not during the prosecution's rebuttal to defense testimony. Funk agreed, and ordered Mrs. Henderson's answer stricken. Talbot, wanting the jury to be allowed to consider Ludwig's alleged threat, fought for Mrs. Henderson's answer to be included, explaining that the state did not know the existence of her testimony until after the state had introduced its evidence.

Parker disagreed. "That is clearly a shifting of position and should not be allowed."

The judge sided with Parker. Albin's alleged threat to kill Cecilia if she left him was thrown out.[15]

Next, Jarrett returned to the witness stand. Talbot asked him about a conversation he had with Ludwig in the hospital. "I will ask you if in that conversation he said to you, 'I lay down on the bed, face down, and when I came to I was cut and don't know how it happened.'" Jarrett said "yes." He also confirmed that Ludwig said his wife had oil in a can or dish upstairs for cleaning a black skirt.

Under Parker's cross-examination, Jarrett clarified that Ludwig said he personally didn't have any oil upstairs, and that Ludwig did not say that he saw his wife cleaning a skirt. "I did not write down what he said to me then," Jarrett explained. "I am stating my naked memory of what he said. I was interested in gathering evidence in the case."[16]

Arthur Householder, a Mishawaka constable, testified that he was a hospital guard for the thirty-eight days Ludwig was there. "In one talk Ludwig said to me that his wife did the cutting," referring to the wounds with which Ludwig was found.

Householder admitted under cross-examination that he was "pumping" Ludwig occasionally. He said he remembered Parker visiting Ludwig in the hospital. "This talk in which he said that his wife did the cutting occurred after you were there." Householder said he recalled Ludwig telling Parker that he hadn't said anything to the guard.[17]

The final witness, James Edward Girton, testified that he was the night guard in the hospital one evening when a nurse, Miss McElroy (previously referred to as *Mrs.* McElroy), was tending to Ludwig. "Miss McElroy asked him in my presence, 'Why did you kill your wife?' and he answered, 'Why did she cut me?'" In cross-examination, Girton told Parker that he never questioned Ludwig personally. "I just happened to overhear the remark to Miss McElroy."[18]

As reported the next day by the *South Bend Daily Times,* "a few minutes before 5 o'clock both sides gave notice that their evidence was in."[19]

In three days, twenty-nine witnesses had testified for the state, which also introduced five exhibits during the testimony of Dr. Holtzendorf, the coroner. Twelve witnesses testified for the defense, including the defendant.

Closing arguments were Friday morning. The *Daily Times* reported:

Attorneys Isaac Kane Parks and Burrell J. Cramer fired the opening guns in the state's closing arguments this morning. The former is assisting Prosecutor Talbot in this case. Both attorneys made a strong appeal to the jury, asking that a verdict of guilty be brought in against Ludwig,

so that the tragic death of his wife may be avenged and an example set
to restrain others from the crime of taking human life.

Attorney Will G. Crabill was the first to address the jury for the defense. He began his plea immediately after the noon adjournment. Following him Attorney Samuel Parker will argue the case for the defense
and Prosecutor Talbot will close the arguments for the state. The case
will go to the jury at 5 o'clock this evening.[20]

As Ed Jernigan wrote in Friday's *Mishawaka Enterprise:* "The verdict will be awaited with great interest."[21]

Judge Funk wanted the jury to begin deliberations immediately instead of the next morning, a Saturday. Maybe he was confident the state
had presented enough evidence that a guilty verdict would be reached
quickly.

He was right. Four and a half hours after entering the jury room, the
twelve men emerged with a verdict, which Foreman John Layton handed
to Judge Funk.[22]

"We, the Jury find the defendant, Albin R. Ludwig, guilty of murder
in the second degree; and further find that he shall be imprisoned in the
State's prison during life."[23]

The finding of second-degree murder saved Ludwig from execution
by hanging, the fate of at least three other Indiana wife murderers convicted that decade of the more serious charge of first-degree murder.[24]
Under Indiana law, first-degree murder meant murder with premeditated malice. The jury determined that Ludwig killed Cecilia with malice but not premeditation, which was second-degree murder. The crime
mandated a sentence of life imprisonment. A disappointed Ludwig
thought his worst-case scenario was a verdict of voluntary manslaughter, "meaning where one acts in defense of himself in taking life."[25]

The *South Bend Daily Times,* which had owned the story since the
day of the crime, reported the outcome in detail the next day at the top
of page 1:

> Albin R. Ludwig is guilty of murder, the jury having so determined at
> 10 o'clock Friday night, when it sent word to Judge Funk, notifying him
> that a verdict had been reached. Court was convened, the attorneys on
> both sides being notified and Ludwig was brought in to hear sentence.

Notwithstanding the lateness of the hour there were a number of people on hand to hear the fate of the accused.

When the jurymen had taken their places, Foreman John Layton was asked by the court if a verdict had been reached, and he replied in the affirmative. The sealed verdict was then turned over to Judge Funk and opened. The verdict was murder in the second degree and imposing life sentence at the Prison North at Michigan City. Ludwig calmly heard the verdict read, but it was no doubt a great disappointment to him as he was confident that the utmost would be a verdict of manslaughter, which provides for a sentence of from two to 14 years.

The first ballot of the jury found Ludwig guilty and seven followed to determine what form of punishment should be [imposed].

The arguments of the state and defense were not closed until after 5 o'clock Friday afternoon, after which Judge Funk read his instructions to the jury. He had prepared five verdicts and the jury returned [(*sic*), the writer probably meant *retired*] a little after 5:30 o'clock.

State's Attorney Talbot's closing argument in rebuttal no doubt carried great weight with the jury and was probably responsible for a verdict being reached in so short a time. The state's attorney made no effort at oratorical splendor, but confined himself to the facts of the case. He first took up the story of the crime as outlined by the defense and picked it over piece by piece until but very little of it remained. He then pointed out the more plausible story, taking the state's evidence, which was mostly circumstantial, and weaving it together until one could almost see in their imagination the crime while it was being committed.

He pointed out the fact that there was but one eye witness, the accused, the only other witness being silent in death. Particular emphasis was placed on certain statements made by Ludwig while at Epworth hospital, which were contradictory to those made on the witness stand.

State's Attorney confined himself entirely to the evidence in the case, refraining altogether from making an attack on the accused, and did not attempt to picture him as a demon as is so often heard in similar trials. That his argument was closely followed by the members of the jury was plainly visible to those who followed the case. . . .

The line of defense adopted by the attorneys for the accused was not at all improbable, and there were many who believed that it would impress a few of the jury to the extent that it would fail to reach an agreement. There were others who felt certain that the very worst would be a verdict of manslaughter. . . .

Sentence will probably be imposed Monday.[26]

The *South Bend Tribune,* which had not covered the case as thoroughly as the competing *Daily Times,* did offer some details about the jury's options in its four-paragraph story that Saturday. The *Tribune* reporter explained that murder in the second degree "is usually the finding that the murder was not premeditated, but rather accomplished on the impulse of the moment. . . . Many thought manslaughter would be the verdict, but it was shown to the evident conviction of the jury that Ludwig intentionally took the life of his wife, though it could not be shown that the act was premeditated."

The *Tribune* said Ludwig "bore up well under the reading of the verdict and accepted his fate without a murmur. Stoicism was his forte all through the proceedings and continued to be until the end." The reporter predicted that Ludwig's sentence of "life" would not be a long one. "It is said that blood poisoning from the self-inflicted wounds, by which he sought to escape through death immediately after the deed for which he was convicted, may set in and that perhaps the proposed amputation of the leg will not be in time to prevent his death."[27]

Even if Ludwig survived his ailments, it was unlikely he would spend the rest of his life in prison. Four other Indiana wife murderers sentenced to life imprisonment that decade were released early. A fifth failed to return to prison after a temporary parole.[28]

The *Tribune* correctly predicted that the verdict would be appealed. "The appeal will be on the ground that some of the evidence for the defense was wrongly excluded during the trial, it is said."[29]

Sentencing didn't come until Wednesday, May 8, when Judge Funk formally imposed the life sentence in the state prison at Michigan City.[30]

Two days before the sentencing, Parker had moved for a new trial, the motion containing thirty-seven separate causes. "The motion for a new trial was taken under advisement by the judge and is based on the proposed introduction of new evidence in the case by the defendant," the *Elkhart Daily Review* reported on May 9.

The new testimony is relative to the blood stains on the stair railing and jamb of the kitchen door, the testimony concerning which in the first trial is believed by the attorneys for the defense to have shown an incriminating circumstance, as it tended to impress the jurors with the idea that Ludwig, after the struggle in which his wife met her death, ran around the house to hunt gasoline with which to set fire to the room.

It is said that the prosecution issued a subpoena for one of the witnesses which the defense purposes [*intends*] to bring in if a new trial is granted, but that the witness could not be found. Attorney Talbot spoke for the state.[31]

Funk overruled the motion on the day of sentencing. "Counsel for the defense took exception to the court's ruling on the motion and were given 60 days in which to file a general bill of exceptions," the *South Bend Daily Times* reported the next day.

"Ludwig then prayed an appeal to the supreme court, which was granted. Ludwig will be taken to Michigan City in a few days."[32]

Ludwig's "commitment" paperwork, directed to the sheriff of St. Joseph County, was written May 11 and signed by Frank P. Christoph, clerk of the Circuit Court of St. Joseph County.[33]

An accompanying document, "Statement of Court Officers," signed by Judge Funk and State's Attorney Talbot, characterized Ludwig's disposition as "Jealous, high tempered."[34]

CHAPTER 17

Prison

ALTHOUGH HIS OFFICIAL arrival date in the Indiana Department of Correction was May 8, the day he was sentenced, thirty-seven-year-old Albin Ludwig remained in the St. Joseph County Jail through the weekend. On Monday, May 13, Officer Swanson escorted him by train to the Indiana State Prison in Michigan City, about forty miles due west of South Bend on the south shore of Lake Michigan.[1] He officially was received at the prison at 9:00 the next morning and assigned the prisoner number of 3701, according to the prison's clothing receipt. Officer A. M. Cooney accepted Ludwig's coat, vest, pants, shirt, undershirt, hat, shoes, collar, and tie with instructions to ship the items to brother Gustave H. Ludwig, 1105 Harrison Street in Elkhart. In return, Albin was handed his prison uniform.[2]

He was assigned to "Reliance," which, from the century-old prison records, appears to be a work assignment.[3]

The mugshots taken when Ludwig reported to prison—one frontal, one profile—show a handsome man with piercing eyes, close-cropped hair, and a light beard, probably from not having shaved for a couple of days. He wore a striped suit, probably corduroy, with short lapels. The top button was stylishly high on the chest. He wore a dark tie and a white shirt with a separate collar, also in the style of the day.

The back of the mugshot includes more descriptions, in handwriting that in places is difficult to read. Albin's occupation is listed as carpenter and plumber, differing from reports of his factory work but perhaps indicating skills that could be used in prison. His build is described as "m hvy," probably medium heavy, which matches his picture. His eyes were medium gray.[4]

On May 27, 1907, Albin R. Ludwig, Prisoner No. 3701, made his "Statement of Prisoner to Board of Commissioners of Paroled Prisoners."

Basic facts were recounted, such as age (thirty-seven), color (white), sentence (life), and crime (murder).

The nature of the crime, he said, was "Charged with killing my wife." "No one" was with him in committing the crime.

What business, occupation, or calling did you follow? "Laborer in a rubber factory."

Were you busy or idle just preceding the crime? "Busy."

He answered that he had no wife and no children.

Are you guilty of the crime? "Self Defence" [sic].

Did you plead guilty? "Not Guilty."

Have you ever been previously convicted of a crime? "No."

Have you ever served a jail or workhouse sentence? "No."

Do you use intoxicants? "Not for the last four years." Ludwig may have intended that answer to coincide with his sale of the Monument Saloon in Elkhart.

Ludwig then handwrote a seven-and-one-half page response, on lined paper, to "Tell your story of the crime." The statement contained no surprises—Ludwig was consistent with the story he told at his trial—other than that he added more details of Cecilia's alleged infidelity that he had learned about at and after the trial:

> At the trial I found out the man with her the night before the crime was a bridge man. He had been in Mishawaka about 4 weeks and had been out a number of afternoons with her when I was at work. After the trial was over I found out she had been going for two years every 2 weeks to a South Bend hotel with a roomer and she had been going with two other man [sic] every week for two years. She would do this while I be at work.[5]

Warden James D. Reid gave a preview of what prison life would be like for Ludwig and other inmates of that era in a 1903 speech in South Bend:

At the time he is received as an inmate of the institution, the prisoner is placed in the second grade. He is clothed in a dark check or plaid suit, and is allowed the privileges belonging to this grade, namely, to write one letter each month, to receive one visit each month from friends or relatives, and reading matter from the library. Three months of continuous good conduct in this grade entitles the prisoner to promotion to the first grade. The object sought in placing the new arrival in the second grade is that he may, in a measure, determine his own future in the institution. His employment is selected for him with great care. His every act is noted. On reaching the first grade he is clothed in a cadet blue uniform with brass buttons and the number of letters he may write and the visitors he may receive is doubled. He must have six months continuous good conduct in the first grade before the board will consider the question of parole. Violations of the rules will receive him to the second grade and if the violation be of a serious nature, he may be reduced to the third grade and wear the old prison stripe.[6]

Ludwig's good conduct likely kept him in the first grade of prisoners. Indiana State Prison archives show only one "Conduct Report" in his name: on August 9, 1915. Officer J. F. Burns wrote that Ludwig's offense was "Laughing and Talking in Chapel yesterday morning when Lines were coming in." Ludwig was reprimanded, a less severe punishment than being placed in solitary.[7]

He was admitted seven times to the prison hospital between 1913 and 1923.[8]

The records don't state whether any of the hospital stays resulted from the injuries he suffered the day Cecilia was killed.

CHAPTER 18

Appeal

CONSIDERING THAT GUSTAVE Ludwig had hired the law firm of Anderson, Parker & Crabill only days before his brother's first appearance in court—nearly two months after Cecilia's death—and that their initial agreement, probably to save Gustave money, was that the South Bend attorneys would not be responsible for tracking down witnesses, the lawyers did not skimp on Albin's appeal.

The ninety-nine-page document, *Albin R. Ludwig, Appellant, vs. The State of Indiana, Appellee,* was filed December 31, 1907, with the Indiana Supreme Court. It included a discussion of the issues, how the issues were decided and what the judgment was, errors relied upon for reversal, a history of the alleged crime and statement of the theories of the parties, seven affidavits, a thirty-four-page condensed recital of the evidence, points and authorities, the argument for the appeal, and a ten-page index.[1]

The appeal noted that, aside from Ludwig's own testimony, the evidence in the case was "wholly circumstantial."

It summarized the state's theory as that Ludwig:

had taken the slop jar upstairs into the front room, off of which was the closet where the body of the deceased was found, and had then gone down stairs and that then he and the deceased got into a quarrel in the dining room or the room just West of it, and that the appellant seized

the potato masher and the deceased ran from him and up stairs and
that he followed her and struck her on the head with the potato masher,
making the jagged wound found after death and rendering her insensible, and that he then dragged her into the closet and then cut his wrists
and throat with the razor and got blood upon his hands and had then
gone down stairs to get oil to throw into the closet and upon his wife's
body with a view to starting a fire there and destroying the evidences of
his crime, and that he had gone into the cellar and started a fire there,
in a bunch of paper and rubbish, and that he then returned to the room
up stairs, where he cut the calves of his legs, and that in going down
stairs and up and in getting the oil he smeared the blood on the stair rail
and made the blood prints of his hand and of his thumb on the casing of
the door, leading from the dining room to the summer kitchen.[2]

The theory of the appellant, Ludwig, was similar to what the jury
heard in his testimony and similar to the statement he wrote upon entering prison. He and Cecilia had agreed to separate. He had given her
a trunk in which to pack her clothes. He felt ill after dinner. He went
upstairs to lie down and took the slop jar with him in case he needed it.
While lying on the bed, he thought of the insurance policy and began a
search.

Not finding it in the dresser drawer where it had been kept, Ludwig
"lit a lamp and commenced to search for it in the trunk, holding the
lamp." While Ludwig was down looking in the trunk, Cecilia

came to the door of the closet and they had some words about the
household property and then she said "What are you doing there?" and
he answered that he was looking for the policy; that then she said she
would fix him anyway and struck at him with the potato masher, which
she had brought from below in anticipation of trouble; that he warded
off the blow and set the lamp down or let it fall and got upon his feet
and caught her by the throat and, in his rage, jammed her head against
one of the hooks and made the scalp wound found later and choked her
until she collapsed and sank down in death; that he had no thought,
purpose or intent of killing her and when he saw what had happened
he was so horrified that he had no realization of what occurred or what
he did; that in the struggle the lamp was upset and broken, or when she

struck at him he let it fall and it broke, in one case or the other causing the fire; that after the homicide he got the razor and cut himself; that he was not down stairs after the wounds were inflicted and that the blood on the door casings and on the stair rail was not put there by him, but by the men who lifted him up and passed him through the window, and that he did not start nor attempt to start any fire in the cellar and did not intentionally start the fire upstairs; that, in short, he was guilty of no higher degree of homicide than manslaughter.[3]

Ludwig's appeal offered fifteen facts in support of its theory, among them that the pieces of lamp were found among the debris in the closet. It also stated that the clothes hooks in the closet "were of such a character that, if the decedent's head had been jammed against one of them with sufficient force, the scalp wound found would have been produced," that the "jagged and irregular wound" found on Cecilia's head could not have been caused by a potato masher, and that Cecilia had a weak heart.[4]

The appeal also claimed the court erred in refusing to give two instructions to the jury requested by the defense and cited eight instances when the court refused to permit witnesses to answer certain defense questions while testifying, several of them involving Ludwig's neighbor Fred Metzler. In one instance, Metzler was asked about Mrs. Ludwig "as to gadding about—going away from home during the three or four weeks immediately prior to her death and in company—being in company with other men." He was not allowed to answer. The appeal claimed Metzler would have testified that "it was her habit, during the time fixed, to leave home immediately after dinner and to stay away the rest of the day and to be out with other men."

Five affidavits regarding evidence discovered after the trial were included in the appeal. So was a counteraffidavit filed by the state.

D. D. Rathbun, a telegraph operator for the Grand Trunk Western Railway Company, solved the mystery of who the "stranger" was on the fire scene. Rathbun revealed in an affidavit that he was the first person to go up the ladder and enter the smoke-filled front room upstairs in the Ludwig home. He described how he "stumbled upon and saw the body of a man on the floor near the windows." At first, he believed the man was dead. Rathbun said his hands became "covered with blood" while handling Albin's body, and, after Albin was taken down the ladder, he and at least one of the other men who had helped went downstairs. "I have no distinct recollection of putting my bloody hand or hands on the rail but have no doubt that I did so."

Rathbun also recounted how at one point in the front room, he noticed some cloth and other matter on the dresser beginning to burn. "This I hastily put on the floor and with my hands swept the covering and whatever was on the dresser into a bunch and threw all out of the west window upstairs."[5]

The significance of Rathbun tossing burning "cloth and other matter" out the window was explained in an affidavit by defense attorneys W. G. Crabill and Samuel Parker, who wrote that "if a fire was found in the cellar later and at a time when the defendant was physically unable to go to the cellar and start the fire, it was the result of burning rubbish thrown by him from the west window upstairs, which might reasonably have blown into the cellar and have been seen by the State's witness."[6]

But the defense still contended that there was no fire in the cellar, citing an affidavit from Bert W. Shaw, the second rescuer up the ladder. Shaw, who did not testify in the trial, stated he went into the cellar twice looking for Cecilia, who still hadn't been found in the smoky house. He saw no fire and no smoldering paper in the cellar either time.[7]

An affidavit submitted by Albin Ludwig asked for a new trial, stating that the new evidence from Rathbun and Shaw was material to his defense. The affidavit summarized Albin's version of the events as he had testified at the trial.[8]

A counteraffidavit by Isaac Kane Parks, an attorney for the prosecution, explained the repeated efforts the state had made to subpoena Rathbun before the grand jury and the trial. At the time, Rathbun was working for the railroad in Michigan.[9]

Was the new evidence sufficient to warrant a new trial? Not according to the Indiana Supreme Court. Chief Justice John H. Gillett wrote the opinion that was filed on July 1, 1908:

The newly-discovered testimony, for which a new trial is sought, satisfactorily accounted for the blood stains upon the stair rail and upon the frame of the door leading to the summer kitchen. Such testimony also tended to show that there was no fire in the cellar, and, if there was, to furnish a possible theory of its accidental presence there—that is, from the throwing out of the upper window, by one of the witnesses, of the covering upon the dresser, which was beginning to burn. There was also an attempt, by affidavit, to show how the matters referred to were used by the prosecuting attorney in his closing argument to show that appellant, after rendering his wife unconscious by a blow upon the head, had dragged her into the closet, and, after inflicting certain of the wounds upon his person, had gone down stairs to set the fire in the basement, and to procure gasoline to pour over his wife's clothing, after which he set fire to her.

After Justice Gillett cited case law on newly discovered evidence, he wrote:

So far as we can perceive, the only effect of the newly-discovered evidence as to the manner in which the blood stains came to be on the stair railing and upon the door-case was to explain, by direct evidence, what might reasonably be conjectured before, as the evidence upon the trial showed that the first man to enter the house was some one who was referred to in the evidence as a stranger. The case against appellant, however, would have been quite as strong with the existence of such blood stains explained, since the hypothesis that appellant went down stairs, after inflicting some of the wounds upon his person, would have involved the objection that other blood marks would, in all probability, have been found upon the gasoline can and elsewhere, if, indeed, his steps would not have been marked by a trail of blood.

Justice Gillett noted that the

killing of a human being in the perpetration of, or attempt to perpetrate, the crime of arson is murder in the first degree. Appellant cannot, however, complain that he has not been convicted of the capital offense, and the question therefore remains whether, in the circumstances of the new evidence being introduced, it could reasonably be expected that the jury might acquit him or find him guilty of manslaughter. The deceased came to her death as the result of the struggle in the closet. It might be conceivable that at the moment she sank to the floor appellant became unconscious, but it passes belief that, after receiving the wound she did, she inflicted the wounds found upon her husband, while he was upon the bed and elsewhere in the room.[10]

The justice determined "that the conclusion of the jury, that appellant was guilty of murder in the second degree, was fully supported."

As for whether a fire was set in the cellar, "the testimony as to the manner of its commission was so trifling that it was likely to fall of its own weight," Gillett wrote. He debunked another issue, writing that he failed "to perceive any ground for the view that the excluded testimony could have in anywise aided appellant."

The judgment of the jury was affirmed.

In the eyes of the chief justice, Albin Ludwig had knocked his wife unconscious with a potato masher, dragged her into the closet, doused her with gasoline, set her on fire, and closed the closet door.

Ludwig got off lucky. Because Cecilia's murder involved arson, he could have been convicted of murder in the first degree.

He was lucky he wasn't sentenced to hang.[11]

CHAPTER 19

Parole

ALBIN LUDWIG APPLIED multiple times for parole.

The *Elkhart Daily Review* carried a one-paragraph story in November 1915 saying that Ludwig had petitioned the pardon board for parole.[1]

It wasn't granted. Cecilia's daughter Lyle, who then was twenty-one, may have testified against Albin's release. "I believe my mom told me that Lyle always went to his parole hearings to try to keep him in prison," a great-granddaughter said in 2017.[2]

Four years later, Ludwig sought "a pardon or at least a parole." Isaac Kane Parks, who assisted Joseph Talbot in prosecuting Ludwig, was "said to be in favor of granting the pardon."[3] The *Daily Review* reported at the time that Ludwig was head of the prison bakery. "His record, friends declare, will assure him of favorable consideration before the board."

The prosecuting attorney in the Sixtieth Judicial Circuit in 1919 was Samuel P. Schwartz. On February 17, he wrote a letter to Edward J. Fogarty, warden of the Indiana State Prison in Michigan City, about a parole application by Ludwig that was to be considered at the March session of the State Board of Pardons. "As you will recall, Ludwig's crime was a most brutal one, and certain people who remember the case and are familiar with the circumstances have come to this office for the purpose of learning what may be done to prevent Ludwig's parole at this time," Schwartz wrote.

He explained that he wasn't familiar with the case and asked Fogarty for its present status.[4]

The warden's response is not in Ludwig's file in the Indiana State Archives, but Schwartz's letter probably influenced the decision. Parole was not granted.

On January 17, 1923, Indiana governor Warren T. McCray commuted Ludwig's sentence from life to a sentence of sixteen years to life, which meant he could be eligible for parole as early as that May. It's unknown what the impetus was for the governor to act at this particular time, but presumably the same people who supported parole for Ludwig had taken their efforts to a higher level.

Executive Order 1016 stated that upon his conviction Ludwig "had no previous criminal history," that he "has maintained a clear record" in prison, and that "after a careful investigation and examination of all the facts in said case," the State Board of Pardons recommended that Ludwig's sentence be commuted.[5]

Ludwig's release after serving only sixteen-plus years of a life term was not uncommon in the early twentieth century. "In 1913, 'life' sentence in the federal system was officially defined as 15 years," wrote political scientist Marie Gottschalk, who has studied mass incarceration, adding: "Many states had comparable rules."[6] Indiana was one of them. Another Indiana wife murderer sentenced to life the same year as Ludwig was paroled after eleven years and two others after fifteen years. And two of those three had been convicted of first-degree murder, a more serious offense than Ludwig's second-degree conviction.[7]

As his release date neared, Ludwig gave written permission to prison physician P. H. Weeks to operate on him on May 28, 1923, for a fistula, an abnormal connection between two hollow spaces.[8]

Ludwig was paroled four days later, on June 1. He signed his parole agreement June 7 and left the prison on June 8.[9] He had been in some sort of custody for sixteen years and eight months, since the day Cecilia died.

The parole agreement Ludwig signed with the Board of Commissioners of Paroled Prisoners of Indiana State Prison listed seven "rules governing prisoners on parole," including that he must not change employment without written permission from the warden, that he report his income and expenses monthly, that he abstain from liquor and "avoid evil associations and improper places of amusement and recreation," and not carry firearms, and that he "respect and obey the laws cheerfully, and conduct himself in all respects as a good citizen."[10]

Albin's new employer was someone who added credibility to the parole application. George H. Whiteman served various roles on the Elkhart police force through the years, from patrolman to superintendent.[11]

It wasn't the first time Whiteman had come to Ludwig's rescue. During the trial, State's Attorney Joseph Talbot had questioned Ludwig about an incident at a dance where Whiteman, then a police sergeant, had pulled Ludwig off Cecilia, whom he was choking on the floor. Ludwig denied the incident happened.

Ludwig was discharged from parole on May 31, 1924.[12] By then, the South Bend newspapers had lost interest in the case. Neither reported on the development.

CHAPTER 20

Life after Prison

IT'S NOT KNOWN for sure what job George Whiteman had waiting when Albin Ludwig was released from prison, but a granddaughter of Cecilia Ludwig's sister Jessie said in a 2017 interview that at some point he worked as a "Jewel Tea Man," a door-to-door purveyor of tea, coffee, and various household goods.[1]

It was hard to find a neighborhood in America where the Jewel Tea Man wasn't a welcome sight.[2] But Albin Ludwig the Jewel Tea Man was not a welcome sight in the neighborhoods where his past was known.

"He would drive down to the houses there," Jessie's granddaughter said. "Mom was just petrified of him."[3]

The 1926 *Polk's Elkhart City Directory* listed Ludwig as one of three men living in the Federation of Labor Hall at 521½ South Main Street, upstairs from the Golden Pheasant Inn, a restaurant at 521 South Main. The directory indicates that Ludwig worked at the restaurant, probably using skills he had learned in the prison bakery. Perhaps Whiteman was a partner in the business.

By 1928, Ludwig may have been in the restaurant business for himself, ironically, just a block south of his old Monument Saloon. Elkhart city directories from 1928 to 1938 list him as operating a restaurant or "lunch room" at 128 South Main and living upstairs. In 1932, the business was Ye Old Inn Restaurant.

In 1940, the seventy-year-old Ludwig had returned to factory work as a metalworker at the Safe Play Company, then a manufacturer of playground devices. During World War II, production shifted to locking devices for the US Navy and metal parts for house trailers.[4] With young men fighting overseas, dependable and able older men like Ludwig had value to factories producing war goods. Elkhart city directories show Ludwig working at Safe Play at least through 1947.

Ludwig no longer was living above a restaurant. The 1940 US Census listed A. R. Ludwig as a lodger in the home of a twenty-nine-year-old unmarried woman in Elkhart. Perhaps she was a coworker who needed a boarder to help make ends meet.

No evidence can be found that Albin Ludwig ever remarried, although Cecilia's daughter believed that he had.

"Lyle did tell me that she saw him once and he was remarried," a great-granddaughter of Lyle related in 2017. "She boldly told the new wife what kind of man he was."[5]

Albin Ludwig filed a Social Security claim on December 10, 1948, when he was seventy-nine years old.[6]

He still was listed in the *Elkhart City Directory* in 1953, a retiree living quietly by himself at 110½ East Franklin in Elkhart.[7]

For all the notoriety of Cecilia Ludwig's death, the death of her second husband and convicted murderer went virtually unnoticed. The only apparent record of Albin Ludwig's death on June 18, 1954, can be found in the published records of an Elkhart funeral home. No death notice for Ludwig appeared in Elkhart's surviving daily newspaper, the *Truth,* and no death date can be found in the Social Security Death Index. Albin's parents and brother are buried in Elkhart's Grace Lawn Cemetery, but Albin is buried in an unmarked grave in Rice Cemetery.[8]

It is possible that Albin Richard Ludwig—a childless eighty-five-year-old man living alone, his cousins embarrassed by his murderous past—died the lonely death of an indigent.

He survived the wife he murdered by almost forty-eight years.

The Modern Woman

MARRIED TWICE, UNAFRAID to sass back to her husbands or gad about town without them or even to flirt with other men, Cecilia Henderson Hornburg Ludwig may have been what in 1906 was called "The Modern Woman."

Newspapers that year reprinted an unattributed article with that title, from the *West Gippsland Gazette* in Australia to London's *Daily Mail* to the *South Bend Daily Times.* Ironically, on Tuesday, September 25, 1906, Cecilia wouldn't have read the "The Modern Woman" story on the "Women's Realm" page of the *Times* because she was murdered earlier that afternoon.

The unknown writer said nothing the modern woman "does or wears or says is like the woman who lived in the 'good old days.'"[1]

Charley Hornburg and Albin Ludwig, traditionalist husbands, were unprepared for marriage with a "modern woman." Both resorted to violence, homicidal violence in Albin's case, to put Cecilia in her place. Unfortunately, at the start of the twentieth century, what today we call domestic violence had been the accepted way of married life for centuries.

A 1982 report on battered women by the United States Commission on Civil Rights traced wife beating in America to British common law, which condoned it as punishment for misbehavior. "As late as 1864, a North Carolina court, in a case in which a man choked his wife, upheld his use of force."

Finally, in 1871 an Alabama court rescinded the legal right of a man to beat his wife, holding that the husband and wife "stand upon the same footing before the law." A North Carolina court followed in 1874, but with a qualification: "If no permanent injury has been inflicted, nor malice, cruelty nor dangerous violence shown by the husband, it is better to draw the curtain, shut out the public gaze, and leave the parties to forget and forgive."[2]

Cecilia, the modern woman, refused to tolerate "cruel and inhumane treatment" by her first husband, escaping the marriage by divorce, easily achieved in a state that had been known as a "divorce mill" earlier in the nineteenth century.[3] For reasons she took to her grave, Cecilia did not seek divorce from Albin Ludwig, perhaps because of the income he provided for her "gadding about." But if Cecilia had lived another few hours, long enough to make good on her threat to move out of their Mishawaka home permanently, a divorce likely would have followed.

In a paper prepared in 1908 for the Century Club of Indianapolis and the Marion County Bar Association, William S. Garber, official reporter in the Marion County Courts, gave several reasons why marriages in that era disintegrated, including one that could have described the Ludwigs' marriage:

> If neither the husband nor wife has yet reached the point of applying for divorce, and laying bare the sores that every human being instinctively seeks to keep covered, though they continue to live together they get farther apart in spirit and interests until the husband seeks in the society of some other woman, or the wife in the society of some other man, that companionship and sympathy which they have failed to find in each other. Then a decree of separation is asked on the ground of infidelity.[4]

Domestic violence resulting in a murder as gruesome as Cecilia Ludwig's death was rare enough to make headlines for months in the northern Indiana of 1906. But even with the resources available to discourage it today, domestic violence resulted in sixty-seven homicides in Indiana in a recent twelve-month period.[5]

The murder of Cecilia Ludwig robbed two children of their mother. Though raised separately, the siblings stayed in occasional contact until William's death in 1969. Lyle, who had been in school on the day her mother was killed, died in 1996, two months short of her one-hundred-second birthday.[6]

Life went on after Cecilia's death for the three other family members who were living in the Ludwig home on the day of the crime: Cecilia's sister Jean Ellsworth and her two children, Lucy (nine) and Charles (not quite seven). Albin complained that Jean, a "modern woman" like her sister, could not be found to testify at his trial. Jean's presence in the Ludwig household that summer may have exacerbated Cecilia's flirtatious tendencies, leading to the fatal showdown between Albin and Cecilia.

In March 2018—nearly 111 years after the trial—Jean's grandson, Chuck Ellsworth, shed some light on the mystery woman of the murder in Mishawaka, her marriages, and her son, Charles, who the *La Porte Argus-Bulletin* reported "was in all probability a witness to the tragedy."[7]

Thanks to Chuck, we now know why Jean Ellsworth and her children were living in the Ludwig home that summer. We know where Jean likely was when Albin was on trial. And we know how she and son Charles spent the rest of their lives—rarely if ever talking about Cecilia Henderson Hornburg Ludwig's murder.

Chuck, the adopted son of Charles Ellsworth, was "pretty much raised" by his grandfather, Jean's first husband, Ora Horace Ellsworth, nicknamed Orie.[8]

As Chuck knew the family history, at the start of the twentieth century, Orie was a respected mining engineer who was in high demand in the goldfields of California. "They worked all over," Chuck said. "They probably were in Railroad Flat longer in one place than anywhere else." A photograph from Railroad Flat dated April 1899 shows Jean, pregnant with Charles, as Orie leans against a scrawny tree, and Orie's father, a white-bearded Horace, holds a bucket.

Orie was a self-taught engineer. "He learned his skills as an apprentice and a lot of reading," Chuck said. "He was an avid reader. He read scholarly stuff. . . . He was a genius. He was a mechanical genius. He never went to school for it."

He also was an amateur geologist who staked a claim on his own mine outside of Railroad Flat.

"Orie took a fair amount of gold out of that mine," Chuck said. "From what I could tell over the years of talking to him, he was pretty stable. He kept his eye on the ball. Jean did not. I think she flitted in and out of Railroad Flat at will."

When Jean showed up in Mishawaka in July 1906 and moved in with Cecilia and Albin, her intent probably was to leave Orie for good, Chuck said. "I think when things started to look flat in Railroad Flat, she took off."

But when Orie took a job at the C&C Mining Works, "a big operation," in Virginia City, Nevada, "I think she came back," Chuck said. "I think Jean went with him. He worked at C&C for a long time. I would say he was there at least until 1920."

Years later, Orie would confide in Chuck that Jean was "a run-around who wouldn't stay home." Whenever Jean left for good, Lucy and Charles stayed with Orie in Virginia City. "He told of raising the kids in that wild town."

At some point, Orie and Jean divorced. Orie remarried. His bride, Anna, was "his true love," Chuck said. Anna died of a stroke in Orie's arms about 1934. "He spoke lovingly of her over the years he raised me." Jean remarried too. Her new husband, William Jones Leigh, was a fellow Scottish immigrant who went by Billy. Both couples lived in California.

As studious as father Orie was, Charles was not. "Charles had no use for school," Chuck said. "Charles, in his later years, told about growing up in Virginia City, being chased out of the Fourth Ward School at thirteen, and sliding down the drain pipe. The end of his formal education."

If Charles was affected by witnessing all or part of a murder at a tender age, it didn't impact his success in life, even with an early end to his education.

"Charles made a nice living as a very young cowboy capturing and wrangling the wild horses in the hills around Virginia and Carson cities," Chuck said. "He was a master with a rope and lariat. Because of this skill, Charles did mention that shortly before he enlisted in the army and went to France as an artilleryman in World War I, he met Will Rogers."

Eventually, Charles settled in California. His career was as a mechanic and owner of gas stations—"He was a terrific mechanic," Chuck said—but his avocation was boat racing. In the 1940s, Chuck said, his father set a world's speed record in a race on Salton Sea in California.

Charles married Floreta Pearl Boyd in 1935. The next year, Orie moved in with Charles and Flo, who adopted Chuck as a newborn in 1944.

Although Jean abandoned Charles and his sister at a young age, Charles helped his mother as she grew older. Chuck remembered that in 1952 or 1953, Charles and Flo bought Jean and Billy a bungalow in Belmont Shore, California, a suburb of Long Beach, where they also lived. Young Chuck was close enough that he could ride his bicycle to his grandmother's house after school and eat a snack—"I recall her being a very good cook"—although mother Flo worried the snacks would spoil his dinner.

When they visited, Chuck recalled, Jean "was cordial enough, but standoffish."

Jean, like her sister Cecilia, was a tall woman. "Jean must have been five-nine, five-ten," Chuck said. "I was a kid—she towered above me."

Jean's husband died a couple of years later. When Charles and Flo moved elsewhere in California, they moved Jean into another house nearby.

Orie Ellsworth died on July 10, 1974. His first wife, Jean, died November 30, 1974.

Their son Charles died on April 20, 1997, at the age of ninety-seven. Their daughter Lucy died on December 3, 1999, at the age of 102. Lucy's final home was in South Bend, just a few miles from Mishawaka and the scene of the September 25, 1906, tragedy that sent her screaming to the back porch of neighbor Alice McNabb. Lucy didn't witness the murder, but she probably was the last person alive who saw the events that followed.

Despite all the stories Chuck heard from Orie and Charles growing up, the first he knew about his father being in the house at the murder of his great-aunt Cecilia was when he was tracked down for this book.

"The murder in Indiana was never spoken of," he said. "Knowing Charles, if he wanted a secret kept, he would tell everybody to keep their mouths shut. He was the patriarch of the family. He was the boss. There was no mistaking that."

The true story of what happened to Cecilia Henderson Hornburg Ludwig on that warm afternoon in 1906 died nine decades later with Charles Ellsworth, the last living person to see her alive, a man who could keep a secret.

Acknowledgments

I MENTIONED IN THE preface how Fern Eddy Schultz, state-appointed historian for La Porte County, Indiana, supplied the first newspaper clippings about my great-grandmother's murder when my research began in 1996. She also mailed detailed genealogical records of the Henderson family, including the divorce decree from Cecilia's first marriage to my great-grandfather.

One other favor by Fern back in 1996 was to connect me with a second cousin once removed, Paula Steiner, granddaughter of Cecilia's sister Jessie. Paula also had written Fern about Henderson family history. Paula and I immediately began a correspondence. Not only did she share all her genealogical research, but she also shared photographs. One was the only known photo of Cecilia. Another was of my mother playing with Paula's father as children. I lost track of Paula through the years, but, thanks to Ancestry.com, we reconnected in September 2017 and resumed our correspondence. Paula's help has been invaluable.

My research was hit-and-miss until my retirement from a forty-three-year career in the newspaper industry at the start of 2016.

Fortunately, the internet had matured since my initial work two decades earlier. Now I was blessed with resources such as Ancestry.com, GenealogyBank.com, and Newspapers.com. I thank family friend Tanafra Murray for introducing me to Ancestry.com, which connected me to previously unknown relatives on the Henderson side of the family as well as members of the Ludwig family. Several were willing to share their own research and be quoted as this project progressed. Many thanks to Kent A. Berridge, who helped extensively and connected me with Judy A. Myer; Randi Herrod, who connected me with Chuck Ellsworth, whose father may have witnessed the murder as a child; Linda Ludwig Irish and Gretchen L. Marks, both of whom shared invaluable knowledge of the Ludwig family; and to the anonymous-by-request source, who wrote about the information provided, "I doubt anyone in the family would have issue, but you never know."

Having access to the trial transcript gave life to the people and events surrounding the murder. I thank Michael Vetman, reference archivist for the Indiana State Archives, for tracking down a copy in the Indiana Supreme Court files. My wife and I appreciated Michael's hospitality on our two visits to the archives.

We also welcomed the hospitality shown by supervisor Deanna Juday and her staff on our two visits to the Heritage Center at the Mishawaka-Penn-Harris Library, which has an extensive microfilm collection of Mishawaka and South Bend newspapers.

I'm also grateful for the help Amy Pfifferling-Irons provided at the Elkhart Public Library. Susie Richter, curator of the La Porte County Historical Society Museum, found the plat books we needed. Ellen Anderson of the St. Joseph County Public Library located four important photos, including an early 1900s photo of Mishawaka's Second and Main intersection, where Albin spied on Cecilia, Jean, and the "bridge-man." And I'm grateful for the assistance we received from the St. Joseph County Clerk's Office as we attempted to pinpoint the courtroom where Albin Ludwig was tried for murder.

Four friends—three of them accomplished journalists, two of them published authors, one a library director—read the first draft of the manuscript and offered suggestions, some of them critical, virtually all of them followed. My thanks to Dr. Chad Stebbins, Ron Davis, Marc Wilson, and Cathy Dame. Another friend who read the first draft, media attorney Jean Maneke, provided welcome advice and reassurance that I was on the right track. Also thanks to friend Daun Crawford for loaning a book that prompted me to explain more about why the Henderson and Ludwig families came to America, and to Jessica Hughey for steering me to the appeal decision. And thanks to Shawna Bradley of the *Laclede County Record,* a newspaper my wife and I published two decades ago when it was the *Lebanon Daily Record,* for creating the map of Albin Ludwig's neighborhood.

A special thanks to the terrific publishing team at the Kent State University Press: Susan Wadsworth-Booth, director; Will Underwood, acquiring editor; Mary D. Young, managing editor; Christine Brooks, design and production manager; Richard Fugini, marketing and sales manager; and Valerie Ahwee, copy editor.

Foremost, I thank my partner in life and in business, Helen, my wife of forty-six years and an award-winning journalist in her own right, for her research assistance, copy editing, encouragement, and, especially, patience as this project came to fruition.

GARY SOSNIECKI
August 2019
Lebanon, Missouri

Brothers in Prison

A DECADE AFTER Albin Ludwig entered prison, his older brother would join him behind bars in Michigan City.

In the 1910 federal census, Gustave Ludwig (whose name often was spelled without the final *e*, sometimes by his own pen,[1] but who was best known simply as Gus) claimed his age was forty-five and that he had immigrated to the United States in 1873. In his naturalization application, Gustave claimed to have arrived in 1883.[2] He more likely was forty-two, and the Ludwig family arrived in America in 1884, but there's no reason to believe he lied to the enumerator on purpose. He said his birth year was "about 1865," indicating that he had some doubt about the details of his early life.

The census identified Gustave as a self-employed carpenter—he later would add plumber to his skill set—and a German-born naturalized citizen who claimed his native tongue was English.[3]

Gustave, his wife Minnie, age forty, and his mother, Ida, age seventy-two, lived in their mortgage-free home at 1209 Harrison Street in Elkhart at the time of the census. However, sometimes he used an address around the corner on Oakland Avenue, adjoining property they also owned. Gustave and Minnie had been married for twenty-two years.

Use of the address in identifying Gustave was important for the newspapers because he wasn't the only Gus Ludwig in Elkhart. The other Gus, not believed to be a relative, was a respected theater manager, grocer, and vocalist at society events.[4]

The Gustave Ludwig on Harrison Street, or Oakland Avenue, was not a big-time criminal—or at least he hadn't been caught committing a major crime yet. "He has in the past been energetic and thrifty," the *Elkhart Truth* reported. "Those in a position to know, declare that at the present time he has a sufficient income to keep him for the rest of his life without further labor."[5]

But Ludwig did have a record of lesser offenses. He had been arrested at least four times in Elkhart for somewhat minor transgressions, once for riding a bicycle on the sidewalk. The fine was nine dollars. The second time, he was fined thirteen dollars for "A & B," presumably assault and battery, possibly as the protagonist in a fistfight. He was arrested a third time for laying sewer in a yard without a license. The case was discharged. The fourth time, he was sentenced to probation for trespassing.[6]

A more serious offense occurred on April 16, 1915, when, according to a headline at the top of page 1 in the next day's *Elkhart Daily Review,* Gustave was the "BURGLAR CAUGHT DEAD TO RIGHTS IN LOCAL STORE."

The story, which revealed much about the dark side of Gustave's character, began:

> Chance led to the discovery of Gustave Ludwig of 1209 Harrison street in the act of burglarizing the wareroom of Borneman & Sons' hardware store at 9 o'clock last night. His arrest followed soon afterward.
>
> Several drayloads of supposed plunder were found in his barn.
>
> Ludwig was released this afternoon on a $700 bond [about $14,000 in 2019 dollars] to answer at the term of superior court which convenes next Monday. The law firm of Hughes & Arnold has been retained by Ludwig.
>
> Ludwig has been the suspect of police investigation in years past, and the general belief has been that he might carry off anything he could get his hands on. Many persons believe he is a kleptomaniac. He owns property worth over $10,000.[7] [In 2019 dollars, Gustave's property was worth more than $200,000.[8]]

The story went on to describe how Gustave was discovered on the scene and how he tussled with a police officer attempting to apprehend him: "the officer used his fists to subdue his captive, which was not fully accomplished until the bluecoat had slammed Ludwig against a brick wall and partially stunned him."

Ludwig had used a ladder behind the store's main building to obtain access through a second-story window. "At the foot of the ladder was a bicycle, an overcoat and a short bar, or jimmie."

When taken to the police station, Gustave gave a false name, "Herman Frederick," and false address "but was soon recognized as Ludwig."

After obtaining a search warrant, the police chief, a sergeant, and two officers went to Ludwig's premises. "So much stuff was found in the basement of the barn," the newspaper said, "that a dray was summoned to take a load to the station. One load was taken and it is said there are three or four more loads of plunder in the basement and the barn proper."

The article continued with the subhead: "Enough to Stock Small Store."

Police found "paints, oils, brushes, chisels, locks, braces, vises, stools, shovels, plumbing fixtures, pieces of lead pipe and innumerable small articles. Many of the packages bear Borneman & Sons' name and others have that firm's cost mark. Some articles were not taken from Borneman & Sons' stores. Where they came from had not been learned this morning.[9]

The *Daily Review* quoted E. C. Borneman as saying Ludwig was a suspect when the store was burglarized a year earlier.

But the newspaper cautioned that there was no conclusive proof that the items found in the barn were stolen. "Herman Borneman said today that Ludwig has been buying materials at the Borneman store for several weeks."

The *Daily Review* wrapped up the article by noting that Ludwig had been caught red-handed with a wagon of stolen plaster a few weeks earlier from an Elkhart lumber yard and that he had been prosecuted for the theft of shingles from a citizen several years ago. "He pleaded guilty and paid a fine."

Gustave made page 1 of the *Daily Review* again two days later. This time, a worker for the Elkhart Gas & Fuel Company discovered that the gas meter at Ludwig's home had been bypassed, that the company's gas line was feeding a heating stove in the living room and possibly other rooms without the company being paid.[10]

It wasn't until October 20 that Gustave's burglary case was filed in Superior Court and scheduled to appear on the docket for the court's next term. The *Daily Review* reported: "In explanation of the delay in sending a transcript of the judgment of the lower court to the superior court Judge Lee said he had 'lost track of the case,' having an impression for a long time that it had been finally disposed of." A few weeks later, the competing *Elkhart Truth* reported that the case would be heard by a jury the week of November 22.[11]

But the trial still hadn't been held by May of the next year. On May 12, the *Daily Review* reported that the stolen items that were evidence in the case had been moved from the basement of the Monger Building, where the Superior Court had met previously, at the request of the owner. Now, the items were in storage at Borneman & Sons, the store from which they had been stolen, though "the firm had not been given possession" of them.

"Frequently questions are asked why the trial does not take place," the newspaper wrote.[12]

Later it would be revealed that a legal technicality was holding up the trial, but that became a moot point with Gustave's arrest on another serious charge on Monday night, November 19, 1917.

As reported two days later in the *Elkhart Daily Review:*

> Stolen merchandise including all kinds of articles and said to be valued at possibly $40,000 were found in a house belonging to Gus Ludwig of 612 Oakland avenue Monday night, and Ludwig is under arrest, along with Max Shuman, formerly an Elkhart resident but who until his arrest yesterday was an employee of the American Express Co. in Chicago. Shuman's father is a cousin of Ludwig.[13]

In 2019 dollars, the value of the stolen merchandise exceeded $800,000, indicating this was more than just a petty heist.[14]

The *Daily Review* article continued:

> Ludwig's arrest was made at about 6 o'clock Monday evening by former Sheriff Frank Leader, Captain Jack Northrop of the Elkhart police department, and Marshal Christman of Goshen. At Mr. Leader's request, pending the arrest of Ludwing's [*sic*] alleged partner in crime, the local press refrained from mentioning the case.

Said He Intended to Start a Store

Ludwig was arrested as he drove up to the rear of his residence with a load of plunder.[15] On being taken to the police station and quizzed by his captors he at first claimed he had bought the goods with the intention of starting a store; but when pressed for the "real truth" he broke down and confessed that he had simply acted as a fence for Shuman, who, he said, had been consigning them to him as "Frank Boss, Goshen, Ind." Chicago authorities on Tuesday arrested Shuman, who was brought here at 10 o'clock last night by Officer G. B. Plowman.

The prisoners are to be arraigned in the superior court Friday morning. Inspector Schuler of the American Express Co., arrived here today to conduct the accumulation of evidence. Shuman, who is 23 years old and unmarried, was head of the "bad order" department of the Chicago office, and it was his duty to repack and redirect such packages as had been broken in transit. Mr. Schuler is said to have declared the company has known of thefts for the last two months at least. Another consignment of goods for Boss at Goshen and Ludwig at Elkhart arrived yesterday, showing that Shuman was "doing business as usual" up to the hour of his arrest, if it should prove that he is the guilty confederate of Ludwig. Shuman, it was said this afternoon, had not yet been questioned, and he had given no signs of making a confession. He worked around the Lake Shore depot here until some eighteen months ago.

A separate, boxed article, headlined "SHUMAN CONFESSES," read: "Late this afternoon it was announced that Shuman had confessed to Prosecutor Oscar Jay, adding that 'he alone was responsible' and exonerating Ludwig. He is said to have claimed that he bought the articles at sales of unclaimed consignments."[16]

The next day's *Daily Review* included an interview with Shuman:

Shuman told a Review reporter late yesterday that he was a German, 27 years old, and formerly lived in this city, having been employed at the Sidway Mercantile Co. He declared he had never been in trouble before, and asserted that others in the employ of the express company in the same office were "doing the same thing" and it was under their influence that he fell. He estimated the plunder as worth $25,000, and said he had been collecting it for a period of two months, making shipments nearly every day. Shuman claimed that he stole only because he had the opportunity, and that he had made no plans for the distribution of the goods.

When asked whether or not he wanted to see the Kaiser win the world war he replied that he "didn't care." Chicago papers in their story of his arrest had said he had been watched as a German spy.

Shuman moved from Elkhart to Chicago with his parents eleven years ago. His parents have since died, and he stated that Ludwig was his nearest surviving relative.[17]

Both suspects wasted no time in pleading guilty, which they did the morning of November 23 in Superior Court. But they did so for different crimes. Ludwig pleaded guilty for the two-year-old burglary at Borneman & Sons, receiving a sentence of two to fourteen years in the prison at Michigan City.

According to that day's *Daily Review,* the court heard why that burglary hadn't been prosecuted faster: "although much of the plunder bore the Borneman price marks, that firm was unwilling to assume the responsibility as required by Prosecutor Jay, to file an affidavit against Ludwig charging theft, because the firm was not in possession of any evidence as to the time and manner of the theft of the various articles. As a matter of fact, hardly any of them had ever been missed from the stock."

Shuman, whose name was spelled "Schuman" in the competing *Elkhart Truth,* pleaded guilty to grand larceny—the theft of $1,000 worth of property—in the American Express case. (The "Schuman" spelling probably was correct; Schuman was the maiden name of Ludwig's mother.) He was sentenced to one to fourteen years in the state reformatory in Jeffersonville and fined fifty dollars. The *Daily Review* quoted former sheriff Frank Leader, who worked on the case, as saying "that any estimate of the value of the plunder that is short of $40,000 is too low."[18]

Ludwig left by train for prison in Michigan City at 9:00 Tuesday, December 18, 1917. Dan Roth, a city fireman pressed into service as a deputy sheriff, accompanied him. The *Elkhart Truth* reported that Ludwig and his cousin had remained in Elkhart "to help the express company identify its property should the corporation decide on a course of action. Ludwig, who owns considerable property here, was granted a stay to arrange his business affairs, which he did not complete until an early hour this morning. He and his attorney, E. L. Arnold, and a friend, held a conference which lasted from early last evening until 1:30 o'clock this morning."[19]

Upon Roth's return to Elkhart, the *Truth* reported the escort saying that Ludwig "caused him no trouble and that he expressed his intentions of making an excellent record so that he could seek a pardon after serving the minimum sentence of two years." Ludwig was assigned to work in the carpentry department.[20]

Gustave's mugshot upon entering prison shows him wearing a corduroy suit identical to the one brother Albin wore when he arrived in Michigan City a decade earlier. Gustave wore a white shirt and collar with a dark bowtie. His hair was longer than Albin's, with a part on the left and a neat wave in front. He was clean-shaven. In the photograph, Gustave's head is thrust back, his chin high, as if he were looking up at the camera. He did not smile. Some would say he looked smug.

On the side of the mugshot, Gustave is listed as five feet six and three-quarter inches tall—one-eighth inch taller than brother Albin. On the back, his weight is listed as 163 pounds.[21]

The prison ledger lists Gustave's age as forty-nine, his civil condition as married, and his mental and physical condition both as fair. His education was fair, his religious denomination was Evangelical, and he attended Sunday School. He did not smoke, but he used oral tobacco. He was a moderate drinker who did not use narcotics. His occupation when his crime was committed was plumber.

He admitted to having been arrested before but denied having any convictions.

Character of his associates? "Bad."[22]

Both Gustave and Albin received temporary parole to attend the funeral of their mother, Eva Ida Ludwig, who was found dead in bed at her home on the morning of December 2, 1919, by Gustave's wife, who lived in the adjoining house.[23] She was eighty-one.

Coroner Eugene Holdeman attributed the death to heart failure caused by her age.[24]

He did not speculate on whether having her two sons in prison was a factor in her demise.

The Plight of Joseph Talbot

JOSEPH TALBOT, THE YOUNG, crime-busting state's attorney who sent Albin Ludwig to prison, would face his own legal problems exactly a year after the Ludwig trial. Though he would be exonerated, the accusations of wrongdoing ultimately cost him his job, his health, and his life.

In late April 1908, Charles F. Holler, a South Bend attorney, filed an affidavit asking Circuit Judge Walter Funk to appoint a committee to investigate Talbot on unspecified charges that the prosecutor had violated the duties of an attorney. Such charges could result in Talbot's disbarment.[1]

Holler was a prominent member of the Prohibition Party. He had run unsuccessfully for Indiana attorney general as a Prohibitionist in 1906 and, according to news reports, hoped to be the Prohibition candidate for vice president in 1908.[2] (He was not a vice presidential candidate, though he would run unsuccessfully for state attorney general again in 1910.)

Holler's motivation wasn't believed to be political. Although Holler's accusations weren't made public at the outset, a South Bend dispatch published in the *Star Press* of Muncie speculated:

> Some time ago proceedings were filed by the prosecutor against Holler and Fred C. Gabriel, another local attorney, in connection with an application for divorce by Mrs. Perry Dickson, of Buffalo, N.Y. Judge Funk

refused to sustain the charges which Talbot made and a divorce was subsequently granted Mrs. Dickson.[3]

Funk apparently thought Holler's affidavit involving Talbot had merit because he promptly appointed a committee of six local attorneys to investigate. They were given until May 23 to file a report.[4]

By late June, the report had not been made public. Talbot, a candidate for reelection, was indignant. A June 29 dispatch from South Bend said the prosecutor actually encouraged that "disbarment proceedings be brought against him in open court." Talbot had sent a letter to the committee "demanding that an adverse report be made against him. He wishes to have the matter brought out in open court so the public may have an opportunity to see what the prosecutor has done to warrant the filing of charges against him."

Talbot accused Holler of "false prosecution" and said he wanted to support his allegation in open court.

He wrote:

Charles Holler felt aggrieved at me because in the performance of my official duty I had been compelled to institute against him a criminal prosecution. Smarting under the feeling engendered by the prosecution he filed an affidavit in the Circuit court charging me in general terms with a violation of my duty as an attorney.

The court appointed you a committee to investigate any charge which Mr. Holler might believe a basis for his accusation. I was at that time and am now prosecuting attorney of this county and a candidate for reelection.

If your committee, after further delay, reports in my favor, it will appear to the public I may have been whitewashed. I can not be helped by a report of your committee in my favor. Therefore, I request that you report to the court that disbarment [sic] proceedings be brought against me and that Mr. Holler be allowed to bring into court any evidence of charges he may have and that in public I be given an opportunity before the court and a jury to try any charges against me that Mr. Holler can make.[5]

Finally, on September 15 the committee made its report. Newspaper headlines summarized the story: "FILE SERIOUS CHARGES AGAINST JOSEPH TALBOT," screamed the *La Porte Weekly Herald;* "ATTORNEY IS IN TROUBLE," read the second line of the *Star Press* headline in Muncie; "Prosecutor of South Bend is Charged with Aiding Vicious," was the second line of the *Fort Wayne Sentinel's* headline, the headline writer misusing the adjective *vicious* as a noun.[6]

The September 17 *La Porte Weekly Herald* carried an extensive story, pointing out that, among other local connections to the case, Talbot was a former La Porte attorney. The coverage described the committee's report as "exhaustive," with "35 closely typewritten pages embodying 12 specifications, setting forth the charges to which Mr. Talbot will be called upon to answer."

The report, according to the newspaper, alleged that "Joseph E. Talbot has been guilty of wilful violations of his duties as an attorney."

Among the twelve specifications, Talbot was charged with filing a "spurious" affidavit "for the purpose of deceiving the court"; that in 1904 Talbot, his brother John, and others had conspired to conceal convicts who had escaped from a Michigan prison; that as state's attorney Talbot had employed his brother to appear in court as "deputy prosecuting attorney" despite that John Talbot had been disbarred in January 1906; that while disbarment charges were pending against his predecessor as state's attorney, George A. Kurtz, Joseph Talbot had employed him as a deputy prosecuting attorney; that for a year Talbot and another man had collected twenty-five dollars a month for not prosecuting a woman who operated a brothel; that in another case Talbot and others had conspired to protect a woman who maintained a "disorderly house," operated a gambling device, and sold liquor illegally; and that Talbot had refused to prosecute a man who kept a gambling house.[7]

Talbot, still hoping to be vindicated and reelected, wanted the case tried before the November 3 election. Talbot's attorneys, including Samuel L. Parker, his opposing attorney in the Albin Ludwig trial, argued for an early hearing, suggesting the trial start on October 12. Special Judge Harry B. Tuthill of Michigan City, according to an October 8 report from South Bend, "concluded that the Thursday following the November election would be a time convenient for all, and it was so ordered."[8]

Meanwhile, more specifications were added to Talbot's charges, making fifteen in all. One charged that Talbot and his brother had attempted to influence two jury commissioners in the selection of jurors for Talbot's disbarment trial.[9]

With the trial looming, Talbot, a Democrat, lost his reelection bid to Republican Cyrus E. Pattee, 8,577 to 8,166.[10] A loss by only 411 votes of 16,743 cast showed that much of the electorate wasn't swayed by the committee's allegations.

The trial was not held on November 5 as scheduled. The committee asked for a continuance because the testimony of an important witness couldn't be obtained.[11] On November 12, the next trial date, attorney Harry B. Wair, representing the committee that charged Talbot, moved for a change of venue after being denied yet another continuance.

"It was stated that the committee would be unable to obtain a fair and impartial trial there owing to the undue influence of the defendant over the citizens of St. Joseph county," the next day's *Elkhart Truth* reported. Perhaps the committee was worried that Talbot garnered more than eight thousand votes in the prior week's election despite the accusations against him. The *Truth*, speculating that the case might be moved to Elkhart, wrote that the motion "was entirely unforeseen and took the judge and defense by surprise."[12]

The committee would regret asking for the trial to be moved, considering that it meant a new judge as well as new jurors.

The *Truth* described Talbot as "keenly disappointed" by the delay. Talbot pointed out that the committee's motion for a continuance was the sixth filed by the prosecution since the disbarment proceedings had begun.[13]

On November 20, Judge Tuthill granted the change of venue to superior court in Elkhart, which the *Truth* predicted wouldn't sit well with citizens in Goshen, the county seat, who questioned Elkhart even having a superior court.

"The Talbot case will occupy the attention of the court for the greater part of the term whenever it comes to trial," the *Truth* reported on November 21. "No one estimates that it will take less than three weeks to try the case, and some think that it will take four or five weeks to complete it."

The story continued:

One of the most important charges against Talbot is his alleged action on assisting "Yock" Allison to escape from the officers after he had escaped from the state prison at Jackson, Mich. Allison is a former member of the old Lake Shore gang. He escaped from prison at Jackson on August 9, 1904, and fled to South Bend.

The committee having charge of the disbarment proceedings wishes to have Allison testify as to the truth of the charge that Talbot furnished him with arms and clothing and otherwise assisted him to keep him out of the clutches of the law.

Allison refuses however to testify in the case at all. Even when he was taken into court in Jackson and ordered under penalty of punishment for contempt of court he steadfastly refused to testify or make a deposition.

As the court ruled that he would have to testify, one of the leading attorneys of the state came to his rescue and appealed the case to the supreme court of Michigan. It may take months for the decision to be handed down by the higher court as to whether Allison must testify or not.

In the meantime the committee in charge of the prosecution of Talbot will strive in every way to gain time until the decision is handed down, as they do not care to go [to] trial with the case until Allison's testimony is assured.

The reason Allison gives for not desiring to testify is that by so doing he may incriminate himself. When he was taken to the prison at Jackson he was not prosecuted on the charge of jail-breaking, for which there is a penalty of three years additional imprisonment, but after serving another year was parolled [sic] and is now living an honest life in the city of Jackson.[14]

The Michigan Supreme Court would not rule until a month after the Talbot trial. Allison would not have had to testify.[15]

The trial began on Monday, February 8, with Special Judge Anthony Deahl of Goshen on the bench. By Wednesday, Talbot's defense team was making progress in refuting the charges. The *Elkhart Truth* reported on February 12 that a woman who allegedly had asked Talbot to investigate a gambling house—an investigation Talbot did not conduct—was "restrained from testifying, unless the attorneys for the prosecution find authorities showing that a person may divulge a conversation formerly had with an attorney." The woman was upset that her husband had lost "considerable money" in a gambling game at the house.

"Many people want revenge in different ways and come and report to the prosecutor that they desire investigations to be made," Judge Deahl said after hearing arguments from both sides. "An officer should be protected. Of course he should have discretionary powers but I don't think he should be brought face to face with a witness, who for the first time is brought in at a disbarment proceedings. I will sustain the ruling now but will not allow any of the evidence to be submitted to the members of the jury until further references are found on the subject."

The *Truth* reported that Francis E. Lambert, one of the attorneys for the prosecution, reacted with disappointment: "The final ruling in this question is one of importance to us, and we might as well hang up the white flag if such testimony is excluded as we have other testimony which is dependent upon this question."[16]

The judge's ruling, which in effect pulled the rug out from under the prosecution, was explained further in a subsequent edition of the *Elkhart Daily Review*. The woman's testimony was declared inadmissible, the newspaper said, "on the ground of being privileged because it related to things asked of the defendant as prosecuting attorney and not as a lawyer at the bar."[17]

By Saturday, the *Daily Review* was reporting that the disbarment trial was likely to end at any time. In fact, the court "seemed to be of the opinion that the proper proceeding against a prosecuting attorney who failed in his duty as prosecutor would be by impeachment and not in a suit to disbar."

Nothing in the Indiana constitution or statutes required a prosecuting attorney to be an attorney. "A butcher, a baker or a candlestick maker is just as eligible as the best lawyer in the state," the *Daily Review* explained. In other words, even if Talbot were disbarred, he still could serve as prosecuting attorney.[18]

By the next Tuesday, the newspaper was quoting the prosecution that the trial could end that day or the next.

The prosecution, according to the newspaper, claimed that the rulings of Judge Deahl "had practically eliminated all of their charges but two, and they seemed to apprehend that he would rule against them on getting the evidence in two charges before the jury. Up to the present, the attorneys for the defendant have succeeded in keeping out nearly all of the evidence which the committee had relied on to prove their case."

The story continued:

> At the time of the noon adjournment it looked as if one more of the charges was to be placed in the "discard." The committee had called William Shimp, one of the St. Joseph county jury commissioners, to the stand for the purpose of proving by him that an attempt was made by John W. Talbot, brother of the defendant and his law partner, to pack the jury before which it was expected that the defendant would be tried. As soon as the evidence reached the point where the witness was asked to tell what occurred between him and John W. Talbot about selecting a jury, the defense objected, on the ground that the defendant was not present at the time of the alleged conversation, and therefore the testimony was not competent.[19]

The committee had more problems. That same morning, Talbot's brother, John, had not shown up to testify despite having been subpoenaed. The committee asked for a bench warrant to bring John Talbot to court. The defense countered that as an attorney, Talbot could not be forced to leave his county. Judge Deahl agreed with the defense and also refused to order John Talbot to make a deposition after the defense argued it would delay the trial.[20]

The trial ended on Wednesday, February 17, at 5:30 in the afternoon when the jury declared Talbot not guilty. Closing arguments for Talbot's defense team had taken three hours. The *Daily Review* reported the next day that six attorneys spoke on Talbot's behalf followed by three for the prosecution. Two of Talbot's attorneys then responded to the prosecution's remarks. If any jurors remained uncertain after all those arguments, their decision was made easier when Judge Deahl granted a motion by one of Talbot's attorneys that the judge instruct the jury to find for the defendant, which it did.

"The close of the trial was not attended by any dramatic or unusual incidents, although on its outcome, to a future degree, depended the future career of Mr. Talbot," the next day's *Daily Review* reported. "Of course the defendant and his wife and his aged mother, who has attended the trial every day, did not attempt to conceal their pleasure, but were undemonstrative. The attorneys, the judge, the jurors, the defendant and the audience hurried away, for it was growing late, and the Talbot case was at an end."

In analyzing the trial, the *Daily Review*'s reporter noted that Talbot was found not guilty on points of law. "Whether or not the defendant ever did any of the things charged in the complaint was not determined by the trial."[21]

No longer a prosecutor after losing his reelection bid, Joseph Talbot returned to his law practice. But any respite from his not-guilty verdict was short lived. On March 1, only twelve days after his own trial ended, his brother and disbarred law partner, John W. Talbot, was shot at four times by a former lover.[22] John Talbot's affair with Leona Mason began after she had hired him to obtain a divorce from her husband, a wealthy real estate broker, six years earlier. The woman shot at John Talbot again on June 21 as he was running through the streets of South Bend.[23]

John Talbot was not injured physically in either shooting, but the married father of a son suffered further injury to his already questionable reputation.[24] While Joseph Talbot arranged with attorneys to prosecute Mrs. Mason for the attempted murder of his brother, newspapers were reporting that John Talbot would refuse to testify against her. "Talbot if he had been allowed to have his own way about the affair, would have had the woman released as soon as she was disarmed," according to a June 23 dispatch from South Bend. The same article said Talbot was alleged to have said during a court hearing, "She is too beautiful to prosecute."[25]

As Mrs. Mason's trial neared, the *Indianapolis News* reported on South Bend's latest "Talbot sensation," including public relations campaigns by both John Talbot and his paramour. Talbot attempted to use his position as founder and supreme president of the Order of the Owls, a secret fraternal organization, to bolster his reputation:

After the shooting Talbot distributed hundreds of post cards showing him in the silk and satin robes of "supreme president of the Owls," and copies of a pamphlet containing a laudatory article entitled, "Who is

John Talbot?" It was accompanied by reproductions of letters from the postmaster, a prominent banker, a lawyer and a business man of South Bend, putting their approval on his character.

South Bend citizens awoke a week ago Wednesday to find on their doorsteps another pamphlet based on the question, "Who is John Talbot" but giving a different answer. This was Mrs. Mason's booklet, with the title printed in big type on the cover and surrounded by a black border an inch wide. On the first page was a caricature of the Owls' emblem, three owls sitting on a limb, uttering the query, "Who? Who? Who?" Below the cartoon was the subtitle, "Who is John Talbot? And My Awful Story." Sensational charges, both public and private, were made against Talbot in this pamphlet.[26]

Mrs. Mason also filed an affidavit in court asserting that John Talbot was insane.[27]

At her trial, which lasted eight days, Defense Attorney Charles A. Davey attacked John Talbot's character mercilessly, calling him a "black villain" and the "lowest of individuals God ever let live."[28]

The jury found Mrs. Mason not guilty after deliberating only five minutes or sixteen minutes, depending on the newspaper covering the trial.[29] Her supporters broke out in applause after the verdict was read.

"As I was confident of acquittal, the verdict was no great surprise to me," she told the *Indianapolis Star*, adding, "I would have gone to the penitentiary before I would have allowed Talbot to have hounded me longer."[30]

Joseph Talbot also was back in the news before the end of 1909:

Sensational charges of having been forced into a marriage distasteful to him are preferred by Norman R. Donathen against Joseph E. Talbot, former prosecuting attorney of St. Joseph county. Suit to have the marriage annuled [sic] was filed in the circuit court yesterday afternoon. The filing of the case again brings the name of Talbot into prominence in the court records.

The article continued:

Donathen alleges that he was arrested in the factory of the Studebaker Brothers Manufacturing Company, where he is employed, and that he was taken before Justice W. B. Wright. He alleges that Talbot was there representing himself as a substitute for the prosecuting attorney and that he displayed an affidavit charging Donathen with a statutory offense.

It is also alleged that Talbot made threats of sending Donathen to the penitentiary unless he married a young girl, Goldy Barkman. Donathen further asserts that he was refused an opportunity to consult an attorney. Talbot advised, it is alleged, that Donathen marry the girl, pay her a few dollars each week for a time and then leave this part of the country. Acting on this advice, Donathen says, he was accompanied to the clerk's office for a marriage license and that he married the Barkman girl. Donathen alleges he told the justice he was innocent of the charge, but that an entry of guilty was made. The plaintiff charges fraud against his wife, Talbot and the justice, all of whom, he says, knew Talbot was not qualified to act in the stead of the prosecutor.

The petition states the girl met Donathen on the street two evenings before the marriage was forced on him and threatened to kill him unless he accompanied her home, although he was then with two women and another man. Donathen went with the girl, he says, because he feared not to do so would mean violence on her part. The statutory charge against Donathen was made two days later.[31]

The disposition of the case isn't known, but surely it didn't help Joseph Talbot's mental health. In less than two years, the onetime "rising young attorney of ability and intellect," who successfully prosecuted Albin Ludwig for murder, had faced disbarment, lost reelection as prosecutor, seen his brother's character tarnished after attempted-murder charges were brought against a former lover, and now faced new charges alleging that he forced an unwanted marriage. To the newspapers of the day, the name Talbot and the word *sensational* had become synonymous.

Talbot fell into despair, the depths of which became known to the public after he wandered away from his South Bend home the evening of June 26, 1910, boarded an interurban car, and traveled to Cassopolis and Niles before the conductor ejected him for nonpayment of fare. In reporting the story, the *Elkhart Daily Review* described Talbot as being in "deplorable mental condition."[32]

On July 6, Talbot was found in South Bend with a revolver and hammer while looking for a former sergeant of detectives. "Talbot's mind is said to have been affected for some time," the *Elkhart Truth* reported with the headline, "TALBOT LOSES MIND." Talbot was taken to a private hospital for the insane in Detroit.[33]

Talbot was being treated for a mental disorder at a hospital in Kenosha, Wisconsin, when he died on November 3. He was only thirty-six years old. "His condition was due to overwork and the strain of a trial for irregularities in the office of the state's attorney," a dispatch from South Bend reported.[34] But a 2018 podcast about Talbot's brother John suggested that Joseph "got to the point where he couldn't function because of his syphilis," which at the time was incurable.[35]

Joseph Edward Leo Talbot is buried in Cedar Grove Cemetery in South Bend. His grave is marked by a plaque, placed by the Order of Owls (founded by his brother, John), that describes Talbot as "skilful at his trade, eminent in his profession, fearless, honest and able in office, happy in his home."[36]

A postscript: Leona Mason, acquitted of the attempted murder of John Talbot, remarried her former husband, which apparently was a surprise to Lena A. Joslin, "a young Mishawaka woman of striking beauty," who claimed that Mr. Mason had promised to marry her. About two weeks after Joseph Talbot's death, Joslin filed a breach-of-promise suit against Mason, asking $25,000 for her broken heart.[37]

Notes

At least two transcripts exist of the trial of the *State of Indiana vs. Albin R. Ludwig*. Both were used in the writing of this book. The first is a full *Transcript of Evidence* (but without opening and closing statements) prepared by the official court reporter, Hugh Noel Seymour Home, and filed in St. Joseph Circuit Court on June 3, 1907. The second, a "Condensed Recital of Evidence," appears in the *Brief and Argument for the Appellant* filed on December 31, 1907, with the Indiana Supreme Court by Anderson, Parker & Crabill, attorneys for Albin R. Ludwig. The condensed transcript is prefaced by the statement: "As we shall not contend that the verdict was not sustained by sufficient evidence, we will not make a *complete* summary of the evidence, but will abstract so much of it as will clearly show the pertinency and force of the errors relied upon for reversal." Both documents are stored at the Indiana State Archives in Indianapolis. The author and his wife reviewed the transcripts in person on January 31, 2017, and July 23, 2018. Rules prohibited making photocopies of the fragile, century-old documents, but, with permission, the author and his wife were able to take notes and take cell phone photographs of the entire condensed transcript and key passages of the full transcript. The author discovered that the quotations in the full transcript and the condensed transcript do not always match word-for-word, although the abstract of testimony is in the spirit of the full transcript. As noted below, the author used the full transcript in describing the testimony of major witnesses, the condensed transcript in describing the testimony of minor witnesses, and, in some cases, a combination of both transcripts.

PREFACE

1. Kent A. Berridge, email to author, Apr. 25, 2019.

2. Chuck Ellsworth, emails to author, Apr. 26 and 27, 2019.

3. Email to author, Apr. 25, 2019, from a great-granddaughter of Lyle who asked not to be identified in this book.

4. Gretchen L. Marks, emails to author, Apr. 27 and May 9, 2019.

PROLOGUE

1. *Celia B. Hornburg v. Charles F Hornburg,* 154.

2. "Ludwig, Wife Murderer, Will Survive His Injuries." *La Porte Argus-Bulletin,* Sept. 27, 1906. The *Argus-Bulletin* paraphrased the reporting of Peter Young of the *South Bend Daily Times,* with credit, but Young's Mishawaka Department column in the September 26 *Times* actually read "without a parallel in Mishawaka."

1. THE LAST NIGHT

1. Unless otherwise noted, the narrative of the last evening of Cecilia Ludwig's life is reconstructed from the testimony of Albin Ludwig, James Anderson, Fred Young, Emma Reifsneider, Marcellus Gaze, Veronica Gaze, and Fred Metzler in the trial *State of Indiana vs. Albin R. Ludwig,* St. Joseph County Circuit Court, Apr. 22–26, 1907, either from the *Transcript of Evidence* or from *Brief and Argument for the Appellant, Albin R. Ludwig vs. The State of Indiana* or from Albin Ludwig's handwritten answer to "Tell your story of the crime" in a "Statement of Prisoner to Board of Commissioners of Paroled Prisoners."

2. Various members of the Ellsworth family owned more than two hundred acres adjoining Kingsbury on the northeast. *Platbook of La Porte County, Indiana.*

3. Weather forecast, *Elkhart Truth,* Sept. 24, 1906: "Fair tonight and Tuesday; warmer."

4. Meints, *Indiana Railroad Lines,* 169. Exact distance by rail between Kingsbury and Mishawaka was 29.21 miles.

5. Howard, *A History of St. Joseph County, Indiana,* 1:347–48.

6. "Mishawaka Woolen Company-Ball Band Rubber," The History Museum, South Bend, IN, https://historymuseumsb.org/mishawaka-woolen-company-ball-band-rubber/.

7. Walking distance from the Ludwig house to the intersection of Second and Main was timed by author on July 24, 2018.

8. The Milburn House was misspelled "Milbourn" in the trial transcript. A plaque on its site today reads: "At this site in 1834, Orlando Hurd built the Mishawaka Hotel, noted as the best hotel on the Vistula Road between Toledo and Chicago. Later site of the Milburn House."

9. This confrontation, recounted by Albin Ludwig in his trial, was not recalled by Fred Metzler in his testimony. However, another neighbor, Emma Reifsneider, testified that she heard two men, one of them a Fred, and a woman arguing. It's possible Fred Young, not Fred Metzler, was the second man Reifsneider heard.

2. THE FAMILIES

1. Birth dates and other dates of record are from various census, marriage, and death records and newspaper obituaries from Scotland and the United States available through internet sources (among them, www.Ancestry.com, www.GeneaologyBank.com, and www.Newspapers.com) and newspaper microfilm and are corroborated by descendants who have done their own genealogical research, notably Paula Steiner, whose primary source was the Family History Library, Church of Jesus Christ of Latter-day Saints, Salt Lake City, Utah.

2. It's unknown whether Christina the mother was married to Shaw at the time of the birth or if the child was born out of wedlock; the mother used the name Christina Orr when she married James Henderson a decade later. Daughter Christina's obituary and death certificate in 1939 refer to her as "Christina Shaw Denham," omitting the name of her first husband, a Wade, in favor of her father's. The obituary (*La Porte Daily Herald-Argus,* Apr. 1, 1939, p. 2) refers to her mother as "Mrs. Shaw-Henderson." The death certificate has a question mark and dashes for her father's first name.

3. "Aunt Tina" was written on the back of a photograph by Roy Wheeler, grandson of Jessie Henderson. But Wheeler's daughter, Paula Steiner, remembers Roy referring to her as "Aunt Tinnie." Email correspondence with author, Apr. 23 and 25, 2018.

4. Alchin, "Scottish Immigration to America Timeline"; Knox, "Health in Scotland 1840–1900," The History of the Scottish People.

5. "Declaration of Intention" to be a US citizen, filed by James Henderson in La Porte, IN, Circuit Court, Oct. 4, 1918.

6. Judy A. Myer, interview with author, Aug. 23, 2017.

7. Kent A. Berridge, email to author, Aug. 19, 2017.

8. Paula Steiner, letter to author, Jan. 17, 1997.

9. Grandson Roy Wheeler told his daughter Paula Steiner that the "wealthy man" may have been the owner of the company James worked for before his accident, though Roy didn't know the name or location of the man. Paula Steiner, email to author, Apr. 23, 2018.

10. Census records for 1900 and 1910; Christina Henderson, testimony, *Transcript of Evidence,* 309; *Platbook of La Porte County, Indiana.*

11. The marriage date is listed in a divorce complaint. *Celia B. Hornburg v. Charles F. Hornburg,* 154.

12. *Celia B. Hornburg v. Charles F. Hornburg.*

13. *Celia B. Hornburg v. Charles F. Hornburg.*

14. *Celia B. Hornburg v. Charles F. Hornburg.*

15. Email to author, Aug. 7, 2017, from a great-granddaughter of Lyle who asked not to be identified in this book.

16. Michigan, Marriage Records, 1867–1952. Charley Hornburg was sixty-three when he died on Feb. 3, 1935, in Douglas, Arizona, where he was being treated for tuberculosis. His death certificate said he had suffered from TB for more than thirty years.

17. Ludwig, "Biographical Record as a Citizen."

18. Staatsarchiv Hamburg, *Hamburg Passenger Lists, 1850–1934.*

19. Ludwig, "Biographical Record as a Citizen."

20. Staatsarchiv Hamburg, *Hamburg Passenger Lists, 1850–1934.*

21. Hoyt, "Germans," 162, 168.

22. Bell, "German Immigrants."

23. Hoyt, "Germans," 148.

24. Linda Ludwig Irish's grandfather, Walter Henry Ludwig, was a cousin of Albin Ludwig. Her great-grandfather, Carl Louis Ludwig, was Albin's uncle. In an email to the author on March 8, 2018, she described the "Five Ludwig Brothers from Germany" who settled in the Mishawaka-Elkhart area. The five who came to America were Ernst Siegfried, Karl Christoph, Heinrich Christoph, Carl Louis, and Heinrich Wilhelm Jacob Ludwig. They did not come together.

25. *Elkhart Weekly Review,* July 10, 1897, p. 2. Newspaper articles used both spellings of the father's name. Albin listed it as "William" when he filled out his "Biographical Record as a Citizen" upon entering prison. *Elkhart Daily Review,* Sept. 26, 1906, p. 1.

26. *Elkhart Weekly Truth,* July 15, 1897; *Goshen Democrat,* July 14, 1897.

27. *Elkhart Weekly Truth,* July 15, 1897.

28. *Brief and Argument for the Appellant,* 4; *Elkhart Daily Review,* Sept. 26, 1906.

29. *Elkhart Daily Review,* Nov. 6, 1900.

30. *Elkhart City Directory,* 152.

31. *Elkhart Daily Review,* Jan. 29, 1898, p. 2; Patrick McGuire, *South Bend Tribune,* Dec. 18, 2016; "Elcar Motor Co., Elkhart Buggy Co., Elkhart Carriage & Harness Mfg. Co., Elkhart Carriage and Motor Car Company."

32. *Elkhart Daily Review,* Sept. 26, 1906.

33. Steve Wylder, "The Way We Were," *Elkhart Truth,* Dec. 9, 2001.

34. About $1,450 in 2019 dollars, Inflation Calculator, July 11, 2019, http://www.in2013dollars.com/us/inflation/1903?amount=50; *Elkhart Weekly Review,* Mar. 7, 1903.

35. *Elkhart Daily Review,* Sept. 26, 1906, p. 1.

36. Ludwig, "Tell Your Story of the Crime."

37. Ludwig, "Tell Your Story of the Crime."

38. Kent A. Berridge, email to author, Aug. 19, 2017. Berridge described James, his great-grandfather, as a "giant" at six feet seven. James's wife Christina also was tall at five feet eleven. Cecilia's height is listed as five feet ten on page 5 of the *Brief and Argument for the Appellant.* Indiana State Prison documents, Indiana State Archives, Indianapolis.

39. Michigan, County Marriage Records, 1822–1940, *Michigan, County Marriage Records, 1822–1940.* However, Elkhart is listed as the wedding location in *Brief and Argument for the Appellant,* 4.

3. MARRIAGE AND MISHAWAKA

1. Ludwig, "Tell Your Story of the Crime."

2. Ludwig, "Tell Your Story of the Crime."

3. Author visit, Aug. 26, 2016.

4. *Elkhart Weekly Review,* Feb. 4, 1903, p. 3.

5. *Elkhart Daily Review,* Feb. 23, 1903. p. 3.

6. *Elkhart Daily Review,* Sept. 26, 1906, p. 1.

7. *Elkhart Daily Review,* Sept. 28, 1906, p. 1.

8. *Elkhart Truth,* Sept. 27, 1906, p. 4.

9. *South Bend Tribune,* Oct. 26, 2009.

10. *Directory of South Bend.* Although the neighborhood featured new homes, their occupancy apparently turned over frequently. A 1910 city directory shows only one of the Ludwigs' neighbors still living on East Marion Street (*Hibbard's 1910 City Directory of South Bend*).

11. *Atlas of the Cities of South Bend and Mishawaka, Indiana.*

12. *Brief and Argument for the Appellant,* 5–8.

13. "Battell Center."

14. Walking distances from Ludwig house was timed by the author on July 24, 2018.

15. *Elkhart Daily Review,* Sept. 28, 1906. Gaylor was identified as a real estate broker, with an office at 126 East Second, in the 1905 *Directory of South Bend; Brief and Argument for the Appellant,* 55.

16. *La Porte Daily Herald,* Sept. 27, 1906; "Mishawaka Woolen Company-Ball Band Rubber."

17. *La Porte Daily Herald,* Sept. 27, 1906, p. 1.

18. *Elkhart Daily Review,* July 31, 1905. The legal notice for the sheriff's sale in the July 14, 1905, *Daily Review* listed Albin's mother as well as Albin, Cecilia, and two others as owners of the property, which was at the corner of Harrison Street and Oakland Avenue.

19. Albin's testimony about coming home unexpectedly from work one morning and discovering Cecilia in a closet with one boarder, "Smoke" Meinen, would be a salacious moment in the trial.

20. *South Bend Tribune,* Sept. 25, 1906, p. 1.

21. Ludwig, "Tell Your Story of the Crime."

22. Email to author, Aug. 7, 2017, from a great-granddaughter of Lyle who asked not to be identified in this book.

23. "The influence of Mrs. Ellsworth upon her sister was bad," Albin's defense team wrote in *Brief and Argument for the Appellant,* 5.

24. Ludwig, "Tell Your Story of the Crime."

4. MURDER

1. The Government Forecast in the September 25, 1906, *Elkhart Review* was "fair and warmer." The high temperature on September 25, as reported in the next day's *Review,* was 84°F. Weather conditions for the previous week were from the "Miles Weather Record" in the September 18, 19, 20, 21, 22, and 24, 1906, *Elkhart Truth.*

2. The Heritage Center in the Mishawaka Library has an extensive microfilm collection of the South Bend newspapers and the *Mishawaka Enterprise* for the period of the murder and trial. However, a gap exists for those years in the limited microfilm collection of the shorter-lived *Mishawaka Democrat.* The author is grateful to Heritage Center Supervisor Deanna Juday and staff for their assistance with and encouragement of his research.

3. P. A. Young, Mishawaka Department, *South Bend Daily Times,* Sept. 25, 1906. Further citations of this work are given in the text.

4. *South Bend Daily Times,* Sept. 25, 1906. Further citations of this work are given in the text.

5. The small *n* in "negro" indicates the *Daily Times'* coverage came from a southern journalist. According to journalists Gene Roberts and Hank Klibanoff, use of the lowercase *n* was common in the southern newspapers until 1938, when Ralph McGill became executive editor of the *Atlanta Constitution* and ordered "Negro" to be capitalized. Roberts and Klibanoff, *The Race Beat,* 29–30.

6. Unless otherwise noted, the narrative of the last morning of Cecilia Ludwig's life is reconstructed from the testimony of Albin Ludwig, Milton E. Robbins, Charles R. Patterson, Lester Gitre, Anna Burkhart, Fred Metzler, Benjamin F. Jarrett, Catherine Brand, and David Hull in the trial *State of Indiana vs. Albin R. Ludwig,* St. Joseph County Circuit Court, April 22–26, 1907, either from the *Transcript of Evidence* or from *Brief and Argument for the Appellant,* and from Ludwig's handwritten answer to "Tell Your Story of the Crime."

7. Bien, "Late 19th-Century Gasoline Stoves."

8. *Directory of South Bend.*

9. Davis, "Immigrant Meals from the Late 1800s."

5. A "GREWSOME" SIGHT

1. Alice McNabb, testimony, *Brief and Argument for the Appellant,* 49.

2. David Hull, testimony, *Brief and Argument for the Appellant,* 42–43.

3. Robert F. Schellenberg, testimony, *Brief and Argument for the Appellant,* 56–57.

4. P. A. Young, Mishawaka Department, *South Bend Daily Times,* Sept. 25, 1906. Location of call box from *Hibbard's 1910 City Directory of South Bend,* 539. However, the Ludwigs' next-door neighbor Catherine Brand testified that her daughter, Mrs. John Wilson, went to the home of Charles R. Patterson, two houses to the west, to report the fire on the Pattersons' telephone (*Transcript of Evidence,* 243). Albert Buysse's testimony in the trial *State of Indiana vs. Albin R. Ludwig.* Ledger, *Daily Report of Fires in Mishawaka,* 1906, examined by author at the Heritage Center of the Mishawaka-Penn-Harris Public Library, Mishawaka, IN, on Aug. 26, 2016. The handwritten ledger also states: "Supposed fire started after murder."

5. Buysse testimony, 45.

6. Alvia J. Bruce, testimony, *Brief and Argument for the Appellant,* 67–69.

7. Bruce, testimony, *Brief and Argument for the Appellant,* 67–69.

8. Bruce, testimony, *Brief and Argument for the Appellant,* 67–69.

9. Bruce, testimony, *Brief and Argument for the Appellant,* 67–69.

10. C. N. Crabill affidavit, *Brief and Argument for the Appellant,* 30.

11. Although the reporter is not identified with a byline, the author assumes

that Young wrote the page 1 story. His office was in Mishawaka, so he would have been closer to the fire scene than a reporter coming from the main office in South Bend.

12. On August 26, 2016, the owner of the house at the address listed in most of the newspaper reports of the crime graciously allowed the author to enter the home and see the closet where the murder allegedly occurred. Subsequent research casts doubts that this was the Ludwig home.

13. Beacon Health System, "Memorial Hospital of South Bend History"; P. A. Young, Mishawaka Department, *South Bend Daily Times,* Sept. 26, 1906.

14. Holtzendorf and Stroup would testify before the grand jury and at the trial. Doane testified before the grand jury but not at the trial.

15. Henry C. Holtzendorf, testimony, *Brief and Argument for the Appellant,* 50–51.

16. Holtzendorf, testimony, *Brief and Argument for the Appellant,* 50–51.

17. Judy A. Myer, interview with author, Aug. 23, 2017.

18. Myer, interview with author, Aug. 23, 2017.

19. *Mishawaka Enterprise,* Sept. 28, 1906, p. 1.

20. *La Porte Argus-Bulletin,* Sept. 26, 1906, p. 1.

21. *Elkhart Daily Review,* Oct. 4, 1906, p. 1.

22. "About Us."

23. Author visit, Kingsbury Cemetery, Aug. 26, 2016.

24. Celia Ludwig, Case 9–121, Probate Records.

6. HORRORS AND SHOCKING FEATURES

1. "Auntie Can't Hurt Uncle, but Uncle Can Hurt Auntie," the *Elkhart Weekly Review,* Apr. 27, 1907, p. 1, reported Jean Ellsworth's daughter telling a neighbor; P. A. Young, Mishawaka Department, *South Bend Daily Times,* Sept. 26, 1906.

2. P. A. Young, Mishawaka Department, *South Bend Daily Times,* Sept. 26, 1906.

3. P. A. Young, Mishawaka Department, *South Bend Daily Times,* Sept. 26, 1906.

4. *La Porte Daily Herald,* Sept. 26, 1906, p. 1.

5. *Pictorial and Biographical Memoirs of Elkhart and St. Joseph Counties, Indiana,* 343–44.

6. *Mishawaka Enterprise,* Sept. 28, 1906, p. 1.

7. *Mishawaka Enterprise,* Sept. 28, 1906, p. 1.

7. MISHAWAKA GROWS—AND GOSSIPS

1. P. A. Young, Mishawaka Department, *South Bend Daily Times,* Sept. 26, 1906, reprinted in *Elkhart Truth,* Sept. 27, 1906.

2. Young, Mishawaka Department, *South Bend Daily Times,* Sept. 27, 1906.

3. *Mishawaka Enterprise,* Sept. 28, 1906; *South Bend Daily Times,* Sept. 28, 1906.

4. *Mishawaka Enterprise,* Sept. 28, 1906.

5. Young, Mishawaka Department, *South Bend Daily Times,* Sept. 27, 1906.

6. *South Bend Tribune,* Sept. 27, 1906. One of the headlines on the *Tribune* story read, "Ludwig known in other cities as a bad man."

7. Young, Mishawaka Department, *South Bend Daily Times,* Sept. 27, 1906.

8. Young, Mishawaka Department, *South Bend Daily Times,* Sept. 27, 1906.

9. Young, Mishawaka Department, *South Bend Daily Times,* Sept. 27, 1906.

10. *South Bend Tribune,* Sept. 27, 1906.

11. *South Bend Tribune,* Sept. 27, 1906.

12. *South Bend Daily Times,* Sept. 29, 1906, reprinted in *La Porte Daily Herald,* Oct. 1, 1906.

13. *South Bend Daily Times,* Sept. 29, 1906.

14. *Elkhart Truth,* Sept. 27, 1906.

15. *Elkhart Daily Review,* Sept. 28, 1906, p. 1.

16. Young, Mishawaka Department, *South Bend Daily Times,* Sept. 28, 1906.

17. *Uxorcide* is an archaic word for a man who kills his wife.

18. Young, Mishawaka Department, *South Bend Daily Times,* Sept. 28, 1906.

19. *South Bend Daily Times,* Sept. 29, 1906.

20. *La Porte Daily Herald,* Oct. 1, 1906.

21. "Miles Weather Record," *Elkhart Truth,* Oct. 1, 1906.

22. Young, Mishawaka Department, *South Bend Daily Times,* Oct. 1, 1906.

23. Young, Mishawaka Department, *South Bend Daily Times,* Oct. 2, 1906.

24. *La Porte Argus-Bulletin,* Oct. 2, 1906, p. 1. See the epilogue for more on the life of Charles Ellsworth, Cecilia's nephew.

25. *La Porte Argus-Bulletin,* Oct. 2, 1906, p. 1.

26. *Elkhart Daily Review,* Oct. 3, 1906, p. 1.

27. *La Porte Argus-Bulletin,* Oct. 4, 1906, p. 1.

28. *South Bend Tribune,* Oct. 4, 1906, p. 7.

29. *Elkhart Daily Review,* Oct. 4, 1906, p. 1.

30. *Elkhart Daily Review,* Oct. 4, 1906, p. 1.

31. Young, Mishawaka Department, *South Bend Daily Times,* Oct. 8, 1906.

32. *Mishawaka Enterprise,* Oct. 12, 1906, p. 1.

33. *Mishawaka Enterprise,* Oct. 12, 1906, p. 1.

34. *Mishawaka Enterprise,* Oct. 12, 1906, p. 1.

8. CHARGES FILED, ATTORNEYS HIRED

1. *South Bend Daily Times,* Oct. 17, 1906.
2. *Mishawaka Enterprise,* Oct. 26, 1906.
3. *Elkhart Daily Review,* Oct. 22, 1906, p. 5; "Local Brevities," *Elkhart Daily Review,* Oct. 30, 1906, p. 5.
4. Anderson and Cooley, *South Bend and the Men Who Have Made It,* 39.
5. *Mishawaka Enterprise,* Nov. 2, 1906, p. 1.
6. *Mishawaka Enterprise,* Nov. 16, 1906, p. 1.
7. *Elkhart Daily Review,* Nov. 20, 1906, p. 1.
8. Samuel Parker and W. G. Crabill affidavit, *Brief and Argument for the Appellant,* 31–32.
9. Howard, *A History of St. Joseph County, Indiana,* 1:519, 2:1141.
10. *Elkhart Weekly Review,* Dec. 1, 1906, p. 4.
11. *Elkhart Weekly Review,* Dec. 5, 1906, p. 11; *Elkhart Truth,* Dec. 6, 1906, p. 1; *Elkhart Daily Review,* Dec. 7, 1906, p. 1.

9. GRAND JURY INDICTS

1. *Mishawaka Enterprise,* Feb. 8, 1907.
2. *Elkhart Daily Review,* Feb. 4, 1907, p. 1.
3. *Elkhart Daily Review,* Feb. 4, 1907, p. 1.
4. *Detroit Free Press,* Dec. 29, 1906, p. 6.
5. *Mishawaka Enterprise,* February 8, 1907. "Etsel" Snyder was spelled "Estel" in the February 16 *Elkhart Weekly Review.*
6. *Elkhart Daily Review,* Feb. 8, 1907, p. 1; *Mishawaka Enterprise,* Feb. 8, 1907.
7. *Elkhart Daily Review,* Feb. 16, 1907, p. 1; Indictment No. 727, *State of Indiana vs. Alvin [sic] Ludwig,* St. Joseph Circuit Court, Feb. Term, 1907.
8. Indictment No. 727, *State of Indiana vs. Alvin [sic] Ludwig,* St. Joseph Circuit Court, Feb. Term, 1907.
9. *Elkhart Truth,* Feb. 27, 1907, p. 8.

10. TRIAL BEGINS

1. Nomination Form, National Register of Historic Places Inventory, *Historic Resources of Downtown South Bend,* Third St. Joseph County Courthouse, Apr. 26, 1985, p. 38.

2. *Elkhart Weekly Review,* Mar. 16, 1907, p. 5.

3. *Elkhart Daily Review,* Mar. 28, 1907, p. 5.

4. *Elkhart Daily Review,* Apr. 6, 1907, p. 6.

5. *Elkhart Daily Review,* Apr. 6, 1907, p. 6.

6. *Elkhart Truth,* Apr. 19, 1907, p. 1.

7. *Elkhart Truth,* Apr. 19, 1907, p. 1.

8. *South Bend Daily Times,* Apr. 23, 1907, p. 1.

9. *South Bend Daily Times,* Apr. 23, 1907, p. 1.

10. *Transcript of Evidence,* 7.

11. *South Bend Daily Times,* Apr. 26, 1907.

12. *South Bend Daily Times,* Apr. 26, 1907.

13. Anderson and Cooley, *South Bend and the Men Who Have Made It,* 283.

14. *Indianapolis Star,* Jan. 25, 1907, p. 5.

15. *Elkhart Daily Review,* Feb. 18, 1909, p. 5.

16. *Elkhart Daily Review,* Feb. 18, 1909, p. 5.

17. Anderson and Cooley, *South Bend and the Men Who Have Made It,* 129.

18. If State's Attorney Talbot made an opening statement, it was not reported by the newspapers or recorded in the trial transcript. Theories of the state and the defense can be found in *Brief and Argument for the Appellant,* 15–16. What appears to be defense attorney Parker's complete opening statement, delivered before he called his first witness, can be found in the April 25, 1907, *South Bend Daily Times.*

19. *South Bend Tribune,* Apr. 23, 1907.

20. Fred Young, testimony, *Transcript of Evidence,* 137–72; *South Bend Daily Times,* Apr. 23, 1907, p. 7.

21. *South Bend Daily Times,* Apr. 23, 1907, p. 7.

22. Fred Young, testimony, *South Bend Daily Times,* Apr. 23, 1907, p. 7.

23. Ludwig, "Tell Your Story of the Crime."

24. *South Bend Daily Times,* Apr. 23, 1907, p. 7.

25. *South Bend Daily Times,* Apr. 23, 1907, p. 7.

26. John Gaylor, testimony, *Brief and Argument for the Appellant,* 39; *South Bend Daily Times,* Apr. 23, 1907, p. 7; Inflation Calculator, http://www.in2013 dollars.com/us/inflation/1906?amount=50.

27. James Anderson, testimony, *Transcript of Evidence,* 175–79; *Brief and Argument for the Appellant,* 39–40, 70–71; *South Bend Daily Times,* Apr. 23, 1907, p. 7.

28. Marcellus Gaze, testimony, *Brief and Argument for the Appellant,* 40; *South Bend Daily Times,* Apr. 23, 1907, p. 7.

29. Veronica Gaze, testimony, *Brief and Argument for the Appellant,* 41; *South Bend Daily Times,* Apr. 23, 1907, p. 7.

30. Lester Gitre, testimony, *Brief and Argument for the Appellant,* 41; *South Bend Daily Times,* Apr. 23, 1907, p. 7.

31. Walking distance from Ludwig house to 607 North Bridge Street (now Main Street) was timed by the author on July 24, 2018.

32. Milton E. Robbins, testimony, *Brief and Argument for the Appellant,* 41; *South Bend Daily Times,* Apr. 23, 1907, p. 7.

33. Anna Burkhart, testimony, *Brief and Argument for the Appellant,* 41–42; *South Bend Daily Times,* Apr. 23, 1907, p. 7.

34. *South Bend Daily Times,* Apr. 23, 1907, p. 7.

35. David Hull, testimony, *Brief and Argument for the Appellant,* 42–43; *South Bend Daily Times,* Apr. 23, 1907, p. 7.

36. Catherine Brand, testimony, *Brief and Argument for the Appellant,* 43–44; *South Bend Daily Times,* Apr. 23, 1907, p. 7.

11. "SHE CERTAINLY WAS DEAD"

1. Catherine Brand, testimony, *Transcript of Evidence,* 242–44; *South Bend Daily Times,* Apr. 23, 1907, p. 7.

2. Milton Carter, testimony, *Brief and Argument for the Appellant,* 44; *South Bend Daily Times,* Apr. 23, 1907, p. 7.

3. James L. France, testimony, *Brief and Argument for the Appellant,* 44; *South Bend Daily Times,* Apr. 23, 1907, p. 7.

4. Albert Buysse, testimony, *Transcript of Evidence,* 254–57; *Brief and Argument for the Appellant,* 45–46; *South Bend Daily Times,* Apr. 23, 1907, p. 7.

5. *South Bend Daily Times,* Apr. 23, 1907, p. 7; *South Bend Tribune,* Apr. 23, 1907, p. 5.

6. Albert Buysse, testimony, *South Bend Daily Times,* Apr. 23, 1907, p. 7.

7. Otto Goeller, *Transcript of Evidence,* 280; *Brief and Argument for the Appellant,* 46; *South Bend Daily Times,* Apr. 23, 1907, p. 7.

8. William C. Hose, testimony, *Brief and Argument for the Appellant,* 46–47; *South Bend Daily Times,* Apr. 23, 1907, p. 7.

9. *South Bend Daily Times,* Apr. 23, 1907, p. 7.

10. *South Bend Daily Times,* Apr. 23, 1907, p. 7.

11. James L. France, testimony, *Brief and Argument for the Appellant,* 47; *South Bend Daily Times,* Apr. 24, 1907, p. 1.

12. *South Bend Daily Times,* Apr. 24, 1907, p. 1.

13. Dr. C. A. Dresch, testimony, *Brief and Argument for the Appellant,* 47–48; *South Bend Daily Times,* Apr. 24, 1907, p. 1.

14. *South Bend Daily Times,* Apr. 23, 1907, p. 1.

15. Emma Reifsneider, testimony, *Brief and Argument for the Appellant,* 48–49; *South Bend Daily Times,* Apr. 24, 1907, pp. 1, 6.

16. Emma Reifsneider, testimony, *Brief and Argument for the Appellant,* 48–49; *South Bend Daily Times,* Apr. 24, 1907, pp. 1, 6.

17. Alice McNabb, testimony, *Brief and Argument for the Appellant,* 49.

18. Alice McNabb, testimony, *Brief and Argument for the Appellant,* 49.

19. Alfred Heiney, testimony, *Brief and Argument for the Appellant,* 49–50; *South Bend Daily Times,* Apr. 24, 1907, p. 6.

20. Henry C. Holtzendorf, testimony, *Transcript of Evidence,* 340–46; *Brief and Argument for the Appellant,* 50–51; *South Bend Daily Times,* Apr. 24, 1907, p. 6.

21. *South Bend Daily Times,* Apr. 23, 1907, p. 7.

12. THE STATE RESTS

1. *Hied* is an archaic word meaning *hastened.*

2. P. A. Young, Mishawaka Department, *South Bend Daily Times,* Apr. 24, 1907.

3. Fred C. Metzler, testimony, *Transcript of Evidence,* 348–49; *Brief and Argument for the Appellant,* 51–52, 58; *South Bend Daily Times,* Apr. 24, 1907, p. 6.

4. Fred C. Metzler, testimony, *Brief and Argument for the Appellant,* 52.

5. Loren A. Foust, testimony, *Brief and Argument for the Appellant,* 52.

6. George H. Wilklow, testimony, *Brief and Argument for the Appellant,* 52.

7. Benjamin F. Jarrett, testimony, *Transcript of Evidence,* 362–81, 394; *Brief and Argument for the Appellant,* 50–51, 71–72; *South Bend Daily Times,* Apr. 24, 1907, p. 6.

8. During Coroner Holtzendorf's second direct examination by State's Attorney Talbot, the prosecutor formally tendered in evidence five exhibits. As they appear on p. 396 of the *Transcript of Evidence:* "Said potato masher— Exhibit 'A'—is an ordinary potato masher—slightly scorched; Said bottle of Iodine and Glycerine—Exhibit 'B'—is an ordinary three-ounce bottle, about one-third full of dark brown liquid, with a cork stopper; Said Exhibits 'C' & 'D' are two pieces of an ordinary steel-colored, flat, door key; Said Exhibit 'E'—Razor—is an ordinary razor, with a black handle."

9. The chain of evidence regarding the potato masher, the potential murder weapon, was not questioned by the defense despite two witnesses claiming that they found it on different days. Coroner Holtzendorf testified he found a potato masher at the scene the afternoon of the fire and that he gave

it to the police chief. But Police Chief Jarrett testified that he found the potato masher on the closet floor the day after the fire.

10. Dr. Henry C. Holtzendorf, testimony, *Transcript of Evidence*, 406.

11. James Anderson, testimony, *Brief and Argument for the Appellant*, 55.

12. Charles C. Stroup, testimony, *Transcript of Evidence*, 422–24; *Brief and Argument for the Appellant*, 55–56; *South Bend Daily Times*, Apr. 24, 1907, p. 6.

13. Robert F. Schellenberg, testimony, *Brief and Argument for the Appellant*, 56–57; *South Bend Daily Times*, Apr. 24, 1907, p. 6.

14. *South Bend Daily Times*, Apr. 24, 1907, p. 6; *Elkhart Daily Review*, Apr. 25, 1907, p. 1.

15. Robert F. Schellenberg, testimony, *Brief and Argument for the Appellant*, 56–57; *South Bend Daily Times*, Apr. 24, 1907, p. 6.

13. "WIFE THE AGGRESSOR"

1. *South Bend Daily Times*, Apr. 25, 1907, p. 9.

2. Gustave Ludwig, testimony, *Brief and Argument for the Appellant*, 57–58. (Gustave's first name is misspelled "Gustav" in the brief.)

3. Fred C. Metzler, testimony, *Brief and Argument for the Appellant*, 58.

4. Anna Spies, testimony, *Brief and Argument for the Appellant*, 58.

14. ALBIN TESTIFIES

1. *South Bend Daily Times*, Apr. 23, 1907, p. 7.

2. It's likely the salesman represented Manning, Bowman & Company, which in the early 1900s sold chafing dishes, coffee percolators, and other kitchen and bathroom products (Linz, "Deco Collector," 19).

3. Albin R. Ludwig, testimony, *Transcript of Evidence*, 473–513.

4. Christina Henderson, testimony, *Transcript of Evidence*, 607.

5. Albin R. Ludwig, testimony, *Transcript of Evidence*, 473–513.

15. CROSS-EXAMINATION

1. Albin R. Ludwig, testimony, *Transcript of Evidence*, 513–56.

2. Albin R. Ludwig, testimony, *Transcript of Evidence*, 513–56.

3. Albin R. Ludwig, testimony, *Transcript of Evidence*, 513–56.

4. *South Bend Daily Times*, Apr. 25, 1907, p. 9.

5. *Mishawaka Enterprise*, Apr. 26, 1907, p. 1.

6. Albin R. Ludwig, testimony, *Transcript of Evidence,* 513–56.

7. Albin R. Ludwig, testimony, *Transcript of Evidence,* 513–56.

16. WRAPPING UP

1. *South Bend Daily Times,* Apr. 25, 1907.

2. John Gaylor, testimony, *Brief and Argument for the Appellant,* 66–67.

3. *South Bend Daily Times,* Apr. 25, 1907.

4. Alvia J. Bruce, testimony, *Brief and Argument for the Appellant,* 67–68; *South Bend Daily Times,* Apr. 26, 1907, p. 9.

5. Robert F. Schellenberg, testimony, *Brief and Argument for the Appellant,* 55–56.

6. Alvia J. Bruce, testimony, *Brief and Argument for the Appellant,* 67–68; Alvia J. Bruce, cross-examination, *Brief and Argument for the Appellant,* 68–69.

7. Nettie May Hess, testimony, *Brief and Argument for the Appellant,* 69.

8. Charles R. Patterson, testimony, *Brief and Argument for the Appellant,* 69.

9. Veronica Gaze, testimony, *Brief and Argument for the Appellant,* 69.

10. James Anderson, testimony, *Brief and Argument for the Appellant,* 70.

11. Argument, Point 5, *Brief and Argument for the Appellant,* 81–84.

12. Grace Jarrett, testimony, *Transcript of Evidence,* 599; *Brief and Argument for the Appellant,* 70.

13. Gustave Ludwig, testimony, *Brief and Argument for the Appellant,* 71.

14. James Anderson, testimony, *Brief and Argument for the Appellant,* 71.

15. Christina Henderson, testimony, *Transcript of Evidence,* 607–11; *South Bend Daily Times,* Apr. 26, 1907.

16. Benjamin F. Jarrett, testimony, *Transcript of Evidence,* 611; Benjamin F. Jarrett, testimony, *Brief and Argument for the Appellant,* 71–72; *South Bend Daily Times,* Apr. 26, 1907.

17. Arthur Householder, testimony, *Brief and Argument for the Appellant,* 72.

18. James Edward Girton, testimony, *Transcript of Evidence,* 625; James Edward Girton, testimony, *Brief and Argument for the Appellant,* 72.

19. *South Bend Daily Times,* Apr. 26, 1907.

20. *South Bend Daily Times,* Apr. 26, 1907.

21. *Mishawaka Enterprise,* Apr. 26, 1907.

22. *South Bend Daily Times,* Apr. 27, 1907, p. 1.

23. Verdict, *Transcript of Evidence,* 41.

24. Author's analysis of twelve Indiana men besides Albin Ludwig convicted from 1900 to 1910 of murdering their wives. John Rinkard of Marion was hanged January 16, 1902 (*Indianapolis News,* Jan. 17, 1902, p. 2); Ora Copenhaver of Indianapolis was hanged June 12, 1903 (*South Bend Tribune,*

June 12, 1903, p. 1); and Berkley Smith of Indianapolis was hanged June 30, 1905 (*Rushville Republican,* June 30, 1905, p. 2).

25. *Muncie Evening Press,* Oct. 25, 1909, p. 1.

26. *South Bend Daily Times,* Apr. 27, 1907, p. 1.

27. *South Bend Tribune,* Apr. 27, 1907, p. 1.

28. Author's analysis of twelve Indiana men besides Albin Ludwig convicted from 1900 to 1910 of murdering their wives. Wife murderers sentenced to life who were released early were Alonzo Fisher of Richmond, served eleven years (*Richmond Palladium-Item,* Oct. 9, 1918, p. 8); Anthony Miller of Muncie, served fifteen years (*Star Press,* Aug. 12, 1922, p. 1); John Glasco of Anderson, served ten years (*Star Press,* Oct. 16, 1919, p. 9); and Lewis Fuller of Goshen, served fifteen years (*Journal and Courier,* Feb. 3, 1922, p. 10). William Robinson of Kokomo, sentenced to life in 1909, failed to return from a temporary parole and still was missing ten years later. Prison authorities "have ceased to expect he will ever be returned to their keeping" (*Kokomo Tribune,* Nov. 30, 1935, p. 1).

29. *South Bend Tribune,* Apr. 27, 1907, p. 1.

30. *South Bend Daily Times,* May 9, 1907.

31. *Elkhart Daily Review,* May 9, 1907, p. 1.

32. *South Bend Daily Times,* May 9, 1907.

33. *Commitment* document on file with Indiana State Archives.

34. *Statement of Court Officers* on file with Indiana State Archives.

17. PRISON

1. *Elkhart Daily Review,* May 15, 1907, p. 5.

2. *Indiana State Prison Clothing Receipt,* May 14, 1907.

3. Indiana State Prison register for Prisoner 3701, Albin R. Ludwig.

4. Albin R. Ludwig, Indiana Images.

5. *Statement of Prisoner to Board of Commissioners of Paroled Prisoners.*

6. *South Bend Tribune,* June 8, 1903, p. 1.

7. *Indiana State Prison Conduct Report,* Albin R. Ludwig.

8. Indiana State Prison register for Prisoner 3701, Albin R. Ludwig.

18. APPEAL

1. *Brief and Argument for the Appellant.*

2. *Brief and Argument for the Appellant,* 15.

3. *Brief and Argument for the Appellant,* 15–16.

4. *Brief and Argument for the Appellant,* 17–18.

5. *Brief and Argument for the Appellant,* 23–25.

6. *Brief and Argument for the Appellant,* 31–34.

7. *Brief and Argument for the Appellant,* 25–28.

8. *Brief and Argument for the Appellant,* 34–37.

9. *Brief and Argument for the Appellant,* 37.

10. Gillett, "Ludwig v. State (No. 21,144)," 345–49.

11. Hanging was Indiana's method of capital punishment at the time. Five years later, in 1913, the electric chair became the primary method of execution. Lethal injection, the current method, was first used in 1995 (Indiana, Death Penalty Information Center).

19. PAROLE

1. *Elkhart Daily Review,* Nov. 19, 1915, p. 1.

2. Email to author, Aug. 7, 2017, from a great-granddaughter of Lyle who asked not to be identified in this book.

3. *Elkhart Daily Review,* Feb. 10, 1919, p. 3.

4. Samuel P. Schwartz, letter to Edward J. Fogarty, Feb. 17, 1919, on file with the Indiana State Archives.

5. Gov. Warren T. McCray, Executive Order 1016, Jan. 17, 1923, on file with the Indiana State Archives.

6. Gottschalk, "No Way Out?," 228.

7. Author's analysis of three Indiana men besides Albin Ludwig convicted in 1907 of murdering their wives and sentenced to life imprisonment. Alonzo Fisher of Richmond was paroled after eleven years (*Richmond Palladium-Item,* Oct. 9, 1918, p. 8); Lewis Fuller of Goshen was paroled after fifteen years *(Lafayette Journal and Courier,* Feb. 3, 1922, p. 10); and Anthony Miller of Muncie was paroled after fifteen years (*Muncie Star Press,* Aug. 12, 1922, p. 1). Fisher and Fuller had been convicted of first-degree murder and Miller of second-degree murder.

8. Albin R. Ludwig, letter authorizing operation, May 28, 1923, on file with the Indiana State Archives.

9. Indiana State Prison register for Prisoner 3701, Albin R. Ludwig, on file with the Indiana State Archives; Rules Governing Prisoners on Parole, June 7, 1923, on file with the Indiana State Archives; Clerk's Office, Prisoner Outfit, prisoner No. 3701, Ludwig, June 8, 1923, on file with the Indiana State Archives.

10. Rules Governing Prisoners on Parole, June 7, 1923, on file with the Indiana State Archives.

11. *Elkhart Truth,* Jan. 21, 1910, p. 1.

12. Indiana State Prison register for Prisoner 3701, Albin R. Ludwig, on file with the Indiana State Archives.

20. LIFE AFTER PRISON

1. Judy A. Myer, interview with author, Aug. 23, 2017.

2. Linda Hamer Kennett, "'Jewel Tea Man' Was a Welcome Sight in Neighborhood," *Rushville Republican,* Nov. 8, 2008, https://www.rushvillere-publican.com/news/lifestyles/jewel-tea-man-was-a-welcome-site-in-neigh-borhood/article_0c0d1a07-f787-5ae3-aae8-e1730f14f0a1.html.

3. Judy A. Myer, interview with author, Aug. 23, 2017.

4. *Indianapolis Star,* Dec. 16, 1944, p. 15.

5. Email to author, Aug. 7, 2017, from a great-granddaughter of Lyle who asked not to be identified in this book.

6. *Social Security Applications and Claims Index,* 1936–2007.

7. *Polk's Elkhart City Directory,* 1953, p. 162.

8. *Index to the Records of the Walley-Mills Zimmerman Funeral Home,* Book 23.

EPILOGUE

1. "The Modern Woman," *South Bend Daily Times,* Sept. 25, 1906.

2. *Under the Rule of Thumb,* 2.

3. Staff of the *Indiana Magazine of History,* "The Divorce Mill of the Midwest."

4. Garber, "Divorce in Marion County," 1–16.

5. "Domestic Violence in Indiana."

6. Email to author, Aug. 7, 2017, from a great-granddaughter of Lyle who asked not to be identified in this book.

7. *La Porte Argus-Bulletin,* Oct. 2, 1906, p. 1.

8. Chuck Ellsworth, emails to author, Mar. 5, 2018; interview with author, Mar. 6, 2018.

APPENDIX A

1. Gustave signed his name without the *e* on his naturalization application in 1892. His prison records used Gustave with the *e.*

2. Gustav Ludwig declaration of intention to become a citizen, Elkhart Circuit Court, Nov. 7, 1892.

3. Indiana State Prison register for Prisoner 7142, Gustave Ludwig, on file with the Indiana State Archives.

4. *Elkhart Daily Review*, May 7, 1913, p. 5; *Elkhart Truth*, July 19, 1913, p. 5; *Elkhart Truth*, Oct. 19, 1915, p. 5.

5. *Elkhart Truth*, Nov. 21, 1917, p. 2.

6. Indiana State Prison register for Prisoner 7142, Gustave Ludwig, on file with the Indiana State Archives.

7. *Elkhart Daily Review*, Apr. 17, 1915, p. 1.

8. Both estimates of 2019 values in this newspaper excerpt came from Inflation Calculator, http://www.in2013dollars.com/us/inflation/1917?.

9. *Elkhart Daily Review*, Apr. 17, 1915, p. 1.

10. *Elkhart Daily Review*, Apr. 19, 1915, p. 1.

11. *Elkhart Daily Review*, Oct. 30, 1915, p. 8; *Elkhart Truth*, Nov. 13, 1915, p. 1.

12. *Elkhart Daily Review*, May 12, 1915, p. 5.

13. *Elkhart Daily Review*, Nov. 21, 1917, p. 1.

14. Inflation Calculator, http://www.in2013dollars.com/us/inflation/1917? amount=40000.

15. The *Elkhart Truth* of November 21 gave this colorful account of Ludwig's apprehension:

Some time ago Officer Crisman told Leader of the peculiar machinations of an Elkhartan who he said procured large quantities of express from the American Express company's Goshen depot and hauled them to this city in a one horse wagon. Officer Crisman [of the Goshen police department] said he had learned that the shipments were consigned to Frank Boss of Goshen and he was certain that there was no resident by that name in the county seat. Leader, who had four years' experience as sheriff of the county, "smelt a mouse." He told Officer Crisman to keep close watch on the shipments and to notify him immediately after "Boss" came to Goshen for another consignment. At 4:30 Monday afternoon Crisman telephoned Leader that "Boss" had just left Goshen with a wagon load of express. Leader, who had previously notified Captain Northrop of the possibilities of a big catch, telephoned the captain to meet him at the street car barn on South Main street. Meanwhile, Leader drove his car toward Goshen, passing "Boss," who proved to be Ludwig. About a mile back of Ludwig he came upon Crisman, who was attempting to follow Ludwig on foot. Crisman got into the Leader car and they started back toward Elkhart. They caught up with Ludwig when within a few miles of Elkhart and the latter, seeing the officers, took a circuitous route to a shed near a house he owns at 1205 Harrison street. Captain Northrop got into the Leader automobile near the car barns and the three drove to the Ludwig home. They apprehended Ludwig just as he jumped from his wagon. He was placed under arrest on a charge of suspicion.

16. *Elkhart Daily Review,* Nov. 21, 1917, p. 1.
17. *Elkhart Daily Review,* Nov. 22, 1917, p. 1.
18. *Elkhart Daily Review,* Nov. 23, 1917, p. 1.
19. *Elkhart Truth,* Dec. 18, 1917, p. 7.
20. *Elkhart Truth,* Dec. 20, 1917, p. 14.
21. Gustave Ludwig, Indiana Images, Indiana State Archives.
22. Indiana State Prison register for Prisoner 7142, Gustave Ludwig, on file with the Indiana State Archives.
23. Indiana State Prison registers for Prisoner 7142, Gustave Ludwig, and Prisoner 3701, Albin R. Ludwig, on file with the Indiana State Archives.
24. *Elkhart Truth,* Dec. 2, 1919, p. 2.

APPENDIX B

1. *Muncie Star Press,* Apr. 26, 1908, p. 2.
2. "Past Prohibition Party Candidates . . . IN Vote Records"; *Muncie Star Press,* Apr. 26, 1908, p. 2.
3. *Muncie Star Press,* Apr. 26, 1908, p. 2.
4. *Elkhart Weekly Review,* Apr. 29, 1908, p. 3.
5. *Muncie Star Press,* June 30, 1908, p. 5.
6. *La Porte Weekly Herald,* Sept. 17, 1908, p. 10; *Muncie Star Press,* Sept. 17, 1908, p. 2; *Fort Wayne Sentinel,* Sept. 16, 1908, p. 4.
7. *La Porte Weekly Herald,* Sept. 17, 1908, p. 10.
8. *Noblesville Hamilton County Ledger,* Oct. 9, 1908, p. 5.
9. *Noblesville Hamilton County Ledger,* Oct. 9, 1908, p. 5; *Muncie Star Press,* Oct. 9, 1908, p. 9; *Indianapolis News,* Oct. 24, 1908, p. 2.
10. *Biennial Report of Fred A. Sims.*
11. *Elkhart Truth,* Nov. 13, 1908, p. 1.
12. *Elkhart Truth,* Nov. 13, 1908, p. 1.
13. *Elkhart Truth,* Nov. 13, 1908, p. 4.
14. *Elkhart Truth,* Nov. 21, 1908, p. 1.
15. *Elkhart Truth,* Mar. 19, 1909, p. 1.
16. *Elkhart Truth,* Feb. 12, 1909, p. 1.
17. *Elkhart Daily Review,* Feb. 16, 1909, p. 1.

18. *Elkhart Daily Review,* Feb. 13, 1909, p. 1.

19. *Elkhart Daily Review,* Feb. 16, 1909, p. 1.

20. *Elkhart Daily Review,* Feb. 16, 1909, p. 1.

21. *Elkhart Daily Review,* Feb. 18, 1909, p. 1.

22. *Indianapolis News,* Sept. 30, 1909, p. 14 (incorrect date of incident), and Oct. 16, 1909, p. 9 (correct date).

23. *Indianapolis News,* Sept. 30, 1909, p. 14.

24. John W. Talbot "first achieved notoriety in 1897 when he was tried in the theft of a carload of silk from the Baltimore & Ohio railroad," Malcolm F. Horner wrote in the *South Bend Tribune* (Dec. 15, 1937) after Talbot burned to death in his office.

25. *Plymouth Weekly Republican,* July 1, 1909, p. 1.

26. *Indianapolis News,* Sept. 30, 1909, p. 14.

27. *Indianapolis News,* Sept. 30, 1909, p. 14.

28. *Indianapolis News,* Oct. 16, 1909, p. 9.

29. Five minutes in the *Indianapolis Star,* Oct. 16, 1909, p. 4; sixteen minutes in the *Indianapolis News,* Oct. 16, 1909, p. 9.

30. *Indianapolis Star,* Oct. 16, 1909, p. 4.

31. *Indianapolis News,* Nov. 20, 1909, p. 17.

32. *Elkhart Daily Review,* July 1, 1910, p. 8.

33. *Elkhart Truth,* July 8, 1910, p. 6.

34. *Muncie Star Press,* Nov. 5, 1910, p. 7. Talbot's age was listed as forty-seven in this story, but according to a plaque on his cemetery monument, he was three weeks short of his thirty-seventh birthday when he died.

35. Greta Fisher, "The Greatest South Bend Scoundrel You've Never Heard Of," *South Bend Time Machine,* episode 3, Podcast audio, Mar. 5, 2018.

36. Photo of gravestone, Cedar Grove Cemetery, Notre Dame, IN, https://www.findagrave.com/memorial/128543130/joseph-edward-leo-talbot.

37. *Muncie Star Press,* Nov. 22, 1910, p. 10.

Bibliography

NEWSPAPERS

(All from Indiana unless indicated)
Detroit (MI) Free Press
Elkhart Daily Review
Elkhart Truth
Elkhart Weekly Review
Elkhart Weekly Truth
Flint (MI) Journal
Fort Wayne Sentinel
Goshen Democrat
Indianapolis News
Indianapolis Star
Kokomo Tribune
Lafayette Journal and Courier
La Porte Argus-Bulletin
La Porte Daily Herald
La Porte Daily Herald-Argus
La Porte Weekly Herald
Mishawaka Enterprise
Muncie Evening Press
Muncie Star Press
Noblesville Hamilton County Ledger
Plymouth Weekly Republican
Richmond Palladium-Item
Rushville Republican
South Bend Daily Times
South Bend Tribune

SECONDARY SOURCES

"About Us." First Baptist Church of Kingsbury. http://www.fbckingsbury.org/
    custpage.cfm?frm=66953&sec_id=66953.
Alchin, Linda. "Scottish Immigration to America Timeline." http://www.dates
    andevents.org/us-immigration-timelines/scottish-immigration-america
    -timeline.htm.
Anderson and Cooley. *South Bend and the Men Who Have Made It: Historical,*
    Descriptive, Biographical. South Bend: The Tribune Printing Co., 1901.
Atlas of the Cities of South Bend and Mishawaka, Indiana. South Bend: G. L.
    Hughes, 1923. http://www.historicmapworks.com/Atlas/US/8179/South-
    +Bend+and+Mishawaka+Cities+1923/.
Attestation Paper, 1st Depot Battalion, 1st COH, Canadian Overseas Expedi-
    tionary Force, signed Jan. 9, 1918, by Thomas Orr Henderson, Toronto.
"Battell Center." Mishawaka Parks & Recreation, City of Mishawaka, IN.
    http://mishawaka.in.gov/parks/facility/battell-center.
Beacon Health System. "Memorial Hospital of South Bend History." https://www
    .beaconhealthsystem.org/about-us/memorial-hospital-of-south-bend-history.
Bell, Keith J. "German Immigrants." Immigration to the United States. http://
    immigrationtounitedstates.org/519-german-immigrants.html.
Berridge, Kent A. Emails to author, Aug. 19, 2017; Apr. 25, 2019.
Bien, Laura. "Late 19th-Century Gasoline Stoves: Cooking on a Bomb Used to
    Be Normal." Dusty Diary, May 15, 2009. http://ypsiarchivesdustydiary.blog
    spot.com/2009/05/late-19th-century-gasoline-stoves.html.
Biennial Report of Fred A. Sims, Secretary of State of the State of Indiana for
    the Fiscal Term Ending September 30, 1908. Sixtieth Judicial Circuit.
Brief and Argument for the Appellant, Albin R. Ludwig vs. The State of Indiana.
    Filed with the Supreme Court of Indiana, Dec. 31, 1907.
Celia B. Hornburg v. Charles F Hornburg. Laporte Circuit Court, Feb. Term
    1896, Civil Order Book 15, Nov. 1895–Sept. 1896, p. 154.
Celia Ludwig, Case 9–121, Probate Records, Box 167–68, 1907–9. St. Joseph
    County Circuit Court. Indiana. *Indiana, Wills and Probate Records, 1798–*
    1999. Provo, UT: Ancestry.com Operations, Inc., 2015. https://search.ancestry
    .com/cgi-bin/sse.dll?indiv=1&dbid=9045&h=1283861&tid=&pid=&usePUB=
    true&_phsrc=gmF164&_phstart=successSource.
Clerk's Office. Prisoner Outfit, Prisoner No. 3701, Ludwig, June 8, 1923. On file
    with the Indiana State Archives, Indianapolis.
"Congressional Staff and Management—Historical Overview." http://archives
    .democrats.rules.house.gov/archives/jcoc2s.htm (domain and content changed
    in 2018).

Davis, Niki, "Immigrant Meals from the Late 1800s." Rooted in Foods, Jan. 7, 2016, http://rootedinfoods.com/immigrant-meals-1800s/.

"Declaration of Intention" to be a United States citizen. Filed by Gustave Ludwig in Elkhart, IN, Circuit Court, Nov. 7, 1892.

"Declaration of Intention" to be a United States citizen. Filed by James Henderson in La Porte, IN, Circuit Court, Oct. 4, 1918.

Directory of South Bend, Mishawaka and Rural Route Lists of St. Joseph County, Indiana. South Bend: South Bend Directory Company, 1905.

"Domestic Violence in Indiana." National Coalition Against Domestic Violence. https://www.speakcdn.com/assets/2497/indiana.pdf.

"Elcar Motor Co., Elkhart Buggy Co., Elkhart Carriage & Harness Mfg. Co., Elkhart Carriage and Motor Car Company." CoachBuilt. http://www.coach built.com/bui/e/elkhart/elkhart.htm.

Elkhart City Directory. Elkhart, IN: Elkhart Directory Company, 1903, 1904–5.

Elkhart Remembered. Vol. 1. South Bend: South Bend Tribune, 2004.

Ellsworth, Chuck. Interview by author, Mar. 6, 2018, and emails, Mar. 5, 2018; Apr. 26 and 27, 2019.

Fisher, Greta. "The Greatest South Bend Scoundrel You've Never Heard Of." *South Bend Time Machine,* episode 3, Podcast audio, Mar. 5, 2018. https://www.southbendtribune.com/the-greatest-south-bend-scoundrel-you-ve-never-heard-of/audio_b4dce5fa-208d-11e8-b48d-77651810b39d.html.

Garber, William S. "Divorce in Marion County." [A paper prepared in 1908 for the Century Club of Indianapolis and the Marion County Bar Association.] *Indiana Magazine of History,* Mar. 1910. https://www.jstor.org/stable/2778 5253?seq=1#page_scan_tab_contents.

Gillett, Chief Justice John Henry. "Ludwig v. State (No. 21,144)." In *The Northeastern Reporter* (July 10–Dec. 11, 1908), 85:345–49. St. Paul: West Publishing Co., 1909.

Gottschalk, Marie. "No Way Out? Life Sentences and the Politics of Penal Reform." In *Life Without Parole: America's New Death Penalty?, edited by* Charles Ogletree and Austin Sarat, 227–81. New York: NYU Press, 2012.

Hibbard's 1910 City Directory of South Bend, Mishawaka and River Park Indiana. South Bend: South Bend & Mishawaka Directory Company, 1910.

Howard, Timothy Edward. *A History of St. Joseph County, Indiana.* Vol. 1 and 2. Chicago and New York: The Lewis Publishing Co., 1907.

Hoyt, Giles R. "Germans." *Peopling Indiana: The Ethnic Experience,* edited by Robert M. Taylor Jr. and Connie A. McBirney, 146–81. Indianapolis: Indiana Historical Society, 1996.

Index to the Records of the Walley-Mills Zimmerman Funeral Home, Elkhart, IN, April 1912–October 1988. Book 23.

Indiana. Death Penalty Information Center. https://deathpenaltyinfo.org/indi
     ana-1.
Indiana State Prison Clothing Receipt, May 14, 1907. On file with the Indiana
     State Archives, Indianapolis.
Indiana State Prison Conduct Report, Albin R. Ludwig, Aug. 9, 1915. On file
     with the Indiana State Archives, Indianapolis.
Indiana State Prison register for Prisoner 3701, Albin R. Ludwig. On file with
     the Indiana State Archives, Indianapolis.
Indiana State Prison register for Prisoner 7142, Gustave Ludwig. On file with
     the Indiana State Archives, Indianapolis.
Irish, Linda Ludwig. Email to author, Mar. 8, 2018.
Knox, W. W. "Health in Scotland 1840–1900." The History of the Scottish Peo-
     ple. https://www.scran.ac.uk/scotland/pdf/SP2_1Education.pdf.
Linz, Jim. "Deco Collector: Manning, Bowman & Company." In Trans-Lux, Art
     Deco Society of Washington, Mar. 2003.
Ludwig, Albin R. "Biographical Record as a Citizen," Indiana State Prison,
     May 13, 1907. On file with the Indiana State Archives, Indianapolis.
———. "Tell Your Story of the Crime," Indiana State Prison, May 27, 1907. On
     file with the Indiana State Archives, Indianapolis.
McCray, Gov. Warren T. Executive Order 1016, Jan. 17, 1923. On file with the
     Indiana State Archives, Indianapolis.
Marks, Gretchen A. Emails to author, Apr. 27 and May 9, 2019.
Meints, Graydon M. Indiana Railroad Lines. Bloomington: Indiana Univ.
     Press, 2011.
Michigan, County Marriage Records, 1822–1940. Ancestry.com. Michigan, County
     Marriage Records, 1822–1940. Lehi, UT: Ancestry.com Operations, Inc., 2016.
     https://search.ancestry.com/cgi-bin/sse.dll?indiv=1&dbid=61374&h=432022
     &tid=&pid=&usePUB=true&_phsrc=gmF171&_phstart=successSource.
Michigan, Marriage Records, 1867–1952. Michigan Department of Community
     Health, Division for Vital Records and Health Statistics. Ancestry.com, Mich-
     igan, Marriage Records, 1867–1952. Provo, UT: Ancestry.com Operations, Inc.,
     2015. https://search.ancestry.com/cgi-bin/sse.dll?indiv=1&dbid=9093&h=272
     7353&tid=&pid=&usePUB=true&_phsrc=gmF166&_phstart=successSource.
"Mishawaka Woolen Company-Ball Band Rubber." The History Museum, South
     Bend, IN. https://historymuseumsb.org/mishawaka-woolen-company-ball
     -band-rubber/.
Myer, Judy A. Interview with author, Aug. 23, 2017.
Nomination Form, National Register or Historic Places Inventory. Historic
     Resources of Downtown South Bend. Third St. Joseph County Courthouse,
     Apr. 26, 1985.

"Past Prohibition Party Candidates . . . IN Vote Records." http://www.prohibi tionists.org/history/votes/IN_can.htm.

Pictorial and Biographical Memoirs of Elkhart and St. Joseph Counties, Indiana. Chicago: Goodspeed Brothers, Publishers, 1893.

Platbook of La Porte County, Indiana. Chicago: George A. Ogle & Co., 1892. Reprinted in *Combined 1874, 1907, 1921 Atlases of La Porte County and Plat Book.* Evansville, IN: Whipporwill Publications, 1989. Sponsored by La Porte County Historical Society.

Polk's Elkhart City Directory. Detroit: R. L. Polk & Co., 1926, 1928–38, 1953.

Riebs, George E. *Elkhart: A Pictorial History.* St. Louis: G. Bradley Publishing, Inc., 1990.

Roberts, Gene, and Hank Klibanoff. *The Race Beat: The Press, the Civil Rights Struggle, and the Awakening of a Nation.* New York: Vintage Books, 2006.

Rules Governing Prisoners on Parole, June 7, 1923. On file with the Indiana State Archives, Indianapolis.

Schwartz, Samuel P. Letter to Edward J. Fogarty, Feb. 17, 1919. On file with the Indiana State Archives, Indianapolis.

Social Security Applications and Claims Index. 1936–2007, Ancestry.com, *U.S., Social Security Applications and Claims Index, 1936–2007.* Provo, UT: Ancestry.com Operations, Inc., 2015. https://search.ancestry.com/cgi-bin/sse .dll?_phsrc=gmF175&_phstart=successSource&usePUBJs=true&indiv=1 &dbid=60901&gsfn=Albin&gsln=Ludwig&gskw=Elkhart&new=1&rank=1& uidh=i7m&redir=false&msT=1&gss=angs-d&pcat=36&fh=2&h=4255543& recoff=&ml_rpos=3.

Staatsarchiv Hamburg. *Hamburg Passenger Lists, 1850–1934.* Provo, UT: Ancestry.com Operations, Inc., 2008. https://search.ancestry.com/cgi-bin/sse.dll? indiv=1&dbid=1068&h=4147001&tid=&pid=&usePUB=true&_phsrc=gmF162 &_phstart=successSource.

Staff of the *Indiana Magazine of History.* "The Divorce Mill of the Midwest." Moment of Indiana History. Sept. 5, 2011. https://indianapublicmedia.org/ momentofindianahistory/divorce-mill-midwest/.

"Statement of Prisoner to Board of Commissioners of Paroled Prisoners." Albin R Ludwig, May 27, 1907. On file with the Indiana State Archives, Indianapolis.

Steiner, Paula. Emails to author, Apr. 23 and 25, 2018; letter to author, Jan. 17, 1997.

Transcript of Evidence. State of Indiana vs. Albin R. Ludwig, St. Joseph County Circuit Court, Apr. 22–26, 1907.

Under the Rule of Thumb: Battered Women and the Administration of Justice. A Report of the United States Commission on Civil Rights, Jan. 1982.

Wylder, Steve. "The Way We Were." *Elkhart Truth,* Dec. 9, 2001.

Index